The Gospels

New Revised Standard Version
Updated Edition

Catechesis of
the Good Shepherd
Publications

Catechesis of the Good Shepherd Publications is an imprint of Liturgy Training Publications (LTP). Further information about these publications is available from LTP or from The United States Association of The Catechesis of the Good Shepherd, 7655-A East Main Street, Scottsdale, AZ 85251; 480-874-3759; email: cgs@cgsusa.org. Requests for all other aspects of the Catechesis should be directed to this address.

THE GOSPELS: NEW REVISED STANDARD VERSION, UPDATED EDITION © 2023 Archdiocese of Chicago: Liturgy Training Publications, 3949 South Racine Avenue, Chicago, IL 60609; 800-933-1800; fax: 800-933-7094; email: orders@ltp.org; website: www.LTP.org. All rights reserved.

This book was edited by Michaela I. Tudela. Michael A. Dodd was the production editor, Anna Manhart was the designer, and Kari Nicholls was the production artist.

Cover and interior art by Kathy Ann Sullivan

Biblical Maps © United States Association of the Catechesis of the Good Shepherd

27 26 25 24 23   1 2 3 4 5

Printed in the United States of America

Library of Congress Control Number: 2022950680

ISBN: 978-1-61671-719-3

CGSTG

Contents

✦ ✦ ✦

✤ The Peaceful Kingdom

11 A shoot shall come out from the stump of Jesse,
and a branch shall grow out of his roots.
² The spirit of the LORD shall rest on him,
the spirit of wisdom and understanding,
the spirit of counsel and might,
the spirit of knowledge and the fear of the LORD.
³ His delight shall be in the fear of the LORD.

⁶ The wolf shall live with the lamb;
the leopard shall lie down with the kid;
the calf and the lion will feed together,
and a little child shall lead them.
⁷ The cow and the bear shall graze;
their young shall lie down together;
and the lion shall eat straw like the ox.
⁸ The nursing child shall play over the hole of the asp,
and the weaned child shall put its hand on the
adder's den.
⁹ They will not hurt or destroy
on all my holy mountain,
for the earth will be full of the knowledge of the LORD
as the waters cover the sea.

Isaiah 11:1–3, 6–9 (NRSVUE)

✤ The Lord Our Shepherd

23 The Lord is my shepherd;
  I have everything I need.
² He lets me rest in fields of green grass
  and leads me to quiet pools of fresh water.
³ He gives me new strength.
He guides me in the right paths,
  as he has promised.
⁴ Even if I go through the deepest darkness,
  I will not be afraid, LORD,
  for you are with me.
Your shepherd's rod and staff protect me.

⁵ You prepare a banquet for me,
  where all my enemies can see me;
you welcome me as an honored guest
  and fill my cup to the brim.
⁶ I know that your goodness and love will be with me all
    my life;
  and your house will be my home as long as I live.

Psalm 23:1-6 (GNT)

This book is presented to

_____

on _____

Welcome

✤ ✤ ✤

When we have a book in our hands, we often first ask, "Who has written it?" We know that Jesus lived in Israel over two thousand years ago, that he preached and taught in the synagogues and in the marketplaces and squares, and that Jesus never wrote anything about himself. After Jesus died and rose, his disciples continued to preach by proclaiming Christ's resurrection, spreading his teachings, and recalling many facts about the life of Jesus on earth. This is how the Gospels came to be written.

Sts. Matthew, Mark, Luke, and John were the four evangelists who, inspired by the Holy Spirit, authored the four Gospels. They are called *evangelists* (which means "people who proclaim the Good News") because their books announce the Good News" ("Gospel") of Jesus. The Gospels contain only a small part of what Jesus said and did. Jesus did and said so much more that is not written down. Perhaps the world could not hold all the books that would have to be written to include them all!

The solemn reading of the Scriptures is particularly important in the Church when the community gathers for liturgy. Those assembled for worship show love and deep reverence for the Book of the Gospels. The Book of the Gospels is often carried solemnly in procession, preceded by a light indicating that the Word of God is the light to our path. Sometimes the priest incenses the Book of the Gospels as a sign of honor. Just before the Gospels are proclaimed, we hear the words "The Gospel according to . . ." so that we remember that each evangelist sets forth the one "Gospel of God" according to his own ability, but not in the sense of creating his own story.

For a long time, the Church copied the Book of the Word of God by hand. The task of recopying was, for the most part, entrusted to monks, who prayed before, during, and after their work. In their calligraphy and precious drawings, they expressed their love and veneration for God's Word. In this book, you will find similar expressions of love and veneration in the first letters of every chapter, which have been illuminated with a gift of creation. You will also see flourishes of a grapevine to remind us of Jesus our True Vine.

Each Gospel begins with an introduction to the life of the evangelist and an image representing the evangelist as one of "the four living creatures," an image that comes from the throne-chariot of God, the Merkabah in the vision in the Book of Ezekiel:

As for the appearance of their faces: the four had the face of a human being, the face of a lion on the right side, the face of an ox on the left side, and the face of an eagle. (Ez 1:10)

And in the Book of Revelation:

Around the throne, and on each side of the throne, are four living creatures, full of eyes in front and back: the first living creature like a lion, the second living creature like an ox, the third living creature with a face like a human, and the fourth living creature like a flying eagle. And the four living creatures, each of them with six wings, are full of eyes all around and inside. Day and night without ceasing they sing, "Holy, holy, holy, the Lord God the Almighty, who was and is and is to come."   (Rev 4:6–8)

This connection between "the four living creatures" and the four Gospels was well established and accepted even in the early days of the Church.

To help you find the passages from the infancy narratives, parables, passion narratives, and appearances of the Risen Christ that you may enjoy most, you will find an index of readings on pages 262–263. You will also find maps of the Land of Israel to help you locate many of the places written about in the Gospels.

We received the Gospels written in Greek, and many have worked to translate these precious words into English. As you read these Gospels, you will see that each chapter and verse is numbered; others have worked to do this for us. You may notice that some verses are missing. This is because newer translations are attempting to accurately present what the evangelists originally wrote. So some verses are omitted because most scholars believe these words were not in the original text.

Now that you have some ease and interest in reading, we have prepared this biblical text for your study and meditation. It is important for you to have the Gospel in hand when you listen to its proclamation. We know that what we are searching for does not come from the adult but from the Gospel itself. So we bow our heads to pore over the book we all hold and listen for God's voice in the words. As one child told another as she handed on the Book of the Gospels: "When the counsel of others does not help you, here you will be able to find true counsel."

This Book has been studied with love and reverence throughout the ages by men, women, and children. This Book with which men, women, and children have prayed throughout the centuries is now in your hands.

✦ Gospel of Matthew ✦

St. Matthew, also known as Levi, was the son of Alphaeus. He was one of the twelve apostles. But before Jesus called him to become his apostle (Matthew 9:9), he had been a tax collector. In the time of Jesus, tax collectors were considered sinners and untrustworthy because of their unfair business practices. It came as a great surprise to many when Jesus called Matthew to follow him, and he got up from his tax collection booth and did so.

In his Gospel, Matthew is careful to show that the words and actions of Jesus match the prophecies from the Hebrew Bible. He tries to demonstrate to the people of Israel that Jesus is the perfect fulfillment of the long-expected Messiah. Since family ancestry was important to the Jews, Matthew traces Jesus' family line all the way back to Abraham, the father of the people of Israel. Most scholars agree that this Gospel must have been written in the late first century, during the early period of the Church.

After Jesus' ascension to heaven, the apostles went out to all the world to proclaim the Good News. It is believed that Matthew stayed around Judea when he first began preaching. He may have then traveled to Ethiopia, Parthia, and Persia to continue his mission. According to tradition, Matthew died a martyr while preaching the Gospel somewhere near present-day Egypt.

Matthew is the patron saint of accountants and bank workers. His feast day is September 21 in the West and November 16 in the East.

The winged human represents St. Matthew because his Gospel begins with Jesus' family tree and so points to Jesus' incarnation, his human nature. "This, then," according to St. Irenaeus, "is the Gospel of His humanity; for which reason it is, too, that the character of a humble and meek man is kept up through the whole Gospel." This suggests that we should use the gift of knowledge and the virtues of humility and integrity in following our Good Shepherd.

CHAPTER 1

✤ The Genealogy of Jesus the Messiah

n account of the genealogy of Jesus the Messiah, the son of David, the son of Abraham.

² Abraham was the father of Isaac, and Isaac the father of Jacob, and Jacob the father of Judah and his brothers, ³ and Judah the father of Perez and Zerah by Tamar, and Perez the father of Hezron, and Hezron the father of Aram, ⁴ and Aram the father of Aminadab, and Aminadab the father of Nahshon, and Nahshon the father of Salmon, ⁵ and Salmon the father of Boaz by Rahab, and Boaz the father of Obed by Ruth, and Obed the father of Jesse, ⁶ and Jesse the father of King David.

And David was the father of Solomon by the wife of Uriah, ⁷ and Solomon the father of Rehoboam, and Rehoboam the father of Abijah, and Abijah the father of Asaph, ⁸ and Asaph the father of Jehoshaphat, and Jehoshaphat the father of Joram, and Joram the father of Uzziah, ⁹ and Uzziah the father of Jotham, and Jotham the father of Ahaz, and Ahaz the father of Hezekiah, ¹⁰ and Hezekiah the father of Manasseh, and Manasseh the father of Amos, and Amos the father of Josiah, ¹¹ and Josiah the father of Jechoniah and his brothers, at the time of the deportation to Babylon.

¹² And after the deportation to Babylon: Jechoniah was the father of Salathiel, and Salathiel the father of Zerubbabel, ¹³ and Zerubbabel the father of Abiud, and Abiud the father of Eliakim, and Eliakim the father of Azor, ¹⁴ and Azor the father of Zadok, and Zadok the father of Achim, and Achim the father of Eliud, ¹⁵ and Eliud the father of Eleazar, and Eleazar the father of Matthan, and Matthan the father of Jacob, ¹⁶ and Jacob the father of Joseph the husband of Mary, who bore Jesus, who is called the Messiah.

¹⁷ So all the generations from Abraham to David are fourteen generations; and from David to the deportation to Babylon, fourteen

generations; and from the deportation to Babylon to the Messiah, fourteen generations.

✦ The Birth of Jesus the Messiah

[18] Now the birth of Jesus the Messiah took place in this way. When his mother Mary had been engaged to Joseph, but before they lived together, she was found to be pregnant from the Holy Spirit. [19] Her husband Joseph, being a righteous man and unwilling to expose her to public disgrace, planned to divorce her quietly. [20] But just when he had resolved to do this, an angel of the Lord appeared to him in a dream and said, "Joseph, son of David, do not be afraid to take Mary as your wife, for the child conceived in her is from the Holy Spirit. [21] She will bear a son, and you are to name him Jesus, for he will save his people from their sins." [22] All this took place to fulfill what had been spoken by the Lord through the prophet:

[23] "Look, the virgin shall become pregnant and give birth
          to a son,
     and they shall name him Emmanuel,"

which means, "God is with us." [24] When Joseph awoke from sleep, he did as the angel of the Lord commanded him; he took her as his wife [25] but had no marital relations with her until she had given birth to a son, and he named him Jesus.

CHAPTER 2

✦ The Adoration of the Magi

 **n the time of King Herod,** after Jesus was born in Bethlehem of Judea, magi from the east came to Jerusalem, [2] asking, "Where is the child who has been born king of the Jews? For we observed his star in the east and have come to pay him homage." [3] When King Herod heard this, he was frightened, and all Jerusalem with him, [4] and calling together all the chief priests and scribes of the people, he inquired of them where the Messiah was to be born. [5] They

told him, "In Bethlehem of Judea, for so it has been written by the prophet:

> [6] 'And you, Bethlehem, in the land of Judah,
>   are by no means least among the rulers of Judah,
>   for from you shall come a ruler
>   who is to shepherd my people Israel.'"

[7] Then Herod secretly called for the magi and learned from them the exact time when the star had appeared. [8] Then he sent them to Bethlehem, saying, "Go and search diligently for the child, and when you have found him, bring me word so that I may also go and pay him homage." [9] When they had heard the king, they set out, and there, ahead of them, went the star that they had seen in the east, until it stopped over the place where the child was. [10] When they saw that the star had stopped, they were overwhelmed with joy. [11] On entering the house, they saw the child with Mary his mother, and they knelt down and paid him homage. Then, opening their treasure chests, they offered him gifts of gold, frankincense, and myrrh. [12] And having been warned in a dream not to return to Herod, they left for their own country by another road.

✦ The Flight into Egypt

[13] Now after they had left, an angel of the Lord appeared to Joseph in a dream and said, "Get up, take the child and his mother, and flee to Egypt, and remain there until I tell you, for Herod is about to search for the child, to destroy him." [14] Then Joseph got up, took the child and his mother by night, and went to Egypt [15] and remained there until the death of Herod. This was to fulfill what had been spoken by the Lord through the prophet, "Out of Egypt I have called my son."

✦ The Massacre of the Infants

[16] When Herod saw that he had been tricked by the magi, he was infuriated, and he sent and killed all the children in and around Bethlehem who were two years old or under, according to the time

that he had learned from the magi. **17** Then what had been spoken through the prophet Jeremiah was fulfilled:

> **18** "A voice was heard in Ramah,
>> wailing and loud lamentation,
> Rachel weeping for her children;
>> she refused to be consoled, because they are no more."

✧ The Return from Egypt

19 When Herod died, an angel of the Lord suddenly appeared in a dream to Joseph in Egypt and said, **20** "Get up, take the child and his mother, and go to the land of Israel, for those who were seeking the child's life are dead." **21** Then Joseph got up, took the child and his mother, and went to the land of Israel. **22** But when he heard that Archelaus was ruling Judea in place of his father Herod, he was afraid to go there. And after being warned in a dream, he went away to the district of Galilee. **23** There he made his home in a town called Nazareth, so that what had been spoken through the prophets might be fulfilled, "He will be called a Nazarene."

CHAPTER 3

✧ The Proclamation of John the Baptist

 **n those days John the Baptist** appeared in the wilderness of Judea, proclaiming, **2** "Repent, for the kingdom of heaven has come near." **3** This is the one of whom the prophet Isaiah spoke when he said,

> "The voice of one crying out in the wilderness:
> 'Prepare the way of the Lord,
>> make his paths straight.'"

4 Now John wore clothing of camel's hair with a leather belt around his waist, and his food was locusts and wild honey. **5** Then Jerusalem and all Judea and all the region around the Jordan were going out to him, **6** and they were baptized by him in the River Jordan, confessing their sins.

⁷ But when he saw many of the Pharisees and Sadducees coming for his baptism, he said to them, "You brood of vipers! Who warned you to flee from the coming wrath? ⁸ Therefore, bear fruit worthy of repentance, ⁹ and do not presume to say to yourselves, 'We have Abraham as our ancestor,' for I tell you, God is able from these stones to raise up children to Abraham. ¹⁰ Even now the ax is lying at the root of the trees; therefore every tree that does not bear good fruit is cut down and thrown into the fire.

¹¹ "I baptize you with water for repentance, but one who is coming after me is more powerful than I, and I am not worthy to carry his sandals. He will baptize you with the Holy Spirit and fire. ¹² His winnowing fork is in his hand, and he will clear his threshing floor and will gather his wheat into the granary, but the chaff he will burn with unquenchable fire."

✣ The Baptism of Jesus

¹³ Then Jesus came from Galilee to John at the Jordan, to be baptized by him. ¹⁴ John would have prevented him, saying, "I need to be baptized by you, and do you come to me?" ¹⁵ But Jesus answered him, "Let it be so now, for it is proper for us in this way to fulfill all righteousness." Then he consented. ¹⁶ And when Jesus had been baptized, just as he came up from the water, suddenly the heavens were opened to him and he saw God's Spirit descending like a dove and alighting on him. ¹⁷ And a voice from the heavens said, "This is my Son, the Beloved, with whom I am well pleased."

CHAPTER 4

✦ The Temptation of Jesus

**hen Jesus was led up** by the Spirit into the wilderness to be tested by the devil. **2** He fasted forty days and forty nights, and afterward he was famished. **3** The tempter came and said to him, "If you are the Son of God, command these stones to become loaves of bread." **4** But he answered, "It is written,

> 'One does not live by bread alone,
>> but by every word that comes from the mouth of God.'"

5 Then the devil took him to the holy city and placed him on the pinnacle of the temple, **6** saying to him, "If you are the Son of God, throw yourself down; for it is written,

> 'He will command his angels concerning you,'
>> and 'On their hands they will bear you up,
> so that you will not dash your foot against a stone.'"

7 Jesus said to him, "Again it is written, 'Do not put the Lord your God to the test.'"

8 Again, the devil took him to a very high mountain and showed him all the kingdoms of the world and their glory, **9** and he said to him, "All these I will give you, if you will fall down and worship me." **10** Then Jesus said to him, "Away with you, Satan! for it is written,

> 'Worship the Lord your God,
>> and serve only him.'"

11 Then the devil left him, and suddenly angels came and waited on him.

✦ Jesus Begins His Ministry in Galilee

12 Now when Jesus heard that John had been arrested, he withdrew to Galilee. **13** He left Nazareth and made his home in Capernaum by the sea, in the territory of Zebulun and Naphtali, ¹⁴ so that what had been spoken through the prophet Isaiah might be fulfilled:

> ¹⁵ "Land of Zebulun, land of Naphtali,
>   on the road by the sea, across the Jordan, Galilee
>   of the gentiles —
> ¹⁶ the people who sat in darkness
>   have seen a great light,
> and for those who sat in the region and shadow of death
>   light has dawned."

¹⁷ From that time Jesus began to proclaim, "Repent, for the kingdom of heaven has come near."

✤ Jesus Calls the First Disciples

¹⁸ As he walked by the Sea of Galilee, he saw two brothers, Simon, who is called Peter, and Andrew his brother, casting a net into the sea — for they were fishers. ¹⁹ And he said to them, "Follow me, and I will make you fishers of people." ²⁰ Immediately they left their nets and followed him. ²¹ As he went from there, he saw two other brothers, James son of Zebedee and his brother John, in the boat with their father Zebedee, mending their nets, and he called them. ²² Immediately they left the boat and their father and followed him.

✤ Jesus Ministers to Crowds of People

²³ Jesus went throughout all Galilee, teaching in their synagogues and proclaiming the good news of the kingdom and curing every disease and every sickness among the people. ²⁴ So his fame spread throughout all Syria, and they brought to him all the sick, those who were afflicted with various diseases and pains, people possessed by demons or having epilepsy or afflicted with paralysis, and he cured them. ²⁵ And great crowds followed him from Galilee, the Decapolis, Jerusalem, Judea, and from beyond the Jordan.

CHAPTER 5

✦ The Beatitudes

**hen Jesus saw the crowds,** he went up the mountain, and after he sat down, his disciples came to him. ² And he began to speak and taught them, saying:

³ "Blessed are the poor in spirit, for theirs is the kingdom of heaven.

⁴ "Blessed are those who mourn, for they will be comforted.

⁵ "Blessed are the meek, for they will inherit the earth.

⁶ "Blessed are those who hunger and thirst for righteousness, for they will be filled.

⁷ "Blessed are the merciful, for they will receive mercy.

⁸ "Blessed are the pure in heart, for they will see God.

⁹ "Blessed are the peacemakers, for they will be called children of God.

¹⁰ "Blessed are those who are persecuted for the sake of righteousness, for theirs is the kingdom of heaven.

¹¹ "Blessed are you when people revile you and persecute you and utter all kinds of evil against you falsely on my account. ¹² Rejoice and be glad, for your reward is great in heaven, for in the same way they persecuted the prophets who were before you.

✦ Salt and Light

¹³ "You are the salt of the earth, but if salt has lost its taste, how can its saltiness be restored? It is no longer good for anything but is thrown out and trampled under foot.

¹⁴ "You are the light of the world. A city built on a hill cannot be hid. ¹⁵ People do not light a lamp and put it under the bushel basket; rather, they put it on the lampstand, and it gives light to all

in the house. [16] In the same way, let your light shine before others, so that they may see your good works and give glory to your Father in heaven.

✤ The Law and the Prophets

[17] "Do not think that I have come to abolish the Law or the Prophets; I have come not to abolish but to fulfill. [18] For truly I tell you, until heaven and earth pass away, not one letter, not one stroke of a letter, will pass from the law until all is accomplished. [19] Therefore, whoever breaks one of the least of these commandments and teaches others to do the same will be called least in the kingdom of heaven, but whoever does them and teaches them will be called great in the kingdom of heaven. [20] For I tell you, unless your righteousness exceeds that of the scribes and Pharisees, you will never enter the kingdom of heaven.

✤ Concerning Anger

[21] "You have heard that it was said to those of ancient times, 'You shall not murder,' and 'whoever murders shall be liable to judgment.' [22] But I say to you that if you are angry with a brother or sister, you will be liable to judgment, and if you insult a brother or sister, you will be liable to the council, and if you say, 'You fool,' you will be liable to the hell of fire. [23] So when you are offering your gift at the altar, if you remember that your brother or sister has something against you, [24] leave your gift there before the altar and go; first be reconciled to your brother or sister, and then come and offer your gift. [25] Come to terms quickly with your accuser while you are on the way to court with him, or your accuser may hand you over to the judge and the judge to the guard, and you will be thrown into prison. [26] Truly I tell you, you will never get out until you have paid the last penny.

✤ Concerning Adultery

[27] "You have heard that it was said, 'You shall not commit adultery.' [28] But I say to you that everyone who looks at a woman with lust has already committed adultery with her in his heart. [29] If your

right eye causes you to sin, tear it out and throw it away; it is better for you to lose one of your members than for your whole body to be thrown into hell. ³⁰ And if your right hand causes you to sin, cut it off and throw it away; it is better for you to lose one of your members than for your whole body to go into hell.

✦ Concerning Divorce

³¹ "It was also said, 'Whoever divorces his wife, let him give her a certificate of divorce.' ³² But I say to you that anyone who divorces his wife, except on the ground of sexual immorality, causes her to commit adultery, and whoever marries a divorced woman commits adultery.

✦ Concerning Oaths

³³ "Again, you have heard that it was said to those of ancient times, 'You shall not swear falsely, but carry out the vows you have made to the Lord.' ³⁴ But I say to you: Do not swear at all, either by heaven, for it is the throne of God, ³⁵ or by the earth, for it is his footstool, or by Jerusalem, for it is the city of the great King. ³⁶ And do not swear by your head, for you cannot make one hair white or black. ³⁷ Let your word be 'Yes, Yes' or 'No, No'; anything more than this comes from the evil one.

✦ Concerning Retaliation

³⁸ "You have heard that it was said, 'An eye for an eye and a tooth for a tooth.' ³⁹ But I say to you: Do not resist an evildoer. But if anyone strikes you on the right cheek, turn the other also, ⁴⁰ and if anyone wants to sue you and take your shirt, give your coat as well, ⁴¹ and if anyone forces you to go one mile, go also the second mile. ⁴² Give to everyone who asks of you, and do not refuse anyone who wants to borrow from you.

✦ Love for Enemies

⁴³ "You have heard that it was said, 'You shall love your neighbor and hate your enemy.' ⁴⁴But I say to you: Love your enemies and pray for those who persecute you, ⁴⁵ so that you may be children

of your Father in heaven, for he makes his sun rise on the evil and on the good and sends rain on the righteous and on the unrighteous. **⁴⁶** For if you love those who love you, what reward do you have? Do not even the tax collectors do the same? **⁴⁷** And if you greet only your brothers and sisters, what more are you doing than others? Do not even the gentiles do the same? **⁴⁸** Be perfect, therefore, as your heavenly Father is perfect.

CHAPTER 6

✦ Concerning Almsgiving

eware of practicing your righteousness before others in order to be seen by them, for then you have no reward from your Father in heaven.

² "So whenever you give alms, do not sound a trumpet before you, as the hypocrites do in the synagogues and in the streets, so that they may be praised by others. Truly I tell you, they have received their reward. **³** But when you give alms, do not let your left hand know what your right hand is doing, **⁴** so that your alms may be done in secret, and your Father who sees in secret will reward you.

✦ Concerning Prayer

⁵ "And whenever you pray, do not be like the hypocrites, for they love to stand and pray in the synagogues and at the street corners, so that they may be seen by others. Truly I tell you, they have received their reward. **⁶** But whenever you pray, go into your room and shut the door and pray to your Father who is in secret, and your Father who sees in secret will reward you.

⁷ "When you are praying, do not heap up empty phrases as the gentiles do, for they think that they will be heard because of their many words. **⁸** Do not be like them, for your Father knows what you need before you ask him.

[9] "Pray, then, in this way:

> Our Father in heaven,
> > may your name be revered as holy.
> > [10] May your kingdom come.
> > May your will be done, on earth as it is in heaven.
> > [11] Give us today our daily bread.
> > [12] And forgive us our debts, as we have also forgiven
> > > our debtors.
> > [13] And do not bring us to the time of trial,
> > > but rescue us from the evil one.

[14] "For if you forgive others their trespasses, your heavenly Father will also forgive you, [15] but if you do not forgive others, neither will your Father forgive your trespasses.

✤ Concerning Fasting

[16] "And whenever you fast, do not look somber, like the hypocrites, for they mark their faces to show others that they are fasting. Truly I tell you, they have received their reward. [17] But when you fast, put oil on your head and wash your face, [18] so that your fasting may be seen not by others but by your Father who is in secret, and your Father who sees in secret will reward you.

✤ Concerning Treasures

[19] "Do not store up for yourselves treasures on earth, where moth and rust consume and where thieves break in and steal, [20] but store up for yourselves treasures in heaven, where neither moth nor rust consumes and where thieves do not break in and steal. [21] For where your treasure is, there your heart will be also.

✤ The Eye

[22] "The eye is the lamp of the body. So if your eye is healthy, your whole body will be full of light, [23] but if your eye is unhealthy, your whole body will be full of darkness. If, then, the light in you is darkness, how great is the darkness!

✤ Serving Two Masters

24 "No one can serve two masters, for a slave will either hate the one and love the other or be devoted to the one and despise the other. You cannot serve God and wealth.

✤ Do Not Worry

25 "Therefore I tell you, do not worry about your life, what you will eat or what you will drink, or about your body, what you will wear. Is not life more than food and the body more than clothing? **26** Look at the birds of the air: they neither sow nor reap nor gather into barns, and yet your heavenly Father feeds them. Are you not of more value than they? **27** And which of you by worrying can add a single hour to your span of life? **28** And why do you worry about clothing? Consider the lilies of the field, how they grow; they neither toil nor spin, **29** yet I tell you, even Solomon in all his glory was not clothed like one of these. **30** But if God so clothes the grass of the field, which is alive today and tomorrow is thrown into the oven, will he not much more clothe you—you of little faith? **31** Therefore do not worry, saying, 'What will we eat?' or 'What will we drink?' or 'What will we wear?' **32** For it is the gentiles who seek all these things, and indeed your heavenly Father knows that you need all these things. **33** But seek first for the kingdom of God and his righteousness, and all these things will be given to you as well.

34 "So do not worry about tomorrow, for tomorrow will bring worries of its own. Today's trouble is enough for today.

CHAPTER 7

✤ Judging Others

**o not judge,** so that you may not be judged. [2] For the judgment you give will be the judgment you get, and the measure you give will be the measure you get. [3] Why do you see the speck in your neighbor's eye but do not notice the log in your own eye? [4] Or how can you say to your neighbor, 'Let me take the speck out of your eye,' while the log is in your own eye? [5] You hypocrite, first take the log out of your own eye, and then you will see clearly to take the speck out of your neighbor's eye.

✤ Profaning the Holy

[6] "Do not give what is holy to dogs, and do not throw your pearls before swine, or they will trample them under foot and turn and maul you.

✤ Ask, Search, Knock

[7] "Ask, and it will be given to you; search, and you will find; knock, and the door will be opened for you. [8] For everyone who asks receives, and everyone who searches finds, and for everyone who knocks, the door will be opened. [9] Is there anyone among you who, if your child asks for bread, would give a stone? [10] Or if the child asks for a fish, would give a snake? [11] If you, then, who are evil, know how to give good gifts to your children, how much more will your Father in heaven give good things to those who ask him!

✤ The Golden Rule

[12] "In everything do to others as you would have them do to you, for this is the Law and the Prophets.

✤ The Narrow Gate

[13] "Enter through the narrow gate, for the gate is wide and the road is easy that leads to destruction, and there are many who

take it. **14** For the gate is narrow and the road is hard that leads to life, and there are few who find it.

✤ A Tree and Its Fruit

15 "Beware of false prophets, who come to you in sheep's clothing but inwardly are ravenous wolves. **16** You will know them by their fruits. Are grapes gathered from thorns or figs from thistles? **17** In the same way, every good tree bears good fruit, but the bad tree bears bad fruit. **18** A good tree cannot bear bad fruit, nor can a bad tree bear good fruit. **19** Every tree that does not bear good fruit is cut down and thrown into the fire. **20** Thus you will know them by their fruits.

✤ Concerning Self-Deception

21 "Not everyone who says to me, 'Lord, Lord,' will enter the kingdom of heaven, but only the one who does the will of my Father in heaven. **22** On that day many will say to me, 'Lord, Lord, did we not prophesy in your name, and cast out demons in your name, and do many mighty works in your name?' **23** Then I will declare to them, 'I never knew you; go away from me, you who behave lawlessly.'

✤ Hearers and Doers

24 "Everyone, then, who hears these words of mine and acts on them will be like a wise man who built his house on rock. **25** The rain fell, the floods came, and the winds blew and beat on that house, but it did not fall because it had been founded on rock. **26** And everyone who hears these words of mine and does not act on them will be like a foolish man who built his house on sand. **27** The rain fell, and the floods came, and the winds blew and beat against that house, and it fell—and great was its fall!"

28 Now when Jesus had finished saying these words, the crowds were astounded at his teaching, **29** for he taught them as one having authority and not as their scribes.

CHAPTER 8

✤ Jesus Heals a Man

**hen Jesus had come down** from the mountain, great crowds followed him, ² and there was a man with a skin disease who came to him and knelt before him, saying, "Lord, if you are willing, you can make me clean." ³ He stretched out his hand and touched him, saying, "I am willing. Be made clean!" Immediately his skin disease was cleansed. ⁴ Then Jesus said to him, "See that you say nothing to anyone, but go, show yourself to the priest, and offer the gift that Moses commanded, as a testimony to them."

✤ Jesus Heals a Centurion's Servant

⁵ When he entered Capernaum, a centurion came to him, appealing to him ⁶ and saying, "Lord, my servant is lying at home paralyzed, in terrible distress." ⁷ And he said to him, "I will come and cure him." ⁸ The centurion answered, "Lord, I am not worthy to have you come under my roof, but only speak the word, and my servant will be healed. ⁹ For I also am a man under authority, with soldiers under me, and I say to one, 'Go,' and he goes, and to another, 'Come,' and he comes, and to my slave, 'Do this,' and the slave does it." ¹⁰ When Jesus heard him, he was amazed and said to those who followed him, "Truly I tell you, in no one in Israel have I found such faith. ¹¹ I tell you, many will come from east and west and will take their places at the banquet with Abraham and Isaac and Jacob in the kingdom of heaven, ¹² while the heirs of the kingdom will be thrown into the outer darkness, where there will be weeping and gnashing of teeth." ¹³ And Jesus said to the centurion, "Go; let it be done for you according to your faith." And the servant was healed in that hour.

✤ Jesus Heals Many at Peter's House

¹⁴ When Jesus entered Peter's house, he saw his mother-in-law lying in bed with a fever; ¹⁵ he touched her hand, and the fever

left her, and she got up and began to serve him. **16** That evening they brought to him many who were possessed with demons, and he cast out the spirits with a word and cured all who were sick. **17** This was to fulfill what had been spoken through the prophet Isaiah, "He took our infirmities and bore our diseases."

✢ Would-Be Followers of Jesus

18 Now when Jesus saw great crowds around him, he gave orders to go over to the other side. **19** A scribe then approached and said, "Teacher, I will follow you wherever you go." **20** And Jesus said to him, "Foxes have holes, and birds of the air have nests, but the Son of Man has nowhere to lay his head." **21** Another of his disciples said to him, "Lord, first let me go and bury my father." **22** But Jesus said to him, "Follow me, and let the dead bury their own dead."

✢ Jesus Calms the Storm

23 And when he got into the boat, his disciples followed him. **24** A windstorm suddenly arose on the sea, so great that the boat was being swamped by the waves, but he was asleep. **25** And they went and woke him up, saying, "Lord, save us! We are perishing!" **26** And he said to them, "Why are you afraid, you of little faith?" Then he got up and rebuked the winds and the sea, and there was a dead calm. **27** They were amazed, saying, "What sort of man is this, that even the winds and the sea obey him?"

✢ Jesus Heals Two Men

28 When he came to the other side, to the region of the Gadarenes, two men possessed by demons came out of the tombs and met him. They were so fierce that no one could pass that way. **29** Suddenly they shouted, "What have you to do with us, Son of God? Have you come here to torment us before the time?" **30** Now a large herd of swine was feeding at some distance from them. **31** The demons begged him, "If you cast us out, send us into the herd of swine." **32** And he said to them, "Go!" So they came out and entered the swine; and suddenly, the whole herd stampeded down the steep bank into the sea and drowned in the water. **33** The swineherds ran off, and, going into the town, they told the whole story about what had happened to the men possessed by demons. **34** Then the whole town came out to meet Jesus, and when they saw him they begged him to leave their region.

CHAPTER 9

nd after getting into a boat he crossed the sea and came to his own town.

✤ Jesus Heals a Paralytic

2 And some people were carrying to him a paralyzed man lying on a stretcher. When Jesus saw their faith, he said to the paralytic, "Take heart, child; your sins are forgiven." **3** Then some of the scribes said to themselves, "This man is blaspheming." **4** But Jesus, perceiving their thoughts, said, "Why do you think evil in your hearts? **5** For which is easier: to say, 'Your sins are forgiven,' or to say, 'Stand up and walk'? **6** But so that you may know that the Son of Man has authority on earth to forgive sins"—he then said to the paralytic—"Stand up, take your bed, and go to your home." **7** And he stood up and went to his home. **8** When the crowds saw it, they were filled with awe, and they glorified God, who had given such authority to human beings.

✤ The Call of Matthew

9 As Jesus was walking along, he saw a man called Matthew sitting at the tax-collection station, and he said to him, "Follow me." And he got up and followed him.

10 And as he sat at dinner in the house, many tax collectors and sinners came and were sitting with Jesus and his disciples. **11** When the Pharisees saw this, they said to his disciples, "Why does your teacher eat with tax collectors and sinners?" **12** But when he heard this, he said, "Those who are well have no need of a physician, but those who are sick. **13** Go and learn what this means, 'I desire mercy, not sacrifice.' For I have not come to call the righteous but sinners."

✦ A Question about Fasting

14 Then the disciples of John came to him, saying, "Why do we and the Pharisees fast often, but your disciples do not fast?" **15** And Jesus said to them, "The wedding attendants cannot mourn as long as the bridegroom is with them, can they? The days will come when the bridegroom is taken away from them, and then they will fast. **16** No one sews a piece of unshrunk cloth on an old cloak, for the patch pulls away from the cloak, and a worse tear is made. **17** Neither is new wine put into old wineskins; otherwise, the skins burst, and the wine is spilled, and the skins are ruined, but new wine is put into fresh wineskins, and so both are preserved."

✦ A Girl Restored to Life and a Woman Healed

18 While he was saying these things to them, suddenly a leader came in and knelt before him, saying, "My daughter has just died, but come and lay your hand on her, and she will live." **19** And Jesus got up and followed him, with his disciples. **20** Then suddenly a woman who had been suffering from a flow of blood for twelve years came up behind him and touched the fringe of his cloak, **21** for she was saying to herself, "If I only touch his cloak, I will be made well." **22** Jesus turned, and seeing her he said, "Take heart, daughter; your faith has made you well." And the woman was made well from that moment. **23** When Jesus came to the leader's house and saw the flute players and the crowd making a commotion, **24** he said, "Go away; for the girl is not dead but sleeping." And they laughed at him. **25** But when the crowd had been put outside, he went in and took her by the hand, and the girl got up. **26** And the report of this spread through all of that district.

✦ Jesus Heals Two Blind Men

27 As Jesus went on from there, two blind men followed him, crying loudly, "Have mercy on us, Son of David!" **28** When he entered the house, the blind men came to him, and Jesus said to them, "Do you have faith that I can do this?" They said to him, "Yes, Lord." ²⁹ Then he touched their eyes and said, "According to your faith, let it be done to you." ³⁰ And their eyes were opened. Then Jesus sternly ordered them, "See that no one knows of this." ³¹ But they went away and spread the news about him through all of that district.

✢ Jesus Heals One Who Was Mute

³² After they had gone away, a demon-possessed man who was mute was brought to him. ³³ And when the demon had been cast out, the one who had been mute spoke, and the crowds were amazed and said, "Never has anything like this been seen in Israel." ³⁴ But the Pharisees were saying, "By the ruler of the demons he casts out the demons."

✢ The Harvest Is Plentiful, the Laborers Few

³⁵ Then Jesus went about all the cities and villages, teaching in their synagogues and proclaiming the good news of the kingdom and curing every disease and every sickness. ³⁶ When he saw the crowds, he had compassion for them because they were harassed and helpless, like sheep without a shepherd. ³⁷ Then he said to his disciples, "The harvest is plentiful, but the laborers are few; ³⁸ therefore ask the Lord of the harvest to send out laborers into his harvest."

CHAPTER 10

✢ The Twelve Apostles

hen Jesus summoned his twelve disciples and gave them authority over unclean spirits, to cast them out, and to cure every disease and every sickness. ² These are the names of the twelve apostles: first, Simon, also known as Peter, and his brother Andrew; James son of Zebedee and his brother John; ³ Philip and Bartholomew; Thomas and Matthew the tax collector; James son of Alphaeus, and Thaddaeus; **⁴** Simon the Cananaean, and Judas Iscariot, the one who betrayed him.

✤ The Mission of the Twelve

⁵ These twelve Jesus sent out with the following instructions: "Do not take a road leading to gentiles, and do not enter a Samaritan town, **⁶** but go rather to the lost sheep of the house of Israel. **⁷** As you go, proclaim the good news, 'The kingdom of heaven has come near.' **⁸** Cure the sick; raise the dead; cleanse those with a skin disease; cast out demons. You received without payment; give without payment. **⁹** Take no gold, or silver, or copper in your belts, **¹⁰** no bag for your journey, or two tunics, or sandals, or a staff, for laborers deserve their food. **¹¹** Whatever town or village you enter, find out who in it is worthy, and stay there until you leave. **¹²** As you enter the house, greet it. **¹³** If the house is worthy, let your peace come upon it, but if it is not worthy, let your peace return to you. **¹⁴** If anyone will not welcome you or listen to your words, shake off the dust from your feet as you leave that house or town. **¹⁵** Truly I tell you, it will be more tolerable for the land of Sodom and Gomorrah on the day of judgment than for that town.

✤ The Sending Out

¹⁶ "I am sending you out like sheep into the midst of wolves, so be wise as serpents and innocent as doves. **¹⁷** Beware of them, for they will hand you over to councils and flog you in their synagogues, **¹⁸** and you will be dragged before governors and kings because of me, as a testimony to them and the gentiles. **¹⁹** When they hand you over, do not worry about how you are to speak or what you are to say, for what you are to say will be given to you at that time, **²⁰** for it is not you who speak, but the Spirit of your Father speaking through you. **²¹** Sibling will betray sibling to death and a father his child, and children will rise against parents and have them put to death, **²²** and you will be hated by all because of my name. But the one who endures to the end will be saved. **²³** When they persecute you in this town, flee to the next, for truly I tell you,

you will not have finished going through all the towns of Israel before the Son of Man comes.

24 "A disciple is not above the teacher nor a slave above the master; 25 it is enough for the disciple to be like the teacher and the slave like the master. If they have called the master of the house Beelzebul, how much more will they malign those of his household!

✣ Do Not Be Afraid

26 "So have no fear of them, for nothing is covered up that will not be uncovered and nothing secret that will not become known. 27 What I say to you in the dark, tell in the light, and what you hear whispered, proclaim from the housetops. 28 Do not fear those who kill the body but cannot kill the soul; rather fear the one who can destroy both soul and body in hell. 29 Are not two sparrows sold for a penny? Yet not one of them will fall to the ground apart from your Father. 30 And even the hairs of your head are all counted. 31 So do not be afraid; you are of more value than many sparrows.

32 "Everyone, therefore, who acknowledges me before others, I also will acknowledge before my Father in heaven, 33 but whoever denies me before others, I also will deny before my Father in heaven.

✣ Not Peace but a Sword

34 "Do not think that I have come to bring peace to the earth; I have not come to bring peace but a sword.

> 35 For I have come to set a man against his father,
> and a daughter against her mother,
> and a daughter-in-law against her mother-in-law;
> 36 and one's foes will be members of one's own household.

37 Whoever loves father or mother more than me is not worthy of me, and whoever loves son or daughter more than me is not worthy of me, 38 and whoever does not take up the cross and follow me is not worthy of me. 39 Those who find their life will lose it, and those who lose their life for my sake will find it.

✤ A Cup of Cold Water

40 "Whoever welcomes you welcomes me, and whoever welcomes me welcomes the one who sent me. **41** Whoever welcomes a prophet in the name of a prophet will receive a prophet's reward, and whoever welcomes a righteous person in the name of a righteous person will receive the reward of the righteous, **42** and whoever gives even a cup of cold water to one of these little ones in the name of a disciple—truly I tell you, none of these will lose their reward."

CHAPTER 11

ow when Jesus had finished instructing his twelve disciples, he went on from there to teach and proclaim his message in their cities.

✤ Messengers from John the Baptist

2 When John heard in prison what the Messiah was doing, he sent word by his disciples **3** and said to him, "Are you the one who is to come, or are we to wait for another?" **4** Jesus answered them, "Go and tell John what you hear and see: **5** the blind receive their sight, the lame walk, those with a skin disease are cleansed, the deaf hear, the dead are raised, and the poor have good news brought to them. **6** And blessed is anyone who takes no offense at me."

✤ Jesus Praises John the Baptist

7 As they went away, Jesus began to speak to the crowds about John: "What did you go out into the wilderness to look at? A reed shaken by the wind? **8** What, then, did you go out to see? Someone dressed in soft robes? Look, those who wear soft robes are in royal palaces. **9** What, then, did you go out to see? A prophet? Yes, I tell you, and more than a prophet. **10** This is the one about whom it is written,

'See, I am sending my messenger ahead of you,
    who will prepare your way before you.'

[11] "Truly I tell you, among those born of women no one has arisen greater than John the Baptist, yet the least in the kingdom of heaven is greater than he. [12] From the days of John the Baptist until now, the kingdom of heaven has suffered violence, and violent people take it by force. [13] For all the Prophets and the Law prophesied until John came, [14] and if you are willing to accept it, he is Elijah who is to come. [15] Let anyone with ears listen!

[16] "But to what will I compare this generation? It is like children sitting in the marketplaces and calling to one another,

[17] 'We played the flute for you, and you did not dance;
we wailed, and you did not mourn.'

[18] For John came neither eating nor drinking, and they say, 'He has a demon'; [19] the Son of Man came eating and drinking, and they say, 'Look, a glutton and a drunkard, a friend of tax collectors and sinners!' Yet wisdom is vindicated by her deeds."

✤ Woes to Unrepentant Cities

[20] Then he began to reproach the cities in which most of his deeds of power had been done because they did not repent. [21] "Woe to you, Chorazin! Woe to you, Bethsaida! For if the deeds of power done in you had been done in Tyre and Sidon, they would have repented long ago in sackcloth and ashes. [22] But I tell you, on the day of judgment it will be more tolerable for Tyre and Sidon than for you. [23] And you, Capernaum,

will you be exalted to heaven?
No, you will be brought down to Hades.

"For if the deeds of power done in you had been done in Sodom, it would have remained until this day. [24] But I tell you that on the day of judgment it will be more tolerable for the land of Sodom than for you."

✤ Jesus Thanks His Father

[25] At that time Jesus said, "I thank you, Father, Lord of heaven and earth, because you have hidden these things from the wise

and the intelligent and have revealed them to infants; ²⁶ yes, Father, for such was your gracious will. ²⁷ All things have been handed over to me by my Father, and no one knows the Son except the Father, and no one knows the Father except the Son and anyone to whom the Son chooses to reveal him.

²⁸ "Come to me, all you who are weary and are carrying heavy burdens, and I will give you rest. ²⁹ Take my yoke upon you, and learn from me, for I am gentle and humble in heart, and you will find rest for your souls. ³⁰ For my yoke is easy, and my burden is light."

CHAPTER 12

✢ The Lord of the Sabbath

 **t that time Jesus** went through the grain fields on the Sabbath; his disciples were hungry, and they began to pluck heads of grain and to eat. ² When the Pharisees saw it, they said to him, "Look, your disciples are doing what is not lawful to do on the Sabbath." ³ He said to them, "Have you not read what David did when he and his companions were hungry? ⁴ How he entered the house of God, and ate the bread of the Presence, which it was not lawful for him or his companions to eat, but only for the priests? ⁵ Or have you not read in the law that on the Sabbath the priests in the temple break the Sabbath and yet are guiltless? ⁶ I tell you, something greater than the temple is here. ⁷ But if you had known what this means, 'I desire mercy and not sacrifice,' you would not have condemned the guiltless. ⁸ For the Son of Man is lord of the Sabbath."

✢ Jesus Heals The Man with a Withered Hand

⁹ He left that place and entered their synagogue; ¹⁰ a man was there with a withered hand, and they asked him, "Is it lawful to cure on the Sabbath?" so that they might accuse him. ¹¹ He said to them, "Suppose one of you has only one sheep and it falls into a pit on the Sabbath; will you not lay hold of it and lift it out?

¹² How much more valuable is a human being than a sheep! So it is lawful to do good on the Sabbath." ¹³ Then he said to the man, "Stretch out your hand." He stretched it out, and it was restored, as sound as the other. ¹⁴ But the Pharisees went out and conspired against him, how to destroy him.

✤ God's Beloved Servant

¹⁵ When Jesus became aware of this, he departed. Many followed him, and he cured all of them, ¹⁶ and he ordered them not to make him known. ¹⁷ This was to fulfill what had been spoken through the prophet Isaiah:

> ¹⁸ "Here is my servant, whom I have chosen,
>   my beloved, with whom my soul is well pleased.
> I will put my Spirit upon him,
>   and he will proclaim justice to the gentiles.
> ¹⁹ He will not wrangle or cry aloud,
>   nor will anyone hear his voice in the streets.
> ²⁰ He will not break a bruised reed
>   or quench a smoldering wick
> until he brings justice to victory.
>   ²¹ And in his name the gentiles will hope."

✤ The Kingdom of God Has Come

²² Then they brought to him a demon-possessed man who was blind and mute, and he cured him, so that the one who had been mute could speak and see. ²³ All the crowds were amazed and were saying, "Can this be the Son of David?" ²⁴ But when the Pharisees heard it, they said, "It is only by Beelzebul, the ruler of the demons, that this man casts out the demons." ²⁵ He knew what they were thinking and said to them, "Every kingdom divided against itself is laid waste, and no city or house divided against itself will stand. ²⁶ If Satan casts out Satan, he is divided against himself; how then will his kingdom stand? ²⁷ If I cast out demons by Beelzebul, by whom do your own exorcists cast them out? Therefore they will be your judges. ²⁸ But if it is by the Spirit of

God that I cast out demons, then the kingdom of God has come upon you. ²⁹ Or how can one enter a strong man's house and plunder his property without first tying up the strong man? Then indeed the house can be plundered. ³⁰ Whoever is not with me is against me, and whoever does not gather with me scatters. ³¹ Therefore I tell you, people will be forgiven for every sin and blasphemy, but blasphemy against the Spirit will not be forgiven. ³² Whoever speaks a word against the Son of Man will be forgiven, but whoever speaks against the Holy Spirit will not be forgiven, either in this age or in the age to come.

✤ A Tree and Its Fruit

³³ "Either make the tree good, and its fruit good, or make the tree bad, and its fruit bad, for the tree is known by its fruit. ³⁴ You brood of vipers! How can you speak good things when you are evil? For out of the abundance of the heart the mouth speaks. ³⁵ The good person brings good things out of a good treasure, and the evil person brings evil things out of an evil treasure. ³⁶ I tell you, on the day of judgment you will have to give an account for every careless word you utter, ³⁷ for by your words you will be justified, and by your words you will be condemned."

✤ The Sign of Jonah

³⁸ Then some of the scribes and Pharisees said to him, "Teacher, we wish to see a sign from you." ³⁹ But he answered them, "An evil and adulterous generation asks for a sign, but no sign will be given to it except the sign of the prophet Jonah. ⁴⁰ For just as Jonah was three days and three nights in the belly of the sea monster, so for three days and three nights the Son of Man will be in the heart of the earth. ⁴¹ The people of Nineveh will rise up at the judgment with this generation and condemn it, because they repented at the proclamation of Jonah, and indeed something greater than Jonah is here! ⁴² The queen of the South will rise up at the judgment with this generation and condemn it, because she came from the ends of the earth to listen to the wisdom of Solomon, and indeed something greater than Solomon is here!

✤ The Return of the Unclean Spirit

43 "When the unclean spirit has gone out of a person, it wanders through waterless regions looking for a resting place, but it finds none. **44** Then it says, 'I will return to my house from which I came.' When it returns, it finds it empty, swept, and put in order. **45** Then it goes and brings along seven other spirits more evil than itself, and they enter and live there; and the last state of that person is worse than the first. So will it be also with this evil generation."

✤ The True Family of Jesus

46 While he was still speaking to the crowds, his mother and his brothers were standing outside, wanting to speak to him. **47** Someone told him, "Look, your mother and your brothers are standing outside, wanting to speak to you." **48** But to the one who had told him this, Jesus replied, "Who is my mother, and who are my brothers?" **49** And pointing to his disciples, he said, "Here are my mother and my brothers! **50** For whoever does the will of my Father in heaven is my brother and sister and mother."

CHAPTER 13

✤ The Parable of the Sower

That same day Jesus went out of the house and sat beside the sea. **2** Such great crowds gathered around him that he got into a boat and sat there, while the whole crowd stood on the beach. **3** And he told them many things in parables, saying: "Listen! A sower went out to sow. **4** And as he sowed, some seeds fell on a path, and the birds came and ate them up. **5** Other seeds fell on rocky ground, where they did not have much soil, and they sprang up quickly, since they had no depth of soil. **6** But when the sun rose, they were scorched, and since they had no root, they withered away. **7** Other seeds fell among thorns, and the thorns grew up and choked them. **8** Other seeds fell on good soil and brought forth grain, some a hundredfold, some sixty, some thirty. **9** If you have ears, hear!"

✤ The Purpose of the Parables

10 Then the disciples came and asked him, "Why do you speak to them in parables?" **11** He answered, "To you it has been given to know the secrets of the kingdom of heaven, but to them it has not been given. **12** For to those who have, more will be given, and they will have an abundance, but from those who have nothing, even what they have will be taken away. **13** The reason I speak to them in parables is that 'seeing they do not perceive, and hearing they do not listen, nor do they understand.' **14** With them indeed is fulfilled the prophecy of Isaiah that says:

> 'You will indeed listen but never understand,
>   and you will indeed look but never perceive.
> **15** For this people's heart has grown dull,
>   and their ears are hard of hearing,
>   and they have shut their eyes,
>   so that they might not look with their eyes,
>   and hear with their ears
> and understand with their heart and turn—
>   and I would heal them.'

16 "But blessed are your eyes, for they see, and your ears, for they hear. **17** Truly I tell you, many prophets and righteous people longed to see what you see but did not see it and to hear what you hear but did not hear it.

✤ The Parable of the Sower Revisited

18 "Hear, then, the parable of the sower. **19** When anyone hears the word of the kingdom and does not understand it, the evil one comes and snatches away what is sown in the heart; this is what was sown on the path. **20** As for what was sown on rocky ground, this is the one who hears the word and immediately receives it with joy, **21** yet such a person has no root but endures only for a while, and when trouble or persecution arises on account of the word, that person immediately falls away. **22** As for what was sown among thorns, this is the one who hears the word, but the cares of this age and the lure of wealth choke the word, and it yields nothing. ²³ But as for what was sown on good soil, this is the one who hears the word and understands it, who indeed bears fruit and yields in one case a hundredfold, in another sixty, and in another thirty."

✦ The Parable of Weeds among the Wheat

²⁴ He put before them another parable: "The kingdom of heaven may be compared to someone who sowed good seed in his field, ²⁵ but while everybody was asleep an enemy came and sowed weeds among the wheat and then went away. ²⁶ So when the plants came up and bore grain, then the weeds appeared as well. ²⁷ And the slaves of the householder came and said to him, 'Master, did you not sow good seed in your field? Where, then, did these weeds come from?' ²⁸ He answered, 'An enemy has done this.' The slaves said to him, 'Then do you want us to go and gather them?' ²⁹ But he replied, 'No, for in gathering the weeds you would uproot the wheat along with them. ³⁰ Let both of them grow together until the harvest, and at harvest time I will tell the reapers, Collect the weeds first and bind them in bundles to be burned, but gather the wheat into my barn.'"

✦ The Parable of the Mustard Seed

³¹ He put before them another parable: "The kingdom of heaven is like a mustard seed that someone took and sowed in his field; ³² it is the smallest of all the seeds, but when it has grown it is the greatest of shrubs and becomes a tree, so that the birds of the air come and make nests in its branches."

✦ The Parable of the Yeast

³³ He told them another parable: "The kingdom of heaven is like yeast that a woman took and mixed in with three measures of flour until all of it was leavened."

✥ The Use of Parables

34 Jesus told the crowds all these things in parables; without a parable he told them nothing. **35** This was to fulfill what had been spoken through the prophet:

> "'I will open my mouth to speak in parables;
> I will proclaim what has been hidden since
> the foundation."

✥ The Parable of the Weeds Revisited

36 Then he left the crowds and went into the house. And his disciples approached him, saying, "Explain to us the parable of the weeds of the field." **37** He answered, "The one who sows the good seed is the Son of Man; **38** the field is the world, and the good seed are the children of the kingdom; the weeds are the children of the evil one, **39** and the enemy who sowed them is the devil; the harvest is the end of the age, and the reapers are angels. **40** Just as the weeds are collected and burned up with fire, so will it be at the end of the age. **41** The Son of Man will send his angels, and they will collect out of his kingdom all causes of sin and all evildoers, **42** and they will throw them into the furnace of fire, where there will be weeping and gnashing of teeth. **43** Then the righteous will shine like the sun in the kingdom of their Father. Let anyone with ears listen!

✥ The Hidden Treasure, the Precious Pearl, and the Great Net

44 "The kingdom of heaven is like treasure hidden in a field, which a man found and reburied; then in his joy he goes and sells all that he has and buys that field.

45 "Again, the kingdom of heaven is like a merchant in search of fine pearls; **46** on finding one pearl of great value, he went and sold all that he had and bought it.

47 "Again, the kingdom of heaven is like a net that was thrown into the sea and caught fish of every kind; **48** when it was full, they drew it ashore, sat down, and put the good into baskets but threw out the bad. ⁴⁹ So it will be at the end of the age. The angels will come out and separate the evil from the righteous ⁵⁰ and throw them into the furnace of fire, where there will be weeping and gnashing of teeth.

✤ Treasures New and Old

⁵¹ "Have you understood all this?" They answered, "Yes." ⁵² And he said to them, "Therefore every scribe who has become a disciple in the kingdom of heaven is like the master of a household who brings out of his treasure what is new and what is old." ⁵³ When Jesus had finished these parables, he left that place.

✤ The Rejection of Jesus at Nazareth

⁵⁴ He came to his hometown and began to teach the people in their synagogue, so that they were astounded and said, "Where did this man get this wisdom and these deeds of power? ⁵⁵ Is not this the carpenter's son? Is not his mother called Mary? And are not his brothers James and Joseph and Simon and Judas? ⁵⁶ And are not all his sisters with us? Where then did this man get all this?" ⁵⁷ And they took offense at him. But Jesus said to them, "Prophets are not without honor except in their own hometown and in their own house." ⁵⁸ And he did not do many deeds of power there, because of their unbelief.

CHAPTER 14

✤ The Death of John the Baptist

 **t that time Herod the ruler** heard reports about Jesus, ² and he said to his servants, "This is John the Baptist; he has been raised from the dead, and for this reason these powers are at work in him." ³ For Herod had arrested John, bound him, and put him in prison on account of Herodias, his brother Philip's wife, ⁴ because John had been telling him, "It is not lawful for you to have her." ⁵ Though Herod wanted to put him to death, he feared the crowd,

because they regarded him as a prophet. **6** But when Herod's birthday came, the daughter of Herodias danced before the company, and she pleased Herod **7** so much that he promised on oath to grant her whatever she might ask. **8** Prompted by her mother, she said, "Give me the head of John the Baptist here on a platter." **9** The king was grieved, yet out of regard for his oaths and for the guests, he commanded it to be given; **10** he sent and had John beheaded in the prison. **11** His head was brought on a platter and given to the girl, who brought it to her mother. **12** His disciples came and took the body and buried him; then they went and told Jesus.

✣ Jesus Feeds the Five Thousand

13 Now when Jesus heard this, he withdrew from there in a boat to a deserted place by himself. But when the crowds heard it, they followed him on foot from the towns. **14** When he went ashore, he saw a great crowd, and he had compassion for them and cured their sick. **15** When it was evening, the disciples came to him and said, "This is a deserted place, and the hour is now late; send the crowds away so that they may go into the villages and buy food for themselves." **16** Jesus said to them, "They need not go away; you give them something to eat." **17** They replied, "We have nothing here but five loaves and two fish." **18** And he said, "Bring them here to me." **19** Then he ordered the crowds to sit down on the grass. Taking the five loaves and the two fish, he looked up to heaven and blessed and broke the loaves and gave them to the disciples, and the disciples gave them to the crowds. **20** And all ate and were filled, and they took up what was left over of the broken pieces, twelve baskets full. **21** And those who ate were about five thousand men, besides women and children.

✣ Jesus Walks on the Water

22 Immediately he made the disciples get into the boat and go on ahead to the other side, while he dismissed the crowds. **23** And after he had dismissed the crowds, he went up the mountain by himself to pray. When evening came, he was there alone, **24** but by this time the boat, battered by the waves, was far from the land, for the wind was against them. ²⁵ And early in the morning he came walking toward them on the sea. ²⁶ But when the disciples saw him walking on the sea, they were terrified, saying, "It is a ghost!" And they cried out in fear. ²⁷ But immediately Jesus spoke to them and said, "Take heart, it is I; do not be afraid."

²⁸ Peter answered him, "Lord, if it is you, command me to come to you on the water." ²⁹ He said, "Come." So Peter got out of the boat, started walking on the water, and came toward Jesus. ³⁰ But when he noticed the strong wind, he became frightened, and beginning to sink, he cried out, "Lord, save me!" ³¹ Jesus immediately reached out his hand and caught him, saying to him, "You of little faith, why did you doubt?" ³² When they got into the boat, the wind ceased. ³³ And those in the boat worshiped him, saying, "Truly you are the Son of God."

✧ Jesus Heals the Sick in Gennesaret

³⁴ When they had crossed over, they came to land at Gennesaret. ³⁵ After the people of that place recognized him, they sent word to that whole surrounding region, and people brought all who were sick to him ³⁶ and begged him that they might touch even the fringe of his cloak, and all who touched it were healed.

CHAPTER 15

✧ The Tradition of the Elders

 **hen Pharisees and scribes** came to Jesus from Jerusalem and said, ² "Why do your disciples break the tradition of the elders? For they do not wash their hands before they eat." ³ He answered them, "And why do you break the commandment of God for the sake of your tradition? ⁴ For God said, 'Honor your father and your mother,' and, 'Whoever speaks evil of father or mother must surely die.' ⁵ But you say that whoever tells father or mother, 'Whatever support you might have had from me is given to God,' then that

person need not honor the father. ⁶ So, for the sake of your tradition, you nullify the word of God. ⁷ You hypocrites! Isaiah prophesied rightly about you when he said:

⁸ 'This people honors me with their lips,
     but their hearts are far from me;
⁹ in vain do they worship me,
     teaching human precepts as doctrines.'"

✣ Things That Defile

¹⁰ Then he called the crowd to him and said to them, "Listen and understand: ¹¹ it is not what goes into the mouth that defiles a person, but it is what comes out of the mouth that defiles." ¹² Then the disciples approached and said to him, "Do you know that the Pharisees took offense when they heard what you said?" ¹³ He answered, "Every plant that my heavenly Father has not planted will be uprooted. ¹⁴ Let them alone; they are blind guides of the blind. And if one blind person guides another, both will fall into a pit." ¹⁵ But Peter said to him, "Explain this parable to us." ¹⁶ Then he said, "Are you also still without understanding? ¹⁷ Do you not see that whatever goes into the mouth enters the stomach, and goes out into the sewer? ¹⁸ But what comes out of the mouth proceeds from the heart, and this is what defiles. ¹⁹ For out of the heart come evil intentions, murder, adultery, sexual immorality, theft, false witness, slander. ²⁰ These are what defile a person, but to eat with unwashed hands does not defile."

✣ The Canaanite Woman's Faith

²¹ Jesus left that place and went away to the district of Tyre and Sidon. ²² Just then a Canaanite woman from that region came out and started shouting, "Have mercy on me, Lord, Son of David; my daughter is tormented by a demon." ²³ But he did not answer her at all. And his disciples came and urged him, saying, "Send her away, for she keeps shouting after us." ²⁴ He answered, "I was sent only to the lost sheep of the house of Israel." ²⁵ But she came and knelt before him, saying, "Lord, help me." ²⁶ He answered,

"It is not fair to take the children's food and throw it to the dogs."
27 She said, "Yes, Lord, yet even the dogs eat the crumbs that fall from their masters' table." 28 Then Jesus answered her, "Woman, great is your faith! Let it be done for you as you wish." And her daughter was healed from that moment.

✤ Jesus Cures Many People

29 After Jesus had left that place, he passed along the Sea of Galilee, and he went up the mountain, where he sat down. 30 Great crowds came to him, bringing with them the lame, the blind, the maimed, the mute, and many others. They put them at his feet, and he cured them, 31 so that the crowd was amazed when they saw the mute speaking, the maimed whole, the lame walking, and the blind seeing. And they praised the God of Israel.

✤ Jesus Feeds the Four Thousand

32 Then Jesus called his disciples to him and said, "I have compassion for the crowd because they have been with me now for three days and have nothing to eat, and I do not want to send them away hungry, for they might faint on the way." 33 The disciples said to him, "Where are we to get enough bread in the desert to feed so great a crowd?" 34 Jesus asked them, "How many loaves have you?" They said, "Seven, and a few small fish." 35 Then ordering the crowd to sit down on the ground, 36 he took the seven loaves and the fish, and after giving thanks he broke them and gave them to the disciples, and the disciples gave them to the crowds. 37 And all of them ate and were filled, and they took up the broken pieces left over, seven baskets full. 38 Those who had eaten were four thousand men, besides women and children. 39 After sending away the crowds, he got into the boat and went to the region of Magadan.

CHAPTER 16

✣ The Demand for a Sign

he Pharisees and Sadducees came, and to test Jesus they asked him to show them a sign from heaven. [2] He answered them, "When it is evening, you say, 'It will be fair weather, for the sky is red.' [3] And in the morning, 'It will be stormy today, for the sky is red and threatening.' You know how to interpret the appearance of the sky, but you cannot interpret the signs of the times. [4] An evil and adulterous generation asks for a sign, but no sign will be given to it except the sign of Jonah." Then he left them and went away.

✣ The Yeast of the Pharisees and Sadducees

[5] When the disciples reached the other side, they had forgotten to bring any bread. [6] Jesus said to them, "Watch out, and beware of the yeast of the Pharisees and Sadducees." [7] They said to one another, "It is because we have brought no bread." [8] And becoming aware of it, Jesus said, "You of little faith, why are you talking about having no bread? [9] Do you still not perceive? Do you not remember the five loaves for the five thousand and how many baskets you gathered? [10] Or the seven loaves for the four thousand and how many baskets you gathered? [11] How could you fail to perceive that I was not speaking about bread? Beware of the yeast of the Pharisees and Sadducees!" [12] Then they understood that he had not told them to beware of the yeast of bread, but of the teaching of the Pharisees and Sadducees.

✣ Peter's Declaration about Jesus

[13] Now when Jesus came into the district of Caesarea Philippi, he asked his disciples, "Who do people say that the Son of Man is?" [14] And they said, "Some say John the Baptist but others Elijah and still others Jeremiah or one of the prophets." [15] He said to them, "But who do you say that I am?" [16] Simon Peter answered, "You are the Messiah, the Son of the living God." [17] And Jesus

answered him, "Blessed are you, Simon son of Jonah! For flesh and blood has not revealed this to you but my Father in heaven. [18] And I tell you, you are Peter, and on this rock I will build my church, and the gates of Hades will not prevail against it. [19] I will give you the keys of the kingdom of heaven, and whatever you bind on earth will be bound in heaven, and whatever you loose on earth will be loosed in heaven." [20] Then he sternly ordered the disciples not to tell anyone that he was the Messiah.

✤ Jesus Foretells His Death and Resurrection

[21] From that time on, Jesus began to show his disciples that he must go to Jerusalem and undergo great suffering at the hands of the elders and chief priests and scribes and be killed and on the third day be raised. [22] And Peter took him aside and began to rebuke him, saying, "God forbid it, Lord! This must never happen to you." [23] But he turned and said to Peter, "Get behind me, Satan! You are a hindrance to me; for you are setting your mind not on divine things but on human things."

✤ Follow Me

[24] Then Jesus told his disciples, "If any wish to come after me, let them deny themselves and take up their cross and follow me. [25] For those who want to save their life will lose it, and those who lose their life for my sake will find it. [26] For what will it profit them if they gain the whole world but forfeit their life? Or what will they give in return for their life?

[27] "For the Son of Man is to come with his angels in the glory of his Father, and then he will repay everyone for what has been done. [28] Truly I tell you, there are some standing here who will not taste death before they see the Son of Man coming in his kingdom."

CHAPTER 17

✦ The Transfiguration

**ix days later**, **Jesus** took with him Peter and James and his brother John and led them up a high mountain, by themselves. ² And he was transfigured before them, and his face shone like the sun, and his clothes became as bright as light. ³ Suddenly there appeared to them Moses and Elijah, talking with him. ⁴ Then Peter said to Jesus, "Lord, it is good for us to be here; if you wish, I will set up three tents here, one for you, one for Moses, and one for Elijah." ⁵ While he was still speaking, suddenly a bright cloud overshadowed them, and a voice from the cloud said, "This is my Son, the Beloved; with him I am well pleased; listen to him!" ⁶ When the disciples heard this, they fell to the ground and were overcome by fear. ⁷ But Jesus came and touched them, saying, "Get up and do not be afraid." ⁸ And when they raised their eyes, they saw no one except Jesus himself alone.

⁹ As they were coming down the mountain, Jesus ordered them, "Tell no one about the vision until after the Son of Man has been raised from the dead." ¹⁰ And the disciples asked him, "Why, then, do the scribes say that Elijah must come first?" ¹¹ He replied, "Elijah is indeed coming and will restore all things, ¹² but I tell you that Elijah has already come, and they did not recognize him, but they did to him whatever they pleased. So also the Son of Man is about to suffer at their hands." ¹³ Then the disciples understood that he was speaking to them about John the Baptist.

✦ Jesus Heals a Boy

¹⁴ When they came to the crowd, a man came to him, knelt before him, ¹⁵ and said, "Lord, have mercy on my son, for he has epilepsy and suffers terribly; he often falls into the fire and often into the water. ¹⁶ And I brought him to your disciples, but they could not cure him." ¹⁷ Jesus answered, "You faithless and perverse generation,

how much longer must I be with you? How much longer must I put up with you? Bring him here to me." **18** And Jesus rebuked the demon, and it came out of him, and the boy was cured from that moment. **19** Then the disciples came to Jesus privately and said, "Why could we not cast it out?" **20** He said to them, "Because of your little faith. For truly I tell you, if you have faith the size of a mustard seed, you will say to this mountain, 'Move from here to there,' and it will move, and nothing will be impossible for you."

✢ Jesus Again Foretells His Death and Resurrection

22 As they were gathering in Galilee, Jesus said to them, "The Son of Man is going to be betrayed into human hands, **23** and they will kill him, and on the third day he will be raised." And they were greatly distressed.

✢ Jesus and the Temple Tax

24 When they reached Capernaum, the collectors of the temple tax came to Peter and said, "Does your teacher not pay the temple tax?" **25** He said, "Yes, he does." And when he came home, Jesus spoke of it first, asking, "What do you think, Simon? From whom do kings of the earth take toll or tribute? From their children or from others?" **26** When Peter said, "From others," Jesus said to him, "Then the children are free. **27** However, so that we do not give offense to them, go to the sea and cast a hook; take the first fish that comes up, and when you open its mouth, you will find a coin; take that and give it to them for you and me."

CHAPTER **18**

✤ The Greatest in the Kingdom

**t that time the disciples** came to Jesus and asked, "Who is the greatest in the kingdom of heaven?" ² He called a child, whom he put among them, ³ and said, "Truly I tell you, unless you change and become like children, you will never enter the kingdom of heaven. ⁴ Whoever becomes humble like this child is the greatest in the kingdom of heaven. ⁵ Whoever welcomes one such child in my name welcomes me.

✤ Temptations to Sin

⁶ "If any of you cause one of these little ones who believe in me to sin, it would be better for you if a great millstone were fastened around your neck and you were drowned in the depth of the sea. ⁷ Woe to the world because of things that cause sin! Such things are bound to come, but woe to the one through whom they come!

⁸ "If your hand or your foot causes you to sin, cut it off and throw it away; it is better for you to enter life maimed or lame than to have two hands or two feet and to be thrown into the eternal fire. ⁹ And if your eye causes you to sin, tear it out and throw it away; it is better for you to enter life with one eye than to have two eyes and to be thrown into the hell of fire.

✤ The Parable of the Found Sheep

¹⁰ "Take care that you do not despise one of these little ones, for I tell you, in heaven their angels continually see the face of my Father in heaven. ¹² What do you think? If a shepherd has a hundred sheep, and one of them has gone astray, does he not leave the ninety-nine on the mountains and go in search of the one that went astray? ¹³ And if he finds it, truly I tell you, he rejoices over it more than over the ninety-nine that never went astray. ¹⁴ So it is not the will of your Father in heaven that one of these little ones should be lost.

✦ Caring for One Who Sins

15 "If another brother or sister sins against you, go and point out the fault when the two of you are alone. If you are listened to, you have regained that one. **16** But if you are not listened to, take one or two others along with you, so that every word may be confirmed by the evidence of two or three witnesses. **17** If that person refuses to listen to them, tell it to the church, and if the offender refuses to listen even to the church, let such a one be to you as a gentile and a tax collector. **18** Truly I tell you, whatever you bind on earth will be bound in heaven, and whatever you loose on earth will be loosed in heaven. **19** Again, truly I tell you, if two of you agree on earth about anything you ask, it will be done for you by my Father in heaven. **20** For where two or three are gathered in my name, I am there among them."

✦ Forgiveness Seventy-Seven Times

21 Then Peter came and said to him, "Lord, if my brother or sister sins against me, how often should I forgive? As many as seven times?" **22** Jesus said to him, "Not seven times, but, I tell you, seventy-seven times.

✦ The Parable of the Debtors

23 "For this reason the kingdom of heaven may be compared to a king who wished to settle accounts with his slaves. **24** When he began the reckoning, one who owed him ten thousand talents was brought to him, **25** and, as he could not pay, the lord ordered him to be sold, together with his wife and children and all his possessions and payment to be made. **26** So the slave fell on his knees before him, saying, 'Have patience with me, and I will pay you everything.' **27** And out of pity for him, the lord of that slave released him and forgave him the debt. **28** But that same slave, as he went out, came upon one of his fellow slaves who owed him a hundred denarii; and seizing him by the throat he said, 'Pay what you owe.' **29** Then his fellow slave fell down and pleaded with him, 'Have patience with me, and I will pay you.' **30** But he refused; then he went and threw him into prison until he would pay the debt. ³¹ When his fellow slaves saw what had happened, they were greatly distressed, and they went and reported to their lord all that had taken place. ³² Then his lord summoned him and said to him, 'You wicked slave! I forgave you all that debt because you pleaded with me. ³³ Should you not have had mercy on your fellow slave, as I had mercy on you?' ³⁴ And in anger his lord handed him over to be tortured until he would pay his entire debt. ³⁵ So my heavenly Father will also do to every one of you, if you do not forgive your brother or sister from your heart."

CHAPTER 19

✦ Teaching about Divorce

hen Jesus had finished saying these things, he left Galilee and went to the region of Judea beyond the Jordan. ² Large crowds followed him, and he cured them there.

³ Some Pharisees came to him, and to test him they asked, "Is it lawful for a man to divorce his wife for any cause?" ⁴ He answered, "Have you not read that the one who made them at the beginning 'made them male and female,' ⁵ and said, 'For this reason a man shall leave his father and mother and be joined to his wife, and the two shall become one flesh'? ⁶ So they are no longer two but one flesh. Therefore what God has joined together, let no one separate." ⁷ They said to him, "Why then did Moses command us to give a certificate of dismissal and to divorce her?" ⁸ He said to them, "It was because you were so hard-hearted that Moses allowed you to divorce your wives, but from the beginning it was not so. ⁹ And I say to you, whoever divorces his wife, except for sexual immorality, and marries another commits adultery, and he who marries a divorced woman commits adultery."

¹⁰ The disciples said to him, "If such is the case of a man with his wife, it is better not to marry." ¹¹ But he said to them, "Not everyone

can accept this teaching, but only those to whom it is given. 12 For there are eunuchs who have been so from birth, and there are eunuchs who have been made eunuchs by others, and there are eunuchs who have made themselves eunuchs for the sake of the kingdom of heaven. Let anyone accept this who can."

✣ Let the Children Come to Me

13 Then children were being brought to him in order that he might lay his hands on them and pray. The disciples spoke sternly to those who brought them, 14 but Jesus said, "Let the children come to me, and do not stop them; for it is to such as these that the kingdom of heaven belongs." 15 And he laid his hands on them and went on his way.

✣ The Rich Young Man

16 Then someone came to him and said, "Teacher, what good deed must I do to have eternal life?" 17 And he said to him, "Why do you ask me about what is good? There is one who is good. If you wish to enter into life, keep the commandments." 18 He said to him, "Which ones?" And Jesus said, "You shall not murder. You shall not commit adultery. You shall not steal. You shall not bear false witness. 19 Honor your father and mother. Also, you shall love your neighbor as yourself." 20 The young man said to him, "I have kept all these; what do I still lack?" 21 Jesus said to him, "If you wish to be perfect, go, sell your possessions, and give the money to the poor, and you will have treasure in heaven; then come, follow me." 22 When the young man heard this word, he went away grieving, for he had many possessions.

23 Then Jesus said to his disciples, "Truly I tell you, it will be hard for a rich person to enter the kingdom of heaven. 24 Again I tell you, it is easier for a camel to go through the eye of a needle than for someone who is rich to enter the kingdom of God." 25 When the disciples heard this, they were greatly astounded and said, "Then who can be saved?" 26 But Jesus looked at them and said, "For mortals it is impossible, but for God all things are possible."

27 Then Peter said in reply, "Look, we have left everything and followed you. What then will we have?" **28** Jesus said to them, "Truly I tell you, at the renewal of all things, when the Son of Man is seated on the throne of his glory, you who have followed me will also sit on twelve thrones, judging the twelve tribes of Israel. **29** And everyone who has left houses or brothers or sisters or father or mother or wife or children or fields for my name's sake will receive a hundredfold and will inherit eternal life. **30** But many who are first will be last, and the last will be first.

CHAPTER 20

✦ The Parable of the Workers in the Vineyard

 **or the kingdom of heaven** is like a landowner who went out early in the morning to hire laborers for his vineyard. **2** After agreeing with the laborers for a denarius for the day, he sent them into his vineyard. **3** When he went out about nine o'clock, he saw others standing idle in the marketplace, **4** and he said to them, 'You also go into the vineyard, and I will pay you whatever is right.' So they went. **5** When he went out again about noon and about three o'clock, he did the same. **6** And about five o'clock he went out and found others standing around, and he said to them, 'Why are you standing here idle all day?' **7** They said to him, 'Because no one has hired us.' He said to them, 'You also go into the vineyard.' **8** When evening came, the owner of the vineyard said to his manager, 'Call the laborers and give them their pay, beginning with the last and then going to the first.' **9** When those hired about five o'clock came, each of them received a denarius. **10** Now when the first came, they thought they would receive more; but each of them also received a denarius. **11** And when they received it, they grumbled against the landowner, **12** saying, 'These last worked only one hour, and you have made them equal to us who have borne the burden of the day and the scorching heat.' **13** But he replied

to one of them, 'Friend, I am doing you no wrong; did you not agree with me for a denarius? **14** Take what belongs to you and go; I choose to give to this last the same as I give to you. **15** Am I not allowed to do what I choose with what belongs to me? Or are you envious because I am generous?' **16** So the last will be first, and the first will be last."

✢ A Third Time Jesus Foretells His Death and Resurrection

17 While Jesus was going up to Jerusalem, he took the twelve disciples aside by themselves and said to them on the way, **18** "Look, we are going up to Jerusalem, and the Son of Man will be handed over to the chief priests and scribes, and they will condemn him to death; **19** then they will hand him over to the gentiles to be mocked and flogged and crucified, and on the third day he will be raised."

✢ The Request of the Mother of James and John

20 Then the mother of the sons of Zebedee came to him with her sons, and kneeling before him, she asked a favor of him. **21** And he said to her, "What do you want?" She said to him, "Declare that these two sons of mine will sit, one at your right hand and one at your left, in your kingdom." **22** But Jesus answered, "You do not know what you are asking. Are you able to drink the cup that I am about to drink?" They said to him, "We are able." **23** He said to them, "You will indeed drink my cup, but to sit at my right hand and at my left, this is not mine to grant, but it is for those for whom it has been prepared by my Father."

24 When the ten heard it, they were angry with the two brothers. **25** But Jesus called them to him and said, "You know that the rulers of the gentiles lord it over them, and their great ones are tyrants over them. **26** It will not be so among you, but whoever wishes to be great among you must be your servant, **27** and whoever wishes to be first among you must be your slave, **28** just as the Son of Man came not to be served but to serve and to give his life a ransom for many."

✤ Jesus Heals Two Blind Men

29 As they were leaving Jericho, a large crowd followed him. **30** There were two blind men sitting by the roadside. When they heard that Jesus was passing by, they shouted, "Lord, have mercy on us, Son of David!" **31** The crowd sternly ordered them to be quiet, but they shouted even more loudly, "Have mercy on us, Lord, Son of David!" **32** Jesus stood still and called them, saying, "What do you want me to do for you?" **33** They said to him, "Lord, let our eyes be opened." **34** Moved with compassion, Jesus touched their eyes. Immediately they regained their sight and followed him.

CHAPTER 21

✤ Jesus' Triumphal Entry into Jerusalem

 **hen they had come near Jerusalem** and had reached Bethphage, at the Mount of Olives, Jesus sent two disciples, **2** saying to them, "Go into the village ahead of you, and immediately you will find a donkey tied and a colt with her; untie them and bring them to me. **3** If anyone says anything to you, just say this, 'The Lord needs them.' And he will send them immediately." **4** This took place to fulfill what had been spoken through the prophet:

> **5** "Tell the daughter of Zion,
> Look, your king is coming to you,
>   humble and mounted on a donkey,
>   and on a colt, the foal of a donkey."

6 The disciples went and did as Jesus had directed them; **7** they brought the donkey and the colt and put their cloaks on them, and he sat on them. **8** A very large crowd spread their cloaks on the road, and others cut branches from the trees and spread them on the road. **9** The crowds that went ahead of him and that followed were shouting,

"Hosanna to the Son of David!

Blessed is the one who comes in the name of the Lord!

Hosanna in the highest heaven!"

¹⁰ When he entered Jerusalem, the whole city was in turmoil, asking, "Who is this?" ¹¹ The crowds were saying, "This is the prophet Jesus from Nazareth in Galilee."

✢ Jesus Cleanses the Temple

¹² Then Jesus entered the temple and drove out all who were selling and buying in the temple, and he overturned the tables of the money changers and the seats of those who sold doves. ¹³ He said to them, "It is written,

'My house shall be called a house of prayer,'

but you are making it a den of robbers."

¹⁴ The blind and the lame came to him in the temple, and he cured them. ¹⁵ But when the chief priests and the scribes saw the amazing things that he did and heard the children crying out in the temple and saying, "Hosanna to the Son of David," they became angry ¹⁶ and said to him, "Do you hear what these are saying?" Jesus said to them, "Yes; have you never read,

'Out of the mouths of infants and nursing babies

you have prepared praise for yourself'?"

¹⁷ He left them, went out of the city to Bethany, and spent the night there.

✢ Jesus Curses the Fig Tree

¹⁸ In the morning, when he returned to the city, he was hungry. ¹⁹ And seeing a fig tree by the side of the road, he went to it and found nothing at all on it but leaves. Then he said to it, "May no fruit ever come from you again!" And the fig tree withered at once. ²⁰ When the disciples saw it, they were amazed, saying, "How did the fig tree wither at once?" ²¹ Jesus answered them, "Truly I tell you, if you have faith and do not doubt, not only will you do what has been done to the fig tree, but even if you say to this mountain,

'Be lifted up and thrown into the sea,' it will be done. ²² Whatever you ask for in prayer with faith, you will receive."

✣ The Authority of Jesus Questioned

²³ When he entered the temple, the chief priests and the elders of the people came to him as he was teaching and said, "By what authority are you doing these things, and who gave you this authority?" ²⁴ Jesus said to them, "I will also ask you one question; if you tell me the answer, then I will also tell you by what authority I do these things. ²⁵ Did the baptism of John come from heaven, or was it of human origin?" And they argued with one another, "If we say, 'From heaven,' he will say to us, 'Why then did you not believe him?' ²⁶ But if we say, 'Of human origin,' we are afraid of the crowd, for all regard John as a prophet." ²⁷ So they answered Jesus, "We do not know." And he said to them, "Neither will I tell you by what authority I am doing these things.

✣ The Parable of the Two Sons

²⁸ "What do you think? A man had two sons; he went to the first and said, 'Son, go and work in the vineyard today.' ²⁹ He answered, 'I will not,' but later he changed his mind and went. ³⁰ The father went to the second and said the same, and he answered, 'I go, sir,' but he did not go. ³¹ Which of the two did the will of his father?" They said, "The first." Jesus said to them, "Truly I tell you, the tax collectors and the prostitutes are going into the kingdom of God ahead of you. ³² For John came to you in the way of righteousness, and you did not believe him, but the tax collectors and the prostitutes believed him, and even after you saw it you did not change your minds and believe him.

✣ The Parable of the Wicked Tenants

³³ "Listen to another parable. There was a landowner who planted a vineyard, put a fence around it, dug a wine press in it, and built a watchtower. Then he leased it to tenants and went away. ³⁴ When the harvest time had come, he sent his slaves to the tenants to collect his produce. ³⁵ But the tenants seized his slaves and beat

one, killed another, and stoned another. ³⁶ Again he sent other slaves, more than the first; and they treated them in the same way. ³⁷ Then he sent his son to them, saying, 'They will respect my son.' ³⁸ But when the tenants saw the son, they said to themselves, 'This is the heir; come, let us kill him and get his inheritance.' ³⁹ So they seized him, threw him out of the vineyard, and killed him. ⁴⁰ Now when the owner of the vineyard comes, what will he do to those tenants?" ⁴¹ They said to him, "He will put those wretches to a miserable death and lease the vineyard to other tenants who will give him the produce at the harvest time."

⁴² Jesus said to them, "Have you never read in the scriptures:

'The stone that the builders rejected
has become the cornerstone;
this was the Lord's doing,
and it is amazing in our eyes'?

⁴³ Therefore I tell you, the kingdom of God will be taken away from you and given to a people that produces its fruits. ⁴⁴ The one who falls on this stone will be broken to pieces, and it will crush anyone on whom it falls."

⁴⁵ When the chief priests and the Pharisees heard his parables, they realized that he was speaking about them. ⁴⁶ They wanted to arrest him, but they feared the crowds, because they regarded him as a prophet.

CHAPTER 22

✦ The Parable of the Wedding Banquet

nce more Jesus spoke to them in parables, saying: ² "The kingdom of heaven may be compared to a king who gave a wedding banquet for his son. ³ He sent his slaves to call those who had been invited to the wedding banquet, but they would not come. ⁴ Again he sent other slaves, saying, 'Tell those who have been invited:

Look, I have prepared my dinner, my oxen and my fat calves have been slaughtered, and everything is ready; come to the wedding banquet.' **5** But they made light of it and went away, one to his farm, another to his business, **6** while the rest seized his slaves, mistreated them, and killed them. **7** The king was enraged. He sent his troops, destroyed those murderers, and burned their city. **8** Then he said to his slaves, 'The wedding is ready, but those invited were not worthy. **9** Go therefore into the main streets, and invite everyone you find to the wedding banquet.' **10** Those slaves went out into the streets and gathered all whom they found, both good and bad, so the wedding hall was filled with guests.

11 "But when the king came in to see the guests, he noticed a man there who was not wearing a wedding robe, **12** and he said to him, 'Friend, how did you get in here without a wedding robe?' And he was speechless. **13** Then the king said to the attendants, 'Bind him hand and foot, and throw him into the outer darkness, where there will be weeping and gnashing of teeth.' **14** For many are called, but few are chosen."

✦ The Question about Paying Taxes

15 Then the Pharisees went and plotted to entrap him in what he said. **16** So they sent their disciples to him, along with the Herodians, saying, "Teacher, we know that you are sincere, and teach the way of God in accordance with truth, and show deference to no one; for you do not regard people with partiality. **17** Tell us, then, what you think. Is it lawful to pay taxes to Caesar or not?" **18** But Jesus, aware of their malice, said, "Why are you putting me to the test, you hypocrites? **19** Show me the coin used for the tax." And they brought him a denarius. **20** Then he said to them, "Whose head is this, and whose title?" **21** They answered, "Caesar's." Then he said to them, "Give therefore to Caesar the things that are Caesar's, and to God the things that are God's." **22** When they heard this, they were amazed, and they left him and went away.

✦ The Question about the Resurrection

23 The same day some Sadducees came to him saying there is no resurrection, and they asked him a question: **24** "Teacher, Moses said, 'If a man dies childless, his brother shall marry the widow and raise up children for his brother.' **25** Now there were seven brothers among us; the first married, and died childless, leaving the widow to his brother. **26** The second did the same, so also the third, down to the seventh. **27** Last of all, the woman herself died. **28** In the resurrection, then, whose wife of the seven will she be? For all of them had married her."

29 Jesus answered them, "You are wrong because you know neither the scriptures nor the power of God. **30** For in the resurrection people neither marry nor are given in marriage but are like angels of God in heaven. **31** And as for the resurrection of the dead, have you not read what was said to you by God, **32** 'I am the God of Abraham, the God of Isaac, and the God of Jacob'? He is God not of the dead, but of the living." **33** And when the crowd heard it, they were astounded at his teaching.

✦ The Greatest Commandment

34 When the Pharisees heard that he had silenced the Sadducees, they gathered together, **35** and one of them, an expert in the law, asked him a question to test him. **36** "Teacher, which commandment in the law is the greatest?" **37** He said to him, "'You shall love the Lord your God with all your heart, and with all your soul, and with all your mind.' **38** This is the greatest and first commandment. **39** And a second is like it: 'You shall love your neighbor as yourself.' **40** On these two commandments hang all the Law and the Prophets."

✦ The Question about David's Son

41 Now while the Pharisees were gathered together, Jesus asked them this question: **42** "What do you think of the Messiah? Whose son is he?" They said to him, "The son of David." **43** He said to them, "How is it then that David by the Spirit calls him Lord, saying,

⁴⁴ 'The Lord said to my Lord,
"Sit at my right hand,
until I put your enemies under your feet"'?

⁴⁵ If David thus calls him Lord, how can he be his son?" ⁴⁶ No one was able to give him an answer, nor from that day did anyone dare to ask him any more questions.

CHAPTER 23

✣ Jesus Denounces Scribes and Pharisees

 **hen Jesus said to the crowds** and to his disciples, ² "The scribes and the Pharisees sit on Moses' seat; ³ therefore, do whatever they teach you and follow it, but do not do as they do, for they do not practice what they teach. ⁴ They tie up heavy burdens, hard to bear, and lay them on the shoulders of others, but they themselves are unwilling to lift a finger to move them. ⁵ They do all their deeds to be seen by others, for they make their phylacteries broad and their fringes long. ⁶ They love to have the place of honor at banquets and the best seats in the synagogues ⁷ and to be greeted with respect in the marketplaces and to have people call them rabbi. ⁸ But you are not to be called rabbi, for you have one teacher, and you are all brothers and sisters. ⁹ And call no one your father on earth, for you have one Father, the one in heaven. ¹⁰ Nor are you to be called instructors, for you have one instructor, the Messiah. ¹¹ The greatest among you will be your servant. ¹² All who exalt themselves will be humbled, and all who humble themselves will be exalted.

¹³ "But woe to you, scribes and Pharisees, hypocrites! For you lock people out of the kingdom of heaven. For you do not go in yourselves, and when others are going in you stop them. ¹⁵ Woe to you, scribes and Pharisees, hypocrites! For you cross sea and land to make a single convert, and you make the new convert twice as much a child of hell as yourselves.

16 "Woe to you, blind guides who say, 'Whoever swears by the sanctuary is bound by nothing, but whoever swears by the gold of the sanctuary is bound by the oath.' **17** You blind fools! For which is greater, the gold or the sanctuary that has made the gold sacred? **18** And you say, 'Whoever swears by the altar is bound by nothing, but whoever swears by the gift that is on the altar is bound by the oath.' **19** How blind you are! For which is greater, the gift or the altar that makes the gift sacred? **20** So whoever swears by the altar swears by it and by everything on it, **21** and whoever swears by the sanctuary swears by it and by the one who dwells in it, **22** and whoever swears by heaven swears by the throne of God and by the one who is seated upon it.

23 "Woe to you, scribes and Pharisees, hypocrites! For you tithe mint, dill, and cumin, and have neglected the weightier matters of the law: justice and mercy and faith. It is these you ought to have practiced without neglecting the others. **24** You blind guides! You strain out a gnat but swallow a camel!

25 "Woe to you, scribes and Pharisees, hypocrites! For you clean the outside of the cup and of the plate, but inside they are full of greed and self-indulgence. **26** You blind Pharisee! First clean the inside of the cup and of the plate, so that the outside also may become clean.

27 "Woe to you, scribes and Pharisees, hypocrites! For you are like whitewashed tombs, which on the outside look beautiful but inside they are full of the bones of the dead and of all kinds of uncleanness. **28** So you also on the outside look righteous to others, but inside you are full of hypocrisy and lawlessness.

29 "Woe to you, scribes and Pharisees, hypocrites! For you build the tombs of the prophets and decorate the graves of the righteous, **30** and you say, 'If we had lived in the days of our ancestors, we would not have taken part with them in shedding the blood of the prophets.' **31** Thus you testify against yourselves that you are descendants of those who murdered the prophets. **32** Fill up, then, the measure of your ancestors. **33** You snakes, you brood of vipers!

How can you escape the judgment of hell? **34** For this reason I send you prophets, sages, and scribes, some of whom you will kill and crucify, and some you will flog in your synagogues and pursue from town to town, **35** so that upon you may come all the righteous blood shed on earth, from the blood of righteous Abel to the blood of Zechariah son of Barachiah, whom you murdered between the sanctuary and the altar. **36** Truly I tell you, all this will come upon this generation.

✤ The Lament over Jerusalem

37 "Jerusalem, Jerusalem, the city that kills the prophets and stones those who are sent to it! How often have I desired to gather your children together as a hen gathers her brood under her wings, and you were not willing! **38** See, your house is left to you, desolate. **39** For I tell you, you will not see me again until you say, 'Blessed is the one who comes in the name of the Lord.'"

CHAPTER 24

✤ The Destruction of the Temple Foretold

**s Jesus came out of the temple** and was going away, his disciples came to point out to him the buildings of the temple. **2** Then he asked them, "You see all these, do you not? Truly I tell you, not one stone will be left here upon another; all will be thrown down."

✤ Signs of the End of the Age

3 When he was sitting on the Mount of Olives, the disciples came to him privately, saying, "Tell us, when will this be, and what will be the sign of your coming and of the end of the age?" **4** Jesus answered them, "Beware that no one leads you astray. **5** For many will come in my name, saying, 'I am the Messiah!' and they will lead many astray. **6** And you will hear of wars and rumors of wars; see that you are not alarmed, for this must take place, but the end is not yet. **7** For nation will rise against nation and kingdom against kingdom, and there will be famines and earthquakes in various places: ⁸ all this is but the beginning of the birth pangs.

✤ Persecutions Foretold

⁹ "Then they will hand you over to be tortured and will put you to death, and you will be hated by all nations because of my name. ¹⁰ Then many will fall away, and they will betray one another and hate one another. ¹¹ And many false prophets will arise and lead many astray. ¹² And because of the increase of lawlessness, the love of many will grow cold. ¹³ But the one who endures to the end will be saved. ¹⁴ And this good news of the kingdom will be proclaimed throughout the world, as a testimony to all the nations, and then the end will come.

✤ The Coming of False Messiahs

¹⁵ "So when you see the desolating sacrilege, spoken of by the prophet Daniel, standing in the holy place (let the reader understand), ¹⁶ then those in Judea must flee to the mountains; ¹⁷ the one on the housetop must not go down to take things from the house; ¹⁸ the one in the field must not turn back to get a coat. ¹⁹ Woe to those who are pregnant and to those who are nursing infants in those days! ²⁰ Pray that your flight may not be in winter or on a Sabbath. ²¹ For at that time there will be great suffering, such as has not been from the beginning of the world until now, no, and never will be. ²² And if those days had not been cut short, no one would be saved, but for the sake of the elect those days will be cut short. ²³ Then if anyone says to you, 'Look! Here is the Messiah!' or 'There he is!'—do not believe it. ²⁴ For false messiahs and false prophets will appear and produce great signs and wonders, to lead astray, if possible, even the elect. ²⁵ Take note, I have told you beforehand. ²⁶ So, if they say to you, 'Look! He is in the wilderness,' do not go out. If they say, 'Look! He is in the inner rooms,' do not believe it. ²⁷ For as the lightning comes from the east and flashes as far as the west, so will be the coming of the Son of Man. ²⁸ Wherever the corpse is, there the eagles will gather.

✦ The Coming of the Son of Man

29 "Immediately after the suffering of those days

> the sun will be darkened,
>> and the moon will not give its light;
> the stars will fall from heaven,
>> and the powers of heaven will be shaken.

30 Then the sign of the Son of Man will appear in heaven, and then all the tribes of the earth will mourn, and they will see 'the Son of Man coming on the clouds of heaven' with power and great glory. **31** And he will send out his angels with a loud trumpet call, and they will gather his elect from the four winds, from one end of heaven to the other.

✦ The Lesson of the Fig Tree

32 "From the fig tree learn its lesson: as soon as its branch becomes tender and puts forth its leaves, you know that summer is near. **33** So also, when you see all these things, you know that he is near, at the very gates. **34** Truly I tell you, this generation will not pass away until all these things have taken place. **35** Heaven and earth will pass away, but my words will not pass away.

✦ Be Ready

36 "But about that day and hour no one knows, neither the angels of heaven, nor the Son, but only the Father. **37** For as the days of Noah were, so will be the coming of the Son of Man. **38** For as in those days before the flood they were eating and drinking, marrying and giving in marriage, until the day Noah entered the ark, **39** and they knew nothing until the flood came and swept them all away, so, too, will be the coming of the Son of Man. **40** Then two will be in the field; one will be taken, and one will be left. **41** Two women will be grinding meal together; one will be taken, and one will be left. **42** Keep awake, therefore, for you do not know on what day your Lord is coming. **43** But understand this: if the owner of the house had known in what part of the night the thief was coming, he would have stayed awake and would not have let his house be broken into. **44** Therefore you also must be ready, for the Son of Man is coming at an hour you do not expect.

✦ Be Faithful

45 "Who, then, is the faithful and wise slave whom his master has put in charge of his household, to give the other slaves their allowance of food at the proper time? **46** Blessed is that slave whom his master will find at work when he arrives. **47** Truly I tell you, he will put that one in charge of all his possessions. **48** But if that wicked slave says to himself, 'My master is delayed,' **49** and he begins to beat his fellow slaves and eats and drinks with drunkards, **50** the master of that slave will come on a day when he does not expect him and at an hour that he does not know. **51** He will cut him in pieces and put him with the hypocrites, where there will be weeping and gnashing of teeth.

CHAPTER 25

✦ The Parable of the Ten Bridesmaids

Then the kingdom of heaven will be like this. Ten young women took their lamps and went to meet the bridegroom. **2** Five of them were foolish, and five were wise. **3** When the foolish took their lamps, they took no oil with them, **4** but the wise took flasks of oil with their lamps. **5** As the bridegroom was delayed, all of them became drowsy and slept. **6** But at midnight there was a shout, 'Look! Here is the bridegroom! Come out to meet him.' **7** Then all those young women got up and trimmed their lamps. **8** The foolish said to the wise, 'Give us some of your oil, for our lamps are going out.' **9** But the wise replied, 'No! there will not be enough for you and for us; you had better go to the dealers and buy some for yourselves.' **10** And while they went to buy it, the bridegroom came, and those who were ready went with him into the wedding banquet, and the door was shut. **11** Later the other young women came also, saying, 'Lord, lord, open to us.' **12** But he replied, 'Truly I tell you, I do not know you.' **13** Keep awake therefore, for you know neither the day nor the hour.

✣ The Parable of the Talents

14 "For it is as if a man, going on a journey, summoned his slaves and entrusted his property to them; **15** to one he gave five talents, to another two, to another one, to each according to his ability. Then he went away. At once **16** the one who had received the five talents went off at once and traded with them and made five more talents. **17** In the same way, the one who had the two talents made two more talents. **18** But the one who had received the one talent went off and dug a hole in the ground and hid his master's money. **19** After a long time the master of those slaves came and settled accounts with them. **20** Then the one who had received the five talents came forward, bringing five more talents, saying, 'Master, you handed over to me five talents; see, I have made five more talents.' **21** His master said to him, 'Well done, good and trustworthy slave; you have been trustworthy in a few things; I will put you in charge of many things; enter into the joy of your master.' **22** And the one with the two talents also came forward, saying, 'Master, you handed over to me two talents; see, I have made two more talents.' **23** His master said to him, 'Well done, good and trustworthy slave; you have been trustworthy in a few things; I will put you in charge of many things; enter into the joy of your master.' **24** Then the one who had received the one talent also came forward, saying, 'Master, I knew that you were a harsh man, reaping where you did not sow, and gathering where you did not scatter, **25** so I was afraid, and I went and hid your talent in the ground. Here you have what is yours.' **26** But his master replied, 'You wicked and lazy slave! You knew, did you, that I reap where I did not sow, and gather where I did not scatter? **27** Then you ought to have invested my money with the bankers, and on my return I would have received what was my own with interest. **28** So take the talent from him, and give it to the one with the ten talents. **29** For to all those who have, more will be given, and they will have an abundance, but from those who have nothing, even what they have will be taken away. [30] As for this worthless slave, throw him into the outer darkness, where there will be weeping and gnashing of teeth.'

✦ The Judgment of the Nations

[31] "When the Son of Man comes in his glory and all the angels with him, then he will sit on the throne of his glory. [32] All the nations will be gathered before him, and he will separate people one from another as a shepherd separates the sheep from the goats, [33] and he will put the sheep at his right hand and the goats at the left. [34] Then the king will say to those at his right hand, 'Come, you who are blessed by my Father, inherit the kingdom prepared for you from the foundation of the world, [35] for I was hungry and you gave me food, I was thirsty and you gave me something to drink, I was a stranger and you welcomed me, [36] I was naked and you gave me clothing, I was sick and you took care of me, I was in prison and you visited me.' [37] Then the righteous will answer him, 'Lord, when was it that we saw you hungry and gave you food or thirsty and gave you something to drink? [38] And when was it that we saw you a stranger and welcomed you or naked and gave you clothing? [39] And when was it that we saw you sick or in prison and visited you?' [40] And the king will answer them, 'Truly I tell you, just as you did it to one of the least of these brothers and sisters of mine, you did it to me.' [41] Then he will say to those at his left hand, 'You who are accursed, depart from me into the eternal fire prepared for the devil and his angels, [42] for I was hungry and you gave me no food, I was thirsty and you gave me nothing to drink, [43] I was a stranger and you did not welcome me, naked and you did not give me clothing, sick and in prison and you did not visit me.' [44] Then they also will answer, 'Lord, when was it that we saw you hungry or thirsty or a stranger or naked or sick or in prison, and did not take care of you?' [45] Then he will answer them, 'Truly I tell you, just as you did not do it to one of

the least of these, you did not do it to me.' **46** And these will go away into eternal punishment but the righteous into eternal life."

CHAPTER 26

✦ The Plot to Kill Jesus

 **hen Jesus had finished** saying all these things, he said to his disciples, **2** "You know that after two days the Passover is coming, and the Son of Man will be handed over to be crucified."

3 Then the chief priests and the elders of the people gathered in the courtyard of the high priest, who was called Caiaphas, **4** and they conspired to arrest Jesus by stealth and kill him. **5** But they said, "Not during the festival, or there may be a riot among the people."

✦ The Anointing at Bethany

6 Now while Jesus was at Bethany in the house of Simon the leper, **7** a woman came to him with an alabaster jar of very costly ointment, and she poured it on his head as he sat at the table. **8** But when the disciples saw it, they were angry and said, "Why this waste? **9** For this ointment could have been sold for a large sum and the money given to the poor." **10** But Jesus, aware of this, said to them, "Why do you trouble the woman? She has performed a good service for me. **11** For you always have the poor with you, but you will not always have me. **12** By pouring this ointment on my body she has prepared me for burial. **13** Truly I tell you, wherever this good news is proclaimed in the whole world, what she has done will be told in remembrance of her."

✦ Judas Agrees to Betray Jesus

14 Then one of the twelve, who was called Judas Iscariot, went to the chief priests **15** and said, "What will you give me if I betray him to you?" They paid him thirty pieces of silver. **16** And from that moment he began to look for an opportunity to betray him.

✤ The Passover with the Disciples

17 On the first day of Unleavened Bread the disciples came to Jesus, saying, "Where do you want us to make the preparations for you to eat the Passover?" **18** He said, "Go into the city to a certain man and say to him, 'The Teacher says, My time is near; I will keep the Passover at your house with my disciples.'" **19** So the disciples did as Jesus had directed them, and they prepared the Passover meal.

20 When it was evening, he took his place with the twelve disciples, **21** and while they were eating he said, "Truly I tell you, one of you will betray me." **22** And they became greatly distressed and began to say to him one after another, "Surely not I, Lord?" **23** He answered, "The one who has dipped his hand into the bowl with me will betray me. **24** The Son of Man goes as it is written of him, but woe to that one by whom the Son of Man is betrayed! It would have been better for that one not to have been born." **25** Judas, who betrayed him, said, "Surely not I, Rabbi?" He replied, "You have said so."

✤ The Institution of the Lord's Supper

26 While they were eating, Jesus took a loaf of bread, and after blessing it he broke it, gave it to the disciples, and said, "Take, eat; this is my body." **27** Then he took a cup, and after giving thanks he gave it to them, saying, "Drink from it, all of you, **28** for this is my blood of the covenant, which is poured out for many for the forgiveness of sins. **29** I tell you, I will never again drink of this fruit of the vine until that day when I drink it new with you in my Father's kingdom."

30 When they had sung the hymn, they went out to the Mount of Olives.

✤ Peter's Denial Foretold

31 Then Jesus said to them, "You will all fall away because of me this night, for it is written,

'I will strike the shepherd,
    and the sheep of the flock will be scattered.'

³² But after I am raised up, I will go ahead of you to Galilee." ³³ Peter said to him, "Even if all fall away because of you, I will never fall away." ³⁴ Jesus said to him, "Truly I tell you, this very night, before the cock crows, you will deny me three times." ³⁵ Peter said to him, "Even though I must die with you, I will not deny you." And so said all the disciples.

✧ Jesus Prays in Gethsemane

³⁶ Then Jesus went with them to a place called Gethsemane, and he said to his disciples, "Sit here while I go over there and pray." ³⁷ He took with him Peter and the two sons of Zebedee and began to be grieved and agitated. ³⁸ Then he said to them, "My soul is deeply grieved, even to death; remain here, and stay awake with me." ³⁹ And going a little farther, he threw himself on the ground and prayed, "My Father, if it is possible, let this cup pass from me, yet not what I want but what you want." ⁴⁰ Then he came to the disciples and found them sleeping, and he said to Peter, "So, could you not stay awake with me one hour? ⁴¹ Stay awake and pray that you may not come into the time of trial; the spirit indeed is willing, but the flesh is weak." ⁴² Again he went away for the second time and prayed, "My Father, if this cannot pass unless I drink it, your will be done." ⁴³ Again he came and found them sleeping, for their eyes were heavy. ⁴⁴ So leaving them again, he went away and prayed for the third time, saying the same words. ⁴⁵ Then he came to the disciples and said to them, "Are you still sleeping and taking your rest? Now the hour is at hand, and the Son of Man is betrayed into the hands of sinners. ⁴⁶ Get up, let us be going. Look, my betrayer is at hand."

✧ The Betrayal and Arrest of Jesus

⁴⁷ While he was still speaking, Judas, one of the twelve, arrived; with him was a large crowd with swords and clubs, from the chief priests and the elders of the people. ⁴⁸ Now the betrayer had given them a sign, saying, "The one I will kiss is the man; arrest him." ⁴⁹ At once he came up to Jesus and said, "Greetings, Rabbi!" and kissed him. ⁵⁰ Jesus said to him, "Friend, do what you are here to

do." Then they came and laid hands on Jesus and arrested him. [51] Suddenly, one of those with Jesus put his hand on his sword, drew it, and struck the slave of the high priest, cutting off his ear. [52] Then Jesus said to him, "Put your sword back into its place; for all who take the sword will die by the sword. [53] Do you think that I cannot appeal to my Father, and he will at once send me more than twelve legions of angels? [54] But how then would the scriptures be fulfilled, which say it must happen in this way?" [55] At that hour Jesus said to the crowds, "Have you come out with swords and clubs to arrest me as though I were a rebel? Day after day I sat in the temple teaching, and you did not arrest me. [56] But all this has taken place, so that the scriptures of the prophets may be fulfilled." Then all the disciples deserted him and fled.

✦ Jesus before Caiaphas

[57] Those who had arrested Jesus took him to Caiaphas the high priest, where the scribes and the elders had gathered. [58] But Peter was following him at a distance, as far as the courtyard of the high priest, and going inside he sat with the guards in order to see how this would end. [59] Now the chief priests and the whole council were looking for false testimony against Jesus so that they might put him to death, [60] but they found none, though many false witnesses came forward. At last two came forward [61] and said, "This fellow said, 'I am able to destroy the temple of God and to build it in three days.'" [62] The high priest stood up and said, "Have you no answer? What is it that they testify against you?" [63] But Jesus was silent. Then the high priest said to him, "I put you under oath before the living God, tell us if you are the Messiah, the Son of God." [64] Jesus said to him, "You have said so. But I tell you,

> From now on you will see the Son of Man
>> seated at the right hand of Power
>> and coming on the clouds of heaven."

[65] Then the high priest tore his clothes and said, "He has blasphemed! Why do we still need witnesses? You have now heard his

blasphemy. **⁶⁶** What do you think?" They answered, "He deserves death." **⁶⁷** Then they spat in his face and struck him, and some slapped him, **⁶⁸** saying, "Prophesy to us, you Messiah! Who is it that struck you?"

✣ Peter's Denial of Jesus

⁶⁹ Now Peter was sitting outside in the courtyard. A female servant came to him and said, "You also were with Jesus the Galilean." **⁷⁰** But he denied it before all of them, saying, "I do not know what you are talking about." **⁷¹** When he went out to the porch, another female servant saw him, and she said to the bystanders, "This man was with Jesus the Nazarene."**⁷²** Again he denied it with an oath, "I do not know the man." **⁷³** After a little while the bystanders came up and said to Peter, "Certainly you are also one of them, for your accent betrays you." **⁷⁴** Then he began to curse, and he swore an oath, "I do not know the man!" At that moment the cock crowed. **⁷⁵** Then Peter remembered what Jesus had said: "Before the cock crows, you will deny me three times." And he went out and wept bitterly.

CHAPTER 27

✣ Jesus Brought before Pilate

hen morning came, all the chief priests and the elders of the people conferred together against Jesus in order to bring about his death. **²** They bound him, led him away, and handed him over to Pilate the governor.

✣ The End of Judas

³ When Judas, his betrayer, saw that Jesus was condemned, he repented and brought back the thirty pieces of silver to the chief priests and the elders. **⁴** He said, "I have sinned by betraying innocent blood." But they said, "What is that to us? See to it yourself." **⁵** Throwing down the pieces of silver in the temple, he departed, and he went and hanged himself. **6** But the chief priests, taking the pieces of silver, said, "It is not lawful to put them into the treasury, since they are blood money." **7** After conferring together, they used them to buy the potter's field as a place to bury foreigners. **8** For this reason that field has been called the Field of Blood to this day. **9** Then was fulfilled what had been spoken through the prophet Jeremiah, "And they took the thirty pieces of silver, the price of the one on whom a price had been set, on whom some of the people of Israel had set a price, **10** and they gave them for the potter's field, as the Lord commanded me."

✢ Pilate Questions Jesus

11 Now Jesus stood before the governor; and the governor asked him, "Are you the King of the Jews?" Jesus said, "You say so." **12** But when he was accused by the chief priests and elders, he did not answer. **13** Then Pilate said to him, "Do you not hear how many accusations they make against you?" **14** But he gave him no answer, not even to a single charge, so that the governor was greatly amazed.

✢ Barabbas or Jesus?

15 Now at the festival the governor was accustomed to release a prisoner for the crowd, anyone whom they wanted. **16** At that time they had a notorious prisoner, called Jesus Barabbas. **17** So after they had gathered, Pilate said to them, "Whom do you want me to release for you, Jesus Barabbas or Jesus who is called the Messiah?" **18** For he realized that it was out of jealousy that they had handed him over. **19** While he was sitting on the judgment seat, his wife sent word to him, "Have nothing to do with that innocent man, for today I have suffered a great deal because of a dream about him." **20** Now the chief priests and the elders persuaded the crowds to ask for Barabbas and to have Jesus killed. **21** The governor again said to them, "Which of the two do you want me to release for you?" And they said, "Barabbas." **22** Pilate said to them, "Then what should I do with Jesus who is called the Messiah?" All of them said, "Let him be crucified!" **23** Then he asked, "Why, what evil has he done?" But they shouted all the more, "Let him be crucified!"

✦ Pilate Hands Jesus over to Be Crucified

24 So when Pilate saw that he could do nothing but rather that a riot was beginning, he took some water and washed his hands before the crowd, saying, "I am innocent of this man's blood, see to it yourselves." **25** Then the people as a whole answered, "His blood be on us and on our children!" **26** So he released Barabbas for them, and after flogging Jesus he handed him over to be crucified.

✦ The Soldiers Mock Jesus

27 Then the soldiers of the governor took Jesus into the governor's headquarters, and they gathered the whole cohort around him. **28** They stripped him and put a scarlet robe on him, **29** and after twisting some thorns into a crown they put it on his head. They put a reed in his right hand and knelt before him and mocked him, saying, "Hail, King of the Jews!" **30** They spat on him and took the reed and struck him on the head. **31** After mocking him, they stripped him of the robe and put his own clothes on him. Then they led him away to crucify him.

✦ The Crucifixion of Jesus

32 As they went out, they came upon a man from Cyrene named Simon; they compelled this man to carry his cross. **33** And when they came to a place called Golgotha (which means Place of a Skull), **34** they offered him wine to drink, mixed with gall, but when he tasted it, he would not drink it. **35** And when they had crucified him, they divided his clothes among themselves by casting lots; **36** then they sat down there and kept watch over him. **37** Over his head they put the charge against him, which read, "This is Jesus, the King of the Jews."

38 Then two rebels were crucified with him, one on his right and one on his left. **39** Those who passed by derided him, shaking their heads **40** and saying, "You who would destroy the temple and build it in three days, save yourself! If you are the Son of God, come down from the cross." **41** In the same way the chief priests also, along with the scribes and elders, were mocking him, saying, **42** "He saved others; he cannot save himself. He is the King of Israel; let him come down from the cross now, and we will believe in him. **43** He trusts in God; let God deliver him now, if he wants to; for he said, 'I am God's Son.'" **44** The bandits who were crucified with him also taunted him in the same way.

✦ The Death of Jesus

45 From noon on, darkness came over the whole land until three in the afternoon. **46** And about three o'clock Jesus cried with a loud voice, "Eli, Eli, lema sabachthani?" that is, "My God, my God, why have you forsaken me?" **47** When some of the bystanders heard it, they said, "This man is calling for Elijah." **48** At once one of them ran and got a sponge, filled it with sour wine, put it on a stick, and gave it to him to drink. **49** But the others said, "Wait, let us see whether Elijah will come to save him." **50** Then Jesus cried again with a loud voice and breathed his last. **51** At that moment the curtain of the temple was torn in two, from top to bottom. The earth shook, and the rocks were split. **52** The tombs also were opened, and many bodies of the saints who had fallen asleep were raised. **53** After his resurrection they came out of the tombs and entered the holy city and appeared to many. **54** Now when the centurion and those with him, who were keeping watch over Jesus, saw the earthquake and what took place, they were terrified and said, "Truly this man was God's Son!"

55 Many women were also there, looking on from a distance; they had followed Jesus from Galilee, ministering to him. **56** Among them were Mary Magdalene, and Mary the mother of James and Joseph, and the mother of the sons of Zebedee.

✦ The Burial of Jesus

57 When it was evening, there came a rich man from Arimathea named Joseph, who was himself a disciple of Jesus. **58** He went to Pilate and asked for the body of Jesus; then Pilate ordered it to be given to him. **59** So Joseph took the body and wrapped it in a clean linen cloth **⁶⁰** and laid it in his new tomb, which he had hewn in the rock. He then rolled a great stone to the door of the tomb and went away. **⁶¹** Mary Magdalene and the other Mary were there, sitting opposite the tomb.

✤ The Guard at the Tomb

⁶² The next day, that is, after the day of Preparation, the chief priests and the Pharisees gathered before Pilate **⁶³** and said, "Sir, we remember what that impostor said while he was still alive, 'After three days I will rise again.' **⁶⁴** Therefore command the tomb to be made secure until the third day; otherwise his disciples may go and steal him away and tell the people, 'He has been raised from the dead,' and the last deception would be worse than the first." **⁶⁵** Pilate said to them, "You have a guard of soldiers; go, make it as secure as you can." **⁶⁶** So they went with the guard and made the tomb secure by sealing the stone.

CHAPTER 28

✤ The Resurrection of Jesus

 fter the Sabbath, as the first day of the week was dawning, Mary Magdalene and the other Mary went to see the tomb. **²** And suddenly there was a great earthquake, for an angel of the Lord, descending from heaven, came and rolled back the stone and sat on it. **³** His appearance was like lightning, and his clothing white as snow. **⁴** For fear of him the guards shook and became like dead men. **⁵** But the angel said to the women, "Do not be afraid; I know that you are looking for Jesus who was crucified. **⁶** He is not here, for he has been raised, as he said. Come, see the place where he lay. **⁷** Then go quickly and tell his disciples, 'He has been raised from the dead, and indeed he is going ahead of you to Galilee; there you will see him.' This is my message for you." **⁸** So they left the tomb quickly with fear and great joy and ran to tell his disciples. **⁹** Suddenly Jesus met them and said, "Greetings!" And they

came to him, took hold of his feet, and worshiped him. ¹⁰ Then
Jesus said to them, "Do not be afraid; go and tell my brothers and
sisters to go to Galilee; there they will see me."

✦ The Report of the Guard

¹¹ While they were going, some of the guard went into the city
and told the chief priests everything that had happened. ¹² After
the priests had assembled with the elders, they devised a plan to
give a large sum of money to the soldiers, ¹³ telling them, "You
must say, 'His disciples came by night and stole him away while
we were asleep.' ¹⁴ If this comes to the governor's ears, we will
satisfy him and keep you out of trouble." ¹⁵ So they took the money
and did as they were directed. And this story is still told among
the Judeans to this day.

✦ The Commissioning of the Disciples

¹⁶ Now the eleven disciples went to Galilee, to the mountain to
which Jesus had directed them. ¹⁷ When they saw him, they worshiped him, but they doubted. ¹⁸ And Jesus came and said to them,
"All authority in heaven and on earth has been given to me.
¹⁹ Go therefore and make disciples of all nations, baptizing them
in the name of the Father and of the Son and of the Holy Spirit
²⁰ and teaching them to obey everything that I have commanded
you. And remember, I am with you always, to the end of the age."

Gospel of Mark

St. Mark is thought to be the "John Mark" mentioned in the Acts of the Apostles. He was the son of Mary of Jerusalem, who had a large and well-staffed home that the early Christians often used as a meeting place. The apostle Peter came to this home after being miraculously freed from his imprisonment by Herod Antipas in Jerusalem.

Mark became a student and close friend of Peter. Peter even referred to Mark as "his son." Because Mark knew so many languages (Aramaic, Greek, Latin, a Libyan language, and Hebrew), he accompanied Peter on his missionary journeys to Jerusalem, Judea, and Rome. He also joined Paul and Barnabas, his cousin, on their missionary journeys to Antioch and Cyprus, and later to Rome and Asia Minor. Mark lived for years in Alexandria and may have been their first bishop. There, he died a martyr by being dragged through the streets.

It is believed that Mark recorded Peter's eyewitness accounts of his experiences with Jesus. It is possible that Mark was also writing from his own experience when he documented Jesus' arrest in Gethsemane. This is shown by the verses "A certain young man was following him, wearing nothing but a linen cloth. They caught hold of him, but he left the linen cloth and ran off naked" (Mark 14:51–52).

Mark may have provided both Luke and Matthew with basic sources for their Gospels. Most scholars agree that this Gospel had to have been written sometime between the late 50s and 60s, just prior to the Roman destruction of Jerusalem in AD 70.

Mark is the patron saint of Venice (Italy), Egypt, lawyers, painters, interpreters, and lions. His feast day is celebrated on April 25.

Mark's symbol is a winged lion, a sign of courage and royalty, and a fitting image for a friend of the Son of God. Lions also remind us of Christ as our king, and that as Christians we should be courageous in following Jesus, our Good Shepherd.

CHAPTER 1

✦ The Proclamation of John the Baptist

The beginning of the good news of Jesus Christ. **²** As it is written in the prophet Isaiah,

"See, I am sending my messenger ahead of you,
who will prepare your way,
³ the voice of one crying out in the wilderness:
'Prepare the way of the Lord,
make his paths straight,'"

⁴ so John the baptizer appeared in the wilderness, proclaiming a baptism of repentance for the forgiveness of sins. **⁵** And the whole Judean region and all the people of Jerusalem were going out to him and were baptized by him in the River Jordan, confessing their sins. **⁶** Now John was clothed with camel's hair, with a leather belt around his waist, and he ate locusts and wild honey. **⁷** He proclaimed, "The one who is more powerful than I is coming after me; I am not worthy to stoop down and untie the thong of his sandals. **⁸** I have baptized you with water, but he will baptize you with the Holy Spirit."

✦ The Baptism of Jesus

⁹ In those days Jesus came from Nazareth of Galilee and was baptized by John in the Jordan. **¹⁰** And just as he was coming up out of the water, he saw the heavens torn apart and the Spirit descending like a dove upon him. **¹¹** And a voice came from the heavens, "You are my Son, the Beloved; with you I am well pleased."

✦ The Temptation of Jesus

¹² And the Spirit immediately drove him out into the wilderness. **¹³** He was in the wilderness forty days, tested by Satan, and he was with the wild beasts, and the angels waited on him.

✧ The Beginning of the Galilean Ministry

¹⁴ Now after John was arrested, Jesus came to Galilee proclaiming the good news of God ¹⁵ and saying, "The time is fulfilled, and the kingdom of God has come near; repent, and believe in the good news."

✧ Jesus Calls the First Disciples

¹⁶ As Jesus passed along the Sea of Galilee, he saw Simon and his brother Andrew casting a net into the sea, for they were fishers. ¹⁷ And Jesus said to them, "Follow me and I will make you fishers of people." ¹⁸ And immediately they left their nets and followed him. ¹⁹ As he went a little farther, he saw James son of Zebedee and his brother John, who were in their boat mending the nets. ²⁰ Immediately he called them, and they left their father Zebedee in the boat with the hired men and followed him.

✧ The Man with an Unclean Spirit

²¹ They went to Capernaum, and when the Sabbath came, he entered the synagogue and taught. ²² They were astounded at his teaching, for he taught them as one having authority, and not as the scribes. ²³ Just then there was in their synagogue a man with an unclean spirit, ²⁴ and he cried out, "What have you to do with us, Jesus of Nazareth? Have you come to destroy us? I know who you are, the Holy One of God." ²⁵ But Jesus rebuked him, saying, "Be quiet and come out of him!" ²⁶ And the unclean spirit, convulsing him and crying with a loud voice, came out of him. ²⁷ They were all amazed, and they kept on asking one another, "What is this? A new teaching—with authority! He commands even the unclean spirits, and they obey him." ²⁸ At once his fame began to spread throughout the surrounding region of Galilee.

✧ Jesus Heals Many at Simon's House

²⁹ As soon as they left the synagogue, they entered the house of Simon and Andrew, with James and John. ³⁰ Now Simon's mother-in-law was in bed with a fever, and they told him about her at

once. **31** He came and took her by the hand and lifted her up. Then the fever left her, and she began to serve them.

32 That evening, at sunset, they brought to him all who were sick or possessed with demons. **33** And the whole city was gathered around the door. **34** And he cured many who were sick with various diseases and cast out many demons; and he would not permit the demons to speak, because they knew him.

✣ A Preaching Tour in Galilee

35 In the morning, while it was still very dark, he got up and went out to a deserted place, and there he prayed. **36** And Simon and his companions hunted for him. **37** When they found him, they said to him, "Everyone is searching for you." **38** He answered, "Let us go on to the neighboring towns, so that I may proclaim the message there also, for that is what I came out to do." **39** And he went throughout Galilee, proclaiming the message in their synagogues and casting out demons.

✣ Jesus Heals a Man with a Skin Disease

40 A man with a skin disease came to him begging him, and kneeling he said to him, "If you are willing, you can make me clean." **41** Moved with pity, Jesus stretched out his hand and touched him, and said to him, "I am willing. Be made clean!" **42** Immediately the skin disease left him, and he was made clean. **43** After sternly warning him he sent him away at once, **44** saying to him, "See that you say nothing to anyone, but go, show yourself to the priest, and offer for your cleansing what Moses commanded as a testimony to them." **45** But he went out and began to proclaim it freely and to spread the word, so that Jesus could no longer go into a town openly but stayed out in the country, and people came to him from every quarter.

CHAPTER 2

✦ Jesus Heals a Paralytic

**hen he returned** to Capernaum after some days, it was reported that he was at home. **²** So many gathered around that there was no longer room for them, not even in front of the door, and he was speaking the word to them. **³** Then some people came, bringing to him a paralyzed man, carried by four of them. **⁴** And when they could not bring him to Jesus because of the crowd, they removed the roof above him, and after having dug through it, they let down the mat on which the paralytic lay. **⁵** When Jesus saw their faith, he said to the paralytic, "Child, your sins are forgiven." **⁶** Now some of the scribes were sitting there questioning in their hearts, **⁷** "Why does this fellow speak in this way? It is blasphemy! Who can forgive sins but God alone?" **⁸** At once Jesus perceived in his spirit that they were discussing these questions among themselves, and he said to them, "Why do you raise such questions in your hearts? **⁹** Which is easier: to say to the paralytic, 'Your sins are forgiven,' or to say, 'Stand up and take your mat and walk'? **¹⁰** But so that you may know that the Son of Man has authority on earth to forgive sins"—he said to the paralytic— **¹¹** "I say to you, stand up, take your mat and go to your home." **¹²** And he stood up and immediately took the mat and went out before all of them, so that they were all amazed and glorified God, saying, "We have never seen anything like this!"

✦ Jesus Calls Levi

¹³ Jesus went out again beside the sea; the whole crowd gathered around him, and he taught them. **¹⁴** As he was walking along, he saw Levi son of Alphaeus sitting at the tax-collection station, and he said to him, "Follow me." And he got up and followed him.

¹⁵ And as he sat at dinner in Levi's house, many tax collectors and sinners were also sitting with Jesus and his disciples, for there were many who followed him. ¹⁶ When the scribes of the Pharisees saw that he was eating with sinners and tax collectors, they said to his disciples, "Why does he eat with tax collectors and sinners?" ¹⁷ When Jesus heard this, he said to them, "Those who are well have no need of a physician but those who are sick; I have come to call not the righteous but sinners."

✢ A Question about Fasting

¹⁸ Now John's disciples and the Pharisees were fasting, and people came and said to him, "Why do John's disciples and the disciples of the Pharisees fast, but your disciples do not fast?" ¹⁹ Jesus said to them, "The wedding attendants cannot fast while the bridegroom is with them, can they? As long as they have the bridegroom with them, they cannot fast. ²⁰ The days will come when the bridegroom is taken away from them, and then they will fast on that day.

²¹ "No one sews a piece of unshrunk cloth on an old cloak; otherwise, the patch pulls away from it, the new from the old, and a worse tear is made. ²² Similarly, no one puts new wine into old wineskins; otherwise, the wine will burst the skins, and the wine is lost, and so are the skins, but one puts new wine into fresh wineskins."

✢ Lord of the Sabbath

²³ One Sabbath he was going through the grain fields, and as they made their way his disciples began to pluck heads of grain. ²⁴ The Pharisees said to him, "Look, why are they doing what is not lawful on the Sabbath?" ²⁵ And he said to them, "Have you never read what David did when he and his companions were hungry and in need of food, ²⁶ how he entered the house of God when Abiathar was high priest and ate the bread of the Presence, which it is not lawful for any but the priests to eat, and he gave some to his companions?" ²⁷ Then he said to them, "The Sabbath was made for humankind and not humankind for the Sabbath, ²⁸ so the Son of Man is lord even of the Sabbath."

CHAPTER 3

❖ The Man with a Withered Hand

**gain he entered the synagogue,** and a man was there who had a withered hand. **2** They were watching him to see whether he would cure him on the Sabbath, so that they might accuse him. **3** And he said to the man who had the withered hand, "Come forward." **4** Then he said to them, "Is it lawful to do good or to do harm on the Sabbath, to save life or to kill?" But they were silent. **5** He looked around at them with anger; he was grieved at their hardness of heart and said to the man, "Stretch out your hand." He stretched it out, and his hand was restored. **6** The Pharisees went out and immediately conspired with the Herodians against him, how to destroy him.

❖ A Multitude at the Seaside

7 Jesus departed with his disciples to the sea, and a great multitude from Galilee followed him; **8** hearing all that he was doing, they came to him in great numbers from Judea, Jerusalem, Idumea, beyond the Jordan, and the region around Tyre and Sidon. **9** He told his disciples to have a boat ready for him because of the crowd, so that they would not crush him, **10** for he had cured many, so that all who had diseases pressed upon him to touch him. **11** Whenever the unclean spirits saw him, they fell down before him and shouted, "You are the Son of God!" **12** But he sternly ordered them not to make him known.

❖ Jesus Calls the Twelve

13 He went up the mountain and called to him those whom he wanted, and they came to him. **14** And he appointed twelve to be with him and to be sent out to preach **15** and to have authority to cast out demons. **16** So he appointed the twelve: Simon (to whom he gave the name Peter), **17** James son of Zebedee and John the brother of James (to whom he gave the name Boanerges, that is,

Sons of Thunder), [18] and Andrew, and Philip, and Bartholomew, and Matthew, and Thomas, and James son of Alphaeus, and Thaddaeus, and Simon the Cananaean, [19] and Judas Iscariot, who handed him over.

✦ Jesus and Beelzebul

[20] Then he went home, and the crowd came together again, so that they could not even eat. [21] When his family heard it, they went out to restrain him, for people were saying, "He has gone out of his mind." [22] And the scribes who came down from Jerusalem said, "He has Beelzebul, and by the ruler of the demons he casts out demons." [23] And he called them to him and spoke to them in parables, "How can Satan cast out Satan? [24] If a kingdom is divided against itself, that kingdom cannot stand. [25] And if a house is divided against itself, that house will not be able to stand. [26] And if Satan has risen up against himself and is divided, he cannot stand, but his end has come. [27] But no one can enter a strong man's house and plunder his property without first tying up the strong man; then indeed the house can be plundered.

[28] "Truly I tell you, people will be forgiven for their sins and whatever blasphemies they utter, [29] but whoever blasphemes against the Holy Spirit can never have forgiveness but is guilty of an eternal sin"— [30] for they had said, "He has an unclean spirit."

✦ The True Family of Jesus

[31] Then his mother and his brothers came, and standing outside they sent to him and called him. [32] A crowd was sitting around him, and they said to him, "Your mother and your brothers are outside asking for you." [33] And he replied, "Who are my mother and my brothers?" [34] And looking at those who sat around him, he said, "Here are my mother and my brothers! [35] Whoever does the will of God is my brother and sister and mother."

CHAPTER 4

✤ The Parable of the Sower

 **gain he began to teach** beside the sea. Such a very large crowd gathered around him that he got into a boat on the sea and sat there, while the whole crowd was beside the sea on the land. ² He began to teach them many things in parables, and in his teaching he said to them: ³ "Listen! A sower went out to sow. ⁴ And as he sowed, some seed fell on a path, and the birds came and ate it up. ⁵ Other seed fell on rocky ground, where it did not have much soil, and it sprang up quickly, since it had no depth of soil. ⁶ And when the sun rose, it was scorched, and since it had no root it withered away. ⁷ Other seed fell among thorns, and the thorns grew up and choked it, and it yielded no grain. ⁸ Other seed fell into good soil and brought forth grain, growing up and increasing and yielding thirty and sixty and a hundredfold." ⁹ And he said, "If you have ears to hear, then hear!"

✤ The Purpose of the Parables

¹⁰ When he was alone, those who were around him along with the twelve asked him about the parables. ¹¹ And he said to them, "To you has been given the secret of the kingdom of God, but for those outside everything comes in parables, ¹² in order that

'they may indeed look but not perceive,
   and may indeed hear but not understand;
so that they may not turn again and be forgiven.'"

¹³ And he said to them, "Do you not understand this parable? Then how will you understand all the parables? ¹⁴ The sower sows the word. ¹⁵ These are the ones on the path where the word is sown: when they hear, Satan immediately comes and takes away the word that is sown in them. ¹⁶ And these are the ones sown on rocky ground: when they hear the word, they immediately receive it with joy. ¹⁷ But they have no root and endure only for a while;

then, when trouble or persecution arises on account of the word, immediately they fall away. [18] And others are those sown among the thorns: these are the ones who hear the word, [19] but the cares of the age and the lure of wealth and the desire for other things come in and choke the word, and it yields nothing. [20] And these are the ones sown on the good soil: they hear the word and accept it and bear fruit, thirty and sixty and a hundredfold."

✦ A Lamp under a Bushel Basket

[21] He said to them, "Is a lamp brought in to be put under the bushel basket or under the bed and not on the lampstand? [22] For there is nothing hidden, except to be disclosed; nor is anything secret, except to come to light. [23] If you have ears to hear, then hear!" [24] And he said to them, "Pay attention to what you hear; the measure you give will be the measure you get, and it will be added to you. [25] For to those who have, more will be given, and from those who have nothing, even what they have will be taken away."

✦ The Parable of the Growing Seed

[26] He also said, "The kingdom of God is as if someone would scatter seed on the ground [27] and would sleep and rise night and day, and the seed would sprout and grow, he does not know how. [28] The earth produces of itself first the stalk, then the head, then the full grain in the head. [29] But when the grain is ripe, at once he goes in with his sickle because the harvest has come."

✦ The Parable of the Mustard Seed

[30] He also said, "With what can we compare the kingdom of God, or what parable will we use for it? [31] It is like a mustard seed, which, when sown upon the ground, is the smallest of all the seeds on earth, [32] yet when it is sown it grows up and becomes the greatest of all shrubs and puts forth large branches, so that the birds of the air can make nests in its shade."

✦ The Use of Parables

33 With many such parables he spoke the word to them as they were able to hear it; **34** he did not speak to them except in parables, but he explained everything in private to his disciples.

✦ Jesus Calms the Storm

35 On that day, when evening had come, he said to them, "Let us go across to the other side." **36** And leaving the crowd behind, they took him with them in the boat, just as he was. Other boats were with him. **37** A great windstorm arose, and the waves beat into the boat, so that the boat was already being swamped. **38** But he was in the stern, asleep on the cushion, and they woke him up and said to him, "Teacher, do you not care that we are perishing?" **39** And waking up, he rebuked the wind and said to the sea, "Be silent! Be still!" Then the wind ceased, and there was a dead calm. **40** He said to them, "Why are you afraid? Have you still no faith?" **41** And they were filled with great fear and said to one another, "Who then is this, that even the wind and the sea obey him?"

CHAPTER 5

✦ Jesus Heals the Man with an Unclean Spirit

They came to the other side of the sea, to the region of the Gerasenes. **2** And when he had stepped out of the boat, immediately a man out of the tombs with an unclean spirit met him. **3** He lived among the tombs, and no one could restrain him any more, even with a chain, **4** for he had often been restrained with shackles and chains, but the chains he wrenched apart, and the shackles he broke in pieces, and no one had the strength to subdue him. **5** Night and day among the tombs and on the mountains he was always howling and bruising himself with stones. **6** When he saw Jesus from a distance, he ran and bowed down before him, **7** and he shouted at the top of his voice, "What have you to do with me, Jesus, Son of the Most High God? I adjure you by God, do not torment me."

⁸ For he had said to him, "Come out of the man, you unclean spirit!" ⁹ Then Jesus asked him, "What is your name?" He replied, "My name is Legion, for we are many." ¹⁰ He begged him earnestly not to send them out of the region. ¹¹ Now there on the hillside a great herd of swine was feeding, ¹² and the unclean spirits begged him, "Send us into the swine; let us enter them." ¹³ So he gave them permission. And the unclean spirits came out and entered the swine, and the herd, numbering about two thousand, stampeded down the steep bank into the sea and were drowned in the sea.

¹⁴ The swineherds ran off and told it in the city and in the country. Then people came to see what it was that had happened. ¹⁵ They came to Jesus and saw the man possessed by demons sitting there, clothed and in his right mind, the very man who had had the legion, and they became frightened. ¹⁶ Those who had seen what had happened to the man possessed by demons and to the swine reported it. ¹⁷ Then they began to beg Jesus to leave their neighborhood. ¹⁸ As he was getting into the boat, the man who had been possessed by demons begged him that he might be with him. ¹⁹ But Jesus refused and said to him, "Go home to your own people, and tell them how much the Lord has done for you and what mercy he has shown you." ²⁰ And he went away and began to proclaim in the Decapolis how much Jesus had done for him, and everyone was amazed.

✦ A Girl Restored to Life and a Woman Healed

²¹ When Jesus had crossed again in the boat to the other side, a great crowd gathered around him, and he was by the sea. ²² Then one of the leaders of the synagogue, named Jairus, came and, when he saw him, fell at his feet ²³ and pleaded with him repeatedly, "My little daughter is at the point of death. Come and lay your hands on her, so that she may be made well and live." ²⁴ So he went with him.

And a large crowd followed him and pressed in on him. ²⁵ Now there was a woman who had been suffering from a flow of blood for twelve years. ²⁶ She had endured much under many physicians and had spent all that she had, and she was no better but rather grew worse. **27** She had heard about Jesus and came up behind him in the crowd and touched his cloak, **28** for she said, "If I but touch his cloak, I will be made well." **29** Immediately her flow of blood stopped, and she felt in her body that she was healed of her disease. **30** Immediately aware that power had gone forth from him, Jesus turned about in the crowd and said, "Who touched my cloak?" **31** And his disciples said to him, "You see the crowd pressing in on you; how can you say, 'Who touched me?'" **32** He looked all around to see who had done it. **33** But the woman, knowing what had happened to her, came in fear and trembling, fell down before him, and told him the whole truth. **34** He said to her, "Daughter, your faith has made you well; go in peace, and be healed of your disease."

35 While he was still speaking, some people came from the synagogue leader's house to say, "Your daughter is dead. Why trouble the teacher any further?" **36** But overhearing what they said, Jesus said to the synagogue leader, "Do not be afraid; only believe." **37** He allowed no one to follow him except Peter, James, and John, the brother of James. **38** When they came to the synagogue leader's house, he saw a commotion, people weeping and wailing loudly. **39** When he had entered, he said to them, "Why do you make a commotion and weep? The child is not dead but sleeping." **40** And they laughed at him. Then he put them all outside and took the child's father and mother and those who were with him and went in where the child was. **41** Taking her by the hand, he said to her, "Talitha koum," which means, "Little girl, get up!" **42** And immediately the girl stood up and began to walk about (she was twelve years of age). At this they were overcome with amazement. **43** He strictly ordered them that no one should know this and told them to give her something to eat.

Chapter 6

✤ The Rejection of Jesus at Nazareth

**e left that place** and came to his hometown, and his disciples followed him. ² On the Sabbath he began to teach in the synagogue, and many who heard him were astounded. They said, "Where did this man get all this? What is this wisdom that has been given to him? What deeds of power are being done by his hands! ³ Is this not the carpenter, the son of Mary and brother of James and Joses and Judas and Simon, and are not his sisters here with us?" And they took offense at him. ⁴ Then Jesus said to them, "Prophets are not without honor, except in their hometown and among their own kin and in their own house." ⁵ And he could do no deed of power there, except that he laid his hands on a few sick people and cured them. ⁶ And he was amazed at their unbelief.

✤ The Mission of the Twelve

Then he went about among the villages teaching. ⁷ He called the twelve and began to send them out two by two and gave them authority over the unclean spirits. ⁸ He ordered them to take nothing for their journey except a staff: no bread, no bag, no money in their belts, ⁹ but to wear sandals and not to put on two tunics. ¹⁰ He said to them, "Wherever you enter a house, stay there until you leave the place. ¹¹ If any place will not welcome you and they refuse to hear you, as you leave, shake off the dust that is on your feet as a testimony against them." ¹² So they went out and proclaimed that all should repent. ¹³ They cast out many demons and anointed with oil many who were sick and cured them.

✤ The Death of John the Baptist

¹⁴ King Herod heard of it, for Jesus's name had become known. Some were saying, "John the baptizer has been raised from the dead, and for this reason these powers are at work in him." ¹⁵ But others said, "It is Elijah." And others said, "It is a prophet,

like one of the prophets of old." **16** But when Herod heard of it, he said, "John, whom I beheaded, has been raised."

17 For Herod himself had sent men who arrested John, bound him, and put him in prison on account of Herodias, his brother Philip's wife, because Herod had married her. **18** For John had been telling Herod, "It is not lawful for you to have your brother's wife." **19** And Herodias had a grudge against him and wanted to kill him. But she could not, **20** for Herod feared John, knowing that he was a righteous and holy man, and he protected him. When he heard him, he was greatly perplexed, and yet he liked to listen to him. **21** But an opportunity came when Herod on his birthday gave a banquet for his courtiers and officers and for the leaders of Galilee. **22** When his daughter Herodias came in and danced, she pleased Herod and his guests, and the king said to the girl, "Ask me for whatever you wish, and I will give it." **23** And he swore to her, "Whatever you ask me, I will give you, even half of my kingdom." **24** She went out and said to her mother, "What should I ask for?" She replied, "The head of John the baptizer." **25** Immediately she rushed back to the king and requested, "I want you to give me at once the head of John the Baptist on a platter." **26** The king was deeply grieved, yet out of regard for his oaths and for the guests, he did not want to refuse her. **27** Immediately the king sent a soldier of the guard with orders to bring John's head. He went and beheaded him in the prison, **28** brought his head on a platter, and gave it to the girl. Then the girl gave it to her mother. **29** When his disciples heard about it, they came and took his body, and laid it in a tomb.

✢ Jesus Feeds the Five Thousand

30 The apostles gathered around Jesus and told him all that they had done and taught. **31** He said to them, "Come away to a deserted place all by yourselves and rest a while." For many were coming and going, and they had no leisure even to eat. **32** And they went away in the boat to a deserted place by themselves. **33** Now many saw them going and recognized them, and they hurried there on foot from all the towns and arrived ahead of them. 34 As he went ashore, he saw a great crowd, and he had compassion for them, because they were like sheep without a shepherd, and he began to teach them many things. 35 When it grew late, his disciples came to him and said, "This is a deserted place, and the hour is now very late; 36 send them away so that they may go into the surrounding country and villages and buy something for themselves to eat." 37 But he answered them, "You give them something to eat." They said to him, "Are we to go and buy two hundred denarii worth of bread, and give it to them to eat?" 38 And he said to them, "How many loaves have you? Go and see." When they had found out, they said, "Five, and two fish." 39 Then he ordered them to get all the people to sit down in groups on the green grass. 40 So they sat down in groups of hundreds and of fifties. 41 Taking the five loaves and the two fish, he looked up to heaven and blessed and broke the loaves and gave them to his disciples to set before the people, and he divided the two fish among them all. 42 And all ate and were filled, 43 and they took up twelve baskets full of broken pieces and of the fish. 44 Those who had eaten the loaves numbered five thousand men.

✤ Jesus Walks on the Water

45 Immediately he made his disciples get into the boat and go on ahead to the other side, to Bethsaida, while he dismissed the crowd. 46 After saying farewell to them, he went up on the mountain to pray.

47 When evening came, the boat was out on the sea, and he was alone on the land. 48 When he saw that they were straining at the oars against an adverse wind, he came toward them early in the morning, walking on the sea. He intended to pass them by. 49 But when they saw him walking on the sea, they thought it was a ghost and cried out, 50 for they all saw him and were terrified. But immediately he spoke to them and said, "Take heart, it is I; do not be afraid." 51 Then he got into the boat with them, and the

wind ceased. And they were utterly astounded, ⁵² for they did not understand about the loaves, but their hearts were hardened.

✧ Healing the Sick in Gennesaret

⁵³ When they had crossed over, they came to land at Gennesaret and moored the boat. ⁵⁴ When they got out of the boat, people at once recognized him ⁵⁵ and rushed about that whole region and began to bring the sick on mats to wherever they heard he was. ⁵⁶ And wherever he went, into villages or cities or farms, they laid the sick in the marketplaces and begged him that they might touch even the fringe of his cloak, and all who touched it were healed.

CHAPTER 7

✧ The Tradition of the Elders

 **ow when the Pharisees** and some of the scribes who had come from Jerusalem gathered around him, ² they noticed that some of his disciples were eating with defiled hands, that is, without washing them. ³ (For the Pharisees, and all the Jews, do not eat unless they wash their hands, thus observing the tradition of the elders, ⁴ and they do not eat anything from the market unless they wash, and there are also many other traditions that they observe: the washing of cups and pots and bronze kettles and beds.) ⁵ So the Pharisees and the scribes asked him, "Why do your disciples not walk according to the tradition of the elders but eat with defiled hands?" ⁶ He said to them, "Isaiah prophesied rightly about you hypocrites, as it is written,

'This people honors me with their lips,
    but their hearts are far from me;
⁷ in vain do they worship me,
    teaching human precepts as doctrines.'

⁸ You abandon the commandment of God and hold to human tradition."

[9] Then he said to them, "You have a fine way of rejecting the commandment of God in order to keep your tradition! [10] For Moses said, 'Honor your father and your mother,' and, 'Whoever speaks evil of father or mother must surely die.' [11] But you say that if anyone tells father or mother, 'Whatever support you might have had from me is Corban' (that is, an offering to God), [12] then you no longer permit doing anything for a father or mother, [13] thus nullifying the word of God through your tradition that you have handed on. And you do many things like this."

[14] Then he called the crowd again and said to them, "Listen to me, all of you, and understand: [15] there is nothing outside a person that by going in can defile, but the things that come out are what defile."

[17] When he had left the crowd and entered the house, his disciples asked him about the parable. [18] He said to them, "So, are you also without understanding? Do you not see that whatever goes into a person from outside cannot defile, [19] since it enters not the heart but the stomach and goes out into the sewer?" (Thus he declared all foods clean.) [20] And he said, "It is what comes out of a person that defiles. [21] For it is from within, from the human heart, that evil intentions come: sexual immorality, theft, murder, [22] adultery, avarice, wickedness, deceit, debauchery, envy, slander, pride, folly. [23] All these evil things come from within, and they defile a person."

✤ The Syrophoenician Woman's Faith

[24] From there he set out and went away to the region of Tyre. He entered a house and did not want anyone to know he was there. Yet he could not escape notice, [25] but a woman whose little daughter had an unclean spirit immediately heard about him, and she came and bowed down at his feet. [26] Now the woman was a gentile, of Syrophoenician origin. She begged him to cast the demon out of her daughter. [27] He said to her, "Let the children be fed first, for it is not fair to take the children's food and throw it to the dogs." [28] But she answered him, "Sir, even the dogs under the table

eat the children's crumbs." **29** Then he said to her, "For saying that, you may go—the demon has left your daughter." **30** And when she went home, found the child lying on the bed, and the demon gone.

✤ Jesus Cures a Deaf Man

31 Then he returned from the region of Tyre and went by way of Sidon toward the Sea of Galilee, in the region of the Decapolis. **32** They brought to him a deaf man who had an impediment in his speech, and they begged him to lay his hand on him. **33** He took him aside in private, away from the crowd, and put his fingers into his ears, and he spat and touched his tongue. **34** Then looking up to heaven, he sighed and said to him, "Ephphatha," that is, "Be opened." **35** And his ears were opened, his tongue was released, and he spoke plainly. **36** Then Jesus ordered them to tell no one, but the more he ordered them, the more zealously they proclaimed it. **37** They were astounded beyond measure, saying, "He has done everything well; he even makes the deaf to hear and the mute to speak."

CHAPTER 8

✤ Jesus Feeds the Four Thousand

 **n those days** when there was again a great crowd without anything to eat, he called his disciples and said to them, **2** "I have compassion for the crowd because they have been with me now for three days and have nothing to eat. **3** If I send them away hungry to their homes, they will faint on the way—and some of them have come from a great distance." **4** His disciples replied, "How can one feed these people with bread here in the desert?" **5** He asked them, "How many loaves do you have?" They said, "Seven." **6** Then he ordered the crowd to sit down on the ground, and he took the seven loaves, and after giving thanks he broke them and gave them to his disciples to distribute, and they distributed them to the crowd. **7** They had also a few small fish, and after blessing

them he ordered that these, too, should be distributed. **8** They ate and were filled, and they took up the broken pieces left over, seven baskets full. **9** Now there were about four thousand people. And he sent them away. **10** And immediately he got into the boat with his disciples and went to the district of Dalmanutha.

✤ The Demand for a Sign

11 The Pharisees came and began to argue with him, asking him for a sign from heaven, to test him. **12** And he sighed deeply in his spirit and said, "Why does this generation ask for a sign? Truly I tell you, no sign will be given to this generation." **13** And he left them, and getting into the boat again he went across to the other side.

✤ The Yeast of the Pharisees and of Herod

14 Now the disciples had forgotten to bring any bread, and they had only one loaf with them in the boat. **15** And he cautioned them, saying, "Watch out—beware of the yeast of the Pharisees and the yeast of Herod." **16** They said to one another, "It is because we have no bread." **17** And becoming aware of it, Jesus said to them, "Why are you talking about having no bread? Do you still not perceive or understand? Are your hearts hardened? **18** Do you have eyes, and fail to see? Do you have ears, and fail to hear? And do you not remember? **19** When I broke the five loaves for the five thousand, how many baskets full of broken pieces did you collect?" They said to him, "Twelve." **20** "And the seven for the four thousand, how many baskets full of broken pieces did you collect?" And they said to him, "Seven." **21** Then he said to them, "Do you not yet understand?"

✤ Jesus Cures a Blind Man at Bethsaida

22 They came to Bethsaida. Some people brought a blind man to him and begged him to touch him. **23** He took the blind man by the hand and led him out of the village, and when he had put saliva on his eyes and laid his hands on him, he asked him, "Can you see anything?" **24** And the man looked up and said, "I can see people, but they look like trees, walking." **25** Then Jesus laid his hands on his eyes again, and he looked intently, and his sight was restored, and he saw everything clearly. **26** Then he sent him away to his home, saying, "Do not even go into the village."

✤ Peter's Declaration about Jesus

27 Jesus went on with his disciples to the villages of Caesarea Philippi, and on the way he asked his disciples, "Who do people say that I am?" **28** And they answered him, "John the Baptist; and others, Elijah; and still others, one of the prophets." **29** He asked them, "But who do you say that I am?" Peter answered him, "You are the Messiah." **30** And he sternly ordered them not to tell anyone about him.

✤ Jesus Foretells His Death and Resurrection

31 Then he began to teach them that the Son of Man must undergo great suffering and be rejected by the elders, the chief priests, and the scribes and be killed and after three days rise again. **32** He said all this quite openly. And Peter took him aside and began to rebuke him. **33** But turning and looking at his disciples, he rebuked Peter and said, "Get behind me, Satan! For you are setting your mind not on divine things but on human things."

34 He called the crowd with his disciples and said to them, "If any wish to come after me, let them deny themselves and take up their cross and follow me. **35** For those who want to save their life will lose it, and those who lose their life for my sake, and for the sake of the gospel, will save it. **36** For what will it profit them to gain the whole world and forfeit their life? **37** Indeed, what can they give in return for their life? **38** Those who are ashamed of me and of my words in this adulterous and sinful generation, of them the Son of Man will also be ashamed when he comes in the glory of his Father with the holy angels."

CHAPTER 9

nd he said to them, "Truly I tell you, there are some standing here who will not taste death until they see that the kingdom of God has come with power."

✦ The Transfiguration

² Six days later, Jesus took with him Peter and James and John and led them up a high mountain apart, by themselves. And he was transfigured before them, ³ and his clothes became dazzling bright, such as no one on earth could brighten them. ⁴ And there appeared to them Elijah with Moses, who were talking with Jesus. ⁵ Then Peter said to Jesus, "Rabbi, it is good for us to be here; let us set up three tents: one for you, one for Moses, and one for Elijah." ⁶ He did not know what to say, for they were terrified. ⁷ Then a cloud overshadowed them, and from the cloud there came a voice, "This is my Son, the Beloved; listen to him!" ⁸ Suddenly when they looked around, they saw no one with them any more, but only Jesus.

✦ The Coming of Elijah

⁹ As they were coming down the mountain, he ordered them to tell no one about what they had seen, until after the Son of Man had risen from the dead. ¹⁰ So they kept the matter to themselves, questioning what this rising from the dead could mean. ¹¹ Then they asked him, "Why do the scribes say that Elijah must come first?" ¹² He said to them, "Elijah is indeed coming first to restore all things. How then is it written about the Son of Man, that he is to go through many sufferings and be treated with contempt? ¹³ But I tell you that Elijah has come, and they did to him whatever they pleased, as it is written about him."

✦ Jesus Heals a Boy with a Spirit

14 When they came to the disciples, they saw a great crowd around them and some scribes arguing with them. **15** When the whole crowd saw him, they were immediately overcome with awe, and they ran forward to greet him. **16** He asked them, "What are you arguing about with them?" **17** Someone from the crowd answered him, "Teacher, I brought you my son; he has a spirit that makes him unable to speak, **18** and whenever it seizes him, it dashes him down; and he foams and grinds his teeth and becomes rigid, and I asked your disciples to cast it out, but they could not do so." **19** He answered them, "You faithless generation, how much longer must I be with you? How much longer must I put up with you? Bring him to me." **20** And they brought the boy to him. When the spirit saw him, immediately it convulsed the boy, and he fell on the ground and rolled about, foaming at the mouth. **21** Jesus asked the father, "How long has this been happening to him?" And he said, "From childhood. **22** It has often cast him into the fire and into the water, to destroy him; but if you are able to do anything, help us! Have compassion on us!" **23** Jesus said to him, "If you are able! All things can be done for the one who believes." **24** Immediately the father of the child cried out, "I believe; help my unbelief!" **25** When Jesus saw that a crowd came running together, he rebuked the unclean spirit, saying to it, "You spirit that keeps this boy from speaking and hearing, I command you, come out of him, and never enter him again!" **26** After crying out and convulsing him terribly, it came out, and the boy was like a corpse, so that most of them said, "He is dead." **27** But Jesus took him by the hand and lifted him up, and he was able to stand. **28** When he had entered the house, his disciples asked him privately, "Why could we not cast it out?" **29** He said to them, "This kind can come out only through prayer."

✦ Jesus Again Foretells His Death and Resurrection

30 They went on from there and passed through Galilee. He did not want anyone to know it, **31** for he was teaching his disciples, saying to them, "The Son of Man is to be betrayed into human hands, and they will kill him, and three days after being killed, he will rise again." ³² But they did not understand what he was saying and were afraid to ask him.

✤ Who Is the Greatest?

³³ Then they came to Capernaum, and when he was in the house he asked them, "What were you arguing about on the way?" ³⁴ But they were silent, for on the way they had argued with one another who was the greatest. ³⁵ He sat down, called the twelve, and said to them, "Whoever wants to be first must be last of all and servant of all." ³⁶ Then he took a little child and put it among them, and taking it in his arms he said to them, ³⁷ "Whoever welcomes one such child in my name welcomes me, and whoever welcomes me welcomes not me but the one who sent me."

✤ For the Sake of the Name

³⁸ John said to him, "Teacher, we saw someone casting out demons in your name, and we tried to stop him because he was not following us." ³⁹ But Jesus said, "Do not stop him, for no one who does a deed of power in my name will be able soon afterward to speak evil of me. ⁴⁰ Whoever is not against us is for us. ⁴¹ For truly I tell you, whoever gives you a cup of water to drink because you bear the name of Christ will by no means lose the reward.

✤ Temptations to Sin

⁴² "If any of you cause one of these little ones who believe in me to sin, it would be better for you if a great millstone were hung around your neck and you were thrown into the sea. ⁴³ If your hand causes you to sin, cut it off; it is better for you to enter life maimed than to have two hands and to go to hell, to the unquenchable fire. ⁴⁵ And if your foot causes you to sin, cut it off; it is better for you to enter life lame than to have two feet and to be thrown into hell. ⁴⁷ And if your eye causes you to sin, tear it out; it is better for you to enter the kingdom of God with one eye than to have

two eyes and to be thrown into hell, ⁴⁸ where their worm never dies, and the fire is never quenched.

⁴⁹ "For everyone will be salted with fire. ⁵⁰ Salt is good, but if salt has lost its saltiness, how can you season it? Have salt in yourselves, and be at peace with one another."

CHAPTER 10

✤ Concerning Divorce

 **e left that place** and went to the region of Judea and beyond the Jordan. And crowds again gathered around him, and, as was his custom, he again taught them.

² Some, testing him, asked, "Is it lawful for a man to divorce his wife?" ³ He answered them, "What did Moses command you?" ⁴ They said, "Moses allowed a man to write a certificate of dismissal and to divorce her." ⁵ But Jesus said to them, "Because of your hardness of heart he wrote this commandment for you. ⁶ But from the beginning of creation, 'God made them male and female.' ⁷ 'For this reason a man shall leave his father and mother and be joined to his wife, ⁸ and the two shall become one flesh.' So they are no longer two but one flesh. ⁹ Therefore what God has joined together, let no one separate."

¹⁰ Then in the house the disciples asked him again about this matter. ¹¹ He said to them, "Whoever divorces his wife and marries another commits adultery against her, ¹² and if she divorces her husband and marries another, she commits adultery."

✤ Let the Children Come to Me

¹³ People were bringing children to him in order that he might touch them, and the disciples spoke sternly to them. ¹⁴ But when Jesus saw this, he was indignant and said to them, "Let the children come to me; do not stop them, for it is to such as these that the kingdom of God belongs. ¹⁵ Truly I tell you, whoever does not

receive the kingdom of God as a little child will never enter it."
¹⁶ And he took them up in his arms, laid his hands on them, and blessed them.

✦ The Rich Man

¹⁷ As he was setting out on a journey, a man ran up and knelt before him and asked him, "Good Teacher, what must I do to inherit eternal life?" ¹⁸ Jesus said to him, "Why do you call me good? No one is good but God alone. ¹⁹ You know the commandments: 'You shall not murder. You shall not commit adultery. You shall not steal. You shall not bear false witness. You shall not defraud. Honor your father and mother.'" ²⁰ He said to him, "Teacher, I have kept all these since my youth." ²¹ Jesus, looking at him, loved him and said, "You lack one thing; go, sell what you own, and give the money to the poor, and you will have treasure in heaven; then come, follow me." ²² When he heard this, he was shocked and went away grieving, for he had many possessions.

²³ Then Jesus looked around and said to his disciples, "How hard it will be for those who have wealth to enter the kingdom of God!" ²⁴ And the disciples were perplexed at these words. But Jesus said to them again, "Children, how hard it is to enter the kingdom of God! ²⁵ It is easier for a camel to go through the eye of a needle than for someone who is rich to enter the kingdom of God." ²⁶ They were greatly astounded and said to one another, "Then who can be saved?" ²⁷ Jesus looked at them and said, "For mortals it is impossible, but not for God; for God all things are possible."

²⁸ Peter began to say to him, "Look, we have left everything and followed you." ²⁹ Jesus said, "Truly I tell you, there is no one who has left house or brothers or sisters or mother or father or children or fields for my sake and for the sake of the good news ³⁰ who will not receive a hundredfold now in this age—houses, brothers and sisters, mothers and children, and fields, with persecutions—and in the age to come eternal life. ³¹ But many who are first will be last, and the last will be first."

✦ A Third Time Jesus Foretells His Death and Resurrection

³² They were on the road, going up to Jerusalem, and Jesus was walking ahead of them; they were amazed, and those who followed were afraid. He took the twelve aside again and began to tell them what was to happen to him, ³³ saying, "Look, we are going up to Jerusalem, and the Son of Man will be handed over to the chief priests and the scribes, and they will condemn him to death; then they will hand him over to the gentiles; ³⁴ they will mock him and spit upon him and flog him and kill him, and after three days he will rise again."

✦ The Request of James and John

³⁵ James and John, the sons of Zebedee, came forward to him and said to him, "Teacher, we want you to do for us whatever we ask of you." ³⁶ And he said to them, "What is it you want me to do for you?" ³⁷ And they said to him, "Appoint us to sit, one at your right hand and one at your left, in your glory." ³⁸ But Jesus said to them, "You do not know what you are asking. Are you able to drink the cup that I drink or be baptized with the baptism that I am baptized with?" ³⁹ They replied, "We are able." Then Jesus said to them, "The cup that I drink you will drink, and with the baptism with which I am baptized, you will be baptized, ⁴⁰ but to sit at my right hand or at my left is not mine to appoint, but it is for those for whom it has been prepared."

⁴¹ When the ten heard this, they began to be angry with James and John. ⁴² So Jesus called them and said to them, "You know that among the gentiles those whom they recognize as their rulers lord it over them, and their great ones are tyrants over them. ⁴³ But it is not so among you; instead, whoever wishes to become great among you must be your servant, ⁴⁴ and whoever wishes to be first among you must be slave of all. ⁴⁵ For the Son of Man came not to be served but to serve and to give his life a ransom for many."

✦ The Healing of Blind Bartimaeus

46 They came to Jericho. As he and his disciples and a large crowd were leaving Jericho, Bartimaeus son of Timaeus, a blind beggar, was sitting by the roadside. **47** When he heard that it was Jesus of Nazareth, he began to shout out and say, "Jesus, Son of David, have mercy on me!" **48** Many sternly ordered him to be quiet, but he cried out even more loudly, "Son of David, have mercy on me!" **49** Jesus stood still and said, "Call him here." And they called the blind man, saying to him, "Take heart; get up, he is calling you." **50** So throwing off his cloak, he sprang up and came to Jesus. **51** Then Jesus said to him, "What do you want me to do for you?" The blind man said to him, "My teacher, let me see again." **52** Jesus said to him, "Go; your faith has made you well." Immediately he regained his sight and followed him on the way.

CHAPTER 11

✦ Jesus' Triumphal Entry into Jerusalem

When they were approaching Jerusalem, at Bethphage and Bethany, near the Mount of Olives, he sent two of his disciples **2** and said to them, "Go into the village ahead of you, and immediately as you enter it you will find tied there a colt that has never been ridden; untie it and bring it. **3** If anyone says to you, 'Why are you doing this?' just say this, 'The Lord needs it and will send it back here immediately.'" **4** They went away and found a colt tied near a door, outside in the street. As they were untying it, **5** some of the bystanders said to them, "What are you doing, untying the colt?" **6** They told them what Jesus had said, and they allowed them to take it. **7** Then they brought the colt to Jesus and threw their cloaks on it, and he sat on it. **8** Many people spread their cloaks on the road, and others spread leafy branches that they had cut in the fields. **9** Then those who went ahead and those who followed were shouting,

"Hosanna!
Blessed is the one who comes in the name of the Lord!
10 Blessed is the coming kingdom of our ancestor David!
Hosanna in the highest heaven!"

11 Then he entered Jerusalem and went into the temple, and when he had looked around at everything, as it was already late, he went out to Bethany with the twelve.

✧ Jesus Curses the Fig Tree

12 On the following day, when they came from Bethany, he was hungry. 13 Seeing in the distance a fig tree in leaf, he went to see whether perhaps he would find anything on it. When he came to it, he found nothing but leaves, for it was not the season for figs. 14 He said to it, "May no one ever eat fruit from you again." And his disciples heard it.

✧ Jesus Cleanses the Temple

15 Then they came to Jerusalem. And he entered the temple and began to drive out those who were selling and those who were buying in the temple, and he overturned the tables of the money changers and the seats of those who sold doves, 16 and he would not allow anyone to carry anything through the temple. 17 He was teaching and saying, "Is it not written,

'My house shall be called a house of prayer for all
    the nations'?
But you have made it a den of robbers.'"

18 And when the chief priests and the scribes heard it, they kept looking for a way to kill him, for they were afraid of him because the whole crowd was spellbound by his teaching. 19 And when evening came, Jesus and his disciples went out of the city.

✧ The Lesson from the Withered Fig Tree

20 In the morning as they passed by, they saw the fig tree withered away to its roots. 21 Then Peter remembered and said to him, "Rabbi, look! The fig tree that you cursed has withered." 22 Jesus answered

them, "Have faith in God. ²³ Truly I tell you, if you say to this mountain, 'Be taken up and thrown into the sea,' and if you do not doubt in your heart but believe that what you say will come to pass, it will be done for you. ²⁴ So I tell you, whatever you ask for in prayer, believe that you have received it, and it will be yours.

²⁵ "Whenever you stand praying, forgive, if you have anything against anyone, so that your Father in heaven may also forgive you your trespasses."

✧ Jesus' Authority Is Questioned

²⁷ Again they came to Jerusalem. As he was walking in the temple, the chief priests, the scribes, and the elders came to him ²⁸ and said, "By what authority are you doing these things? Who gave you this authority to do them?" ²⁹ Jesus said to them, "I will ask you one question; answer me, and I will tell you by what authority I do these things. ³⁰ Did the baptism of John come from heaven, or was it of human origin? Answer me." ³¹ They argued with one another, "What should we say? If we say, 'From heaven,' he will say, 'Why then did you not believe him?' ³² But shall we say, 'Of human origin'?"—they were afraid of the crowd, for all regarded John as truly a prophet. ³³ So they answered Jesus, "We do not know." And Jesus said to them, "Neither will I tell you by what authority I am doing these things."

CHAPTER 12

✧ The Parable of the Wicked Tenants

**hen he began to speak** to them in parables. "A man planted a vineyard, put a fence around it, dug a pit for the wine press, and built a watchtower; then he leased it to tenants and went away. ² When the season came, he sent a slave to the tenants to collect from them his share of the produce of the vineyard. ³ But they seized him and beat him and sent him away empty-handed.

[4] And again he sent another slave to them; this one they beat over the head and insulted. [5] Then he sent another, and that one they killed. And so it was with many others; some they beat, and others they killed. [6] He had still one other, a beloved son. Finally he sent him to them, saying, 'They will respect my son.' [7] But those tenants said to one another, 'This is the heir; come, let us kill him, and the inheritance will be ours.' [8] So they seized him, killed him, and threw him out of the vineyard. [9] What then will the owner of the vineyard do? He will come and destroy the tenants and give the vineyard to others. [10] Have you not read this scripture:

'The stone that the builders rejected,
    has become the cornerstone;
[11] this was the Lord's doing,
    and it is amazing in our eyes'?"

[12] When they realized that he had told this parable against them, they wanted to arrest him, but they feared the crowd. So they left him and went away.

✢ The Question about Paying Taxes

[13] Then they sent to him some Pharisees and some Herodians to trap him in what he said. [14] And they came and said to him, "Teacher, we know that you are sincere and show deference to no one, for you do not regard people with partiality but teach the way of God in accordance with truth. Is it lawful to pay taxes to Caesar or not? [15] Should we pay them, or should we not?" But knowing their hypocrisy, he said to them, "Why are you putting me to the test? Bring me a denarius and let me see it." [16] And they brought one. Then he said to them, "Whose head is this, and whose title?" They answered, "Caesar's." [17] Jesus said to them, "Give to Caesar the things that are the Caesar's, and to God the things that are God's." And they were utterly amazed at him.

✢ The Question about the Resurrection

[18] Some Sadducees, who say there is no resurrection, came to him and asked him a question, saying, [19] "Teacher, Moses wrote for

us that if a man's brother dies, leaving a wife but no child, the man shall marry the widow and raise up children for his brother. **20** There were seven brothers; the first married and, when he died, left no children, **21** and the second married the widow and died, leaving no children, and the third likewise; **22** none of the seven left children. Last of all the woman herself died. **23** In the resurrection, when they rise, whose wife will she be? For the seven had married her."

24 Jesus said to them, "Is not this the reason you are wrong, that you know neither the scriptures nor the power of God? **25** For when they rise from the dead, they neither marry nor are given in marriage but are like angels in heaven. **26** And as for the dead being raised, have you not read in the book of Moses, in the story about the bush, how God said to him, 'I am the God of Abraham, the God of Isaac, and the God of Jacob'? **27** He is God not of the dead, but of the living; you are quite wrong."

✤ The Greatest Commandment

28 One of the scribes came near and heard them disputing with one another, and seeing that he answered them well he asked him, "Which commandment is the first of all?" **29** Jesus answered, "The first is, 'Hear, O Israel: the Lord our God, the Lord is one; **30** you shall love the Lord your God with all your heart and with all your soul and with all your mind and with all your strength.' **31** The second is this, 'You shall love your neighbor as yourself.' There is no other commandment greater than these." **32** Then the scribe said to him, "You are right, Teacher; you have truly said that 'he is one, and besides him there is no other'; **33** and 'to love him with all the heart and with all the understanding and with all the strength' and 'to love one's neighbor as oneself,'—this is much more important than all whole burnt offerings and sacrifices." **34** When Jesus saw that he answered wisely, he said to him, "You are not far from the kingdom of God." After that no one dared to ask him any question.

✦ The Question about David's Son

35 While Jesus was teaching in the temple, he said, "How can the scribes say that the Messiah is the son of David? **36** David himself, by the Holy Spirit, declared,

'The Lord said to my Lord,
"Sit at my right hand,
until I put your enemies under your feet."'

37 David himself calls him Lord; so how can he be his son?" And the large crowd was listening to him with delight.

✦ Jesus Denounces the Scribes

38 As he taught, he said, "Beware of the scribes, who like to walk around in long robes and to be greeted with respect in the marketplaces **39** and to have the best seats in the synagogues and places of honor at banquets! **40** They devour widows' houses and for the sake of appearance say long prayers. They will receive the greater condemnation."

✦ The Widow's Offering

41 He sat down opposite the treasury and watched the crowd putting money into the treasury. Many rich people put in large sums. **42** A poor widow came and put in two small copper coins, which are worth a penny. **43** Then he called his disciples and said to them, "Truly I tell you, this poor widow has put in more than all those who are contributing to the treasury. **44** For all of them have contributed out of their abundance, but she out of her poverty has put in everything she had, all she had to live on."

Chapter **13**

✤ The Destruction of the Temple Foretold

**s he came out of the temple,** one of his disciples said to him, "Look, Teacher, what large stones and what large buildings!" **2** Then Jesus asked him, "Do you see these great buildings? Not one stone will be left here upon another; all will be thrown down."

3 When he was sitting on the Mount of Olives opposite the temple, Peter, James, John, and Andrew asked him privately, **4** "Tell us, when will this be, and what will be the sign that all these things are about to be accomplished?" **5** Then Jesus began to say to them, "Beware that no one leads you astray. **6** Many will come in my name and say, 'I am he!' and they will lead many astray. **7** When you hear of wars and rumors of wars, do not be alarmed; this must take place, but the end is still to come. **8** For nation will rise against nation and kingdom against kingdom; there will be earthquakes in various places; there will be famines. This is but the beginning of the birth pangs.

✤ Persecution Foretold

9 "As for yourselves, beware, for they will hand you over to councils, and you will be beaten in synagogues, and you will stand before governors and kings because of me, as a testimony to them. **10** And the good news must first be proclaimed to all nations. **11** When they bring you to trial and hand you over, do not worry beforehand about what you are to say, but say whatever is given you at that time, for it is not you who speak but the Holy Spirit. **12** Sibling will betray sibling to death, and a father his child, and children will rise against parents and have them put to death, **13** and you will be hated by all because of my name. But the one who endures to the end will be saved.

✤ The Coming of False Messiahs

14 "But when you see the desolating sacrilege set up where it ought not to be (let the reader understand), then those in Judea must flee to the mountains; **15** the one on the housetop must not go down or enter the house to take anything from the house; **16** the one in the field must not turn back to get a coat. **17** Woe to those who are pregnant and to those who are nursing infants in those days! **18** Pray that it may not be in winter. **19** For in those days there will be suffering, such as has not been from the beginning of the creation that God created until now and never will be. **20** And if the Lord had not cut short those days, no one would be saved, but for the sake of the elect, whom he chose, he has cut short those days. **21** And if anyone says to you at that time, 'Look! Here is the Messiah!' or 'Look! There he is!'—do not believe it. **22** False messiahs and false prophets will appear and produce signs and wonders, to lead astray, if possible, the elect. **23** But be alert; I have already told you everything.

✤ The Coming of the Son of Man

24 "But in those days, after that suffering,

> the sun will be darkened,
>   and the moon will not give its light,
> **25** and the stars will be falling from heaven,
>   and the powers in the heavens will be shaken.

26 Then they will see 'the Son of Man coming in clouds' with great power and glory. **27** Then he will send out the angels and gather his elect from the four winds, from the ends of the earth to the ends of heaven.

✤ The Lesson of the Fig Tree

28 "From the fig tree learn its lesson: as soon as its branch becomes tender and puts forth its leaves, you know that summer is near. **29** So also, when you see these things taking place, you know that he is near, at the very gates. **30** Truly I tell you, this generation will not pass away until all these things have taken place. [31] Heaven and earth will pass away, but my words will not pass away.

✦ Be Ready

[32] "But about that day or hour no one knows, neither the angels in heaven, nor the Son, but only the Father. [33] Beware, keep alert, for you do not know when the time will come. [34] It is like a man going on a journey, when he leaves home and puts his slaves in charge, each with his work, and commands the doorkeeper to be on the watch. [35] Therefore, keep awake, for you do not know when the master of the house will come, in the evening or at midnight or at cockcrow or at dawn, [36] or else he may find you asleep when he comes suddenly. [37] And what I say to you I say to all: Keep awake."

CHAPTER 14

✦ The Plot to Kill Jesus

 **t was two days** before the Passover and the Festival of Unleavened Bread. The chief priests and the scribes were looking for a way to arrest Jesus by stealth and kill him, [2] for they said, "Not during the festival, or there may be a riot among the people."

✦ The Anointing at Bethany

[3] While he was at Bethany in the house of Simon the leper, as he sat at the table, a woman came with an alabaster jar of very costly ointment of nard, and she broke open the jar and poured the ointment on his head. [4] But some were there who said to one another in anger, "Why was the ointment wasted in this way? [5] For this ointment could have been sold for more than three hundred denarii, and the money given to the poor." And they scolded her. [6] But Jesus said, "Let her alone; why do you trouble her? She has performed a good service for me. [7] For you always have the poor with you, and you can show kindness to them whenever you wish, but you will not always have me. [8] She has done what she could; she has

anointed my body beforehand for its burial. **9** Truly I tell you, wherever the good news is proclaimed in the whole world, what she has done will be told in remembrance of her."

✤ Judas Agrees to Betray Jesus

10 Then Judas Iscariot, who was one of the twelve, went to the chief priests in order to betray him to them. **11** When they heard it, they were greatly pleased and promised to give him money. So he began to look for an opportunity to betray him.

✤ The Passover with the Disciples

12 On the first day of Unleavened Bread, when the Passover lamb is sacrificed, his disciples said to him, "Where do you want us to go and make the preparations for you to eat the Passover?" **13** So he sent two of his disciples, saying to them, "Go into the city, and a man carrying a jar of water will meet you; follow him, **14** and wherever he enters, say to the owner of the house, 'The Teacher asks, Where is my guest room where I may eat the Passover with my disciples?' **15** He will show you a large room upstairs, furnished and ready. Make preparations for us there." **16** So the disciples set out and went to the city and found everything as he had told them, and they prepared the Passover meal.

17 When it was evening, he came with the twelve. **18** And when they had taken their places and were eating, Jesus said, "Truly I tell you, one of you will betray me, one who is eating with me." **19** They began to be distressed and to say to him one after another, "Surely, not I?" **20** He said to them, "It is one of the twelve, one who is dipping bread into the bowl with me. **21** For the Son of Man goes as it is written of him, but woe to that one by whom the Son of Man is betrayed! It would have been better for that one not to have been born."

✤ The Institution of the Lord's Supper

22 While they were eating, he took a loaf of bread, and after blessing it he broke it, gave it to them, and said, "Take; this is my body." **23** Then he took a cup, and after giving thanks he gave it to them, and all of them drank from it. ²⁴ He said to them, "This is my blood of the covenant, which is poured out for many. ²⁵ Truly I tell you, I will never again drink of the fruit of the vine until that day when I drink it new in the kingdom of God."

✦ Peter's Denial Foretold

²⁶ When they had sung the hymn, they went out to the Mount of Olives. ²⁷ And Jesus said to them, "You will all fall away, for it is written,

'I will strike the shepherd,
 and the sheep will be scattered.'

²⁸ But after I am raised up, I will go before you to Galilee." ²⁹ Peter said to him, "Even though all fall away, I will not." ³⁰ Jesus said to him, "Truly I tell you, this day, this very night, before the cock crows twice, you will deny me three times." ³¹ But he said vehemently, "Even though I must die with you, I will not deny you." And all of them said the same.

✦ Jesus Prays in Gethsemane

³² They went to a place called Gethsemane, and he said to his disciples, "Sit here while I pray." ³³ He took with him Peter and James and John and began to be distressed and agitated. ³⁴ And he said to them, "My soul is deeply grieved, even to death; remain here, and keep awake." ³⁵ And going a little farther, he threw himself on the ground and prayed that, if it were possible, the hour might pass from him. ³⁶ He said, "Abba, Father, for you all things are possible; remove this cup from me, yet, not what I want, but what you want." ³⁷ He came and found them sleeping, and he said to Peter, "Simon, are you asleep? Could you not keep awake one hour? ³⁸ Keep awake and pray that you may not come into the time of trial; the spirit indeed is willing, but the flesh is weak." ³⁹ And again he went away and prayed, saying the same words. ⁴⁰ And once more he came and found them sleeping, for their eyes were very heavy, and they did not know what to say to him. ⁴¹ He came a third time and said to them, "Are you still sleeping

and taking your rest? Enough! The hour has come; the Son of Man is betrayed into the hands of sinners. ⁴² Get up, let us be going. See, my betrayer is at hand."

✦ The Betrayal and Arrest of Jesus

⁴³ Immediately, while he was still speaking, Judas, one of the twelve, arrived, and with him there was a crowd with swords and clubs, from the chief priests, the scribes, and the elders. ⁴⁴ Now the betrayer had given them a sign, saying, "The one I will kiss is the man; arrest him and lead him away under guard." ⁴⁵ So when he came, he went up to him at once and said, "Rabbi!" and kissed him. ⁴⁶ Then they laid hands on him and arrested him. ⁴⁷ But one of those who stood near drew his sword and struck the slave of the high priest, cutting off his ear. ⁴⁸ Then Jesus said to them, "Have you come out with swords and clubs to arrest me as though I were a rebel? ⁴⁹ Day after day I was with you in the temple teaching, and you did not arrest me. But let the scriptures be fulfilled." ⁵⁰ All of them deserted him and fled.

⁵¹ A certain young man was following him, wearing nothing but a linen cloth. They caught hold of him, ⁵² but he left the linen cloth and ran off naked.

✦ Jesus before Caiaphas

⁵³ They took Jesus to the high priest, and all the chief priests, the elders, and the scribes were assembled. ⁵⁴ Peter had followed him at a distance, right into the courtyard of the high priest, and he was sitting with the guards, warming himself at the fire. ⁵⁵ Now the chief priests and the whole council were looking for testimony against Jesus to put him to death, but they found none. ⁵⁶ For many gave false testimony against him, and their testimony did not agree. ⁵⁷ Some stood up and gave false testimony against him, saying, ⁵⁸ "We heard him say, 'I will destroy this temple that is made with hands, and in three days I will build another, not made with hands.'" ⁵⁹ But even on this point their testimony did not agree. ⁶⁰ Then the high priest stood up before them and asked

Jesus, "Have you no answer? What is it that they testify against you?" ⁶¹ But he was silent and did not answer. Again the high priest asked him, "Are you the Messiah, the Son of the Blessed One?" ⁶² Jesus said, "I am, and

'you will see the Son of Man
seated at the right hand of the Power,'
and 'coming with the clouds of heaven.'"

⁶³ Then the high priest tore his clothes and said, "Why do we still need witnesses? ⁶⁴ You have heard his blasphemy! What is your decision?" All of them condemned him as deserving death. ⁶⁵ Some began to spit on him, to blindfold him, and to strike him, saying to him, "Prophesy!" The guards also took him and beat him.

✣ Peter Denies Jesus

⁶⁶ While Peter was below in the courtyard, one of the female servants of the high priest came by. ⁶⁷ When she saw Peter warming himself, she stared at him and said, "You also were with Jesus, the man from Nazareth." ⁶⁸ But he denied it, saying, "I do not know or understand what you are talking about." And he went out into the forecourt. Then the cock crowed. ⁶⁹ And the female servant, on seeing him, began again to say to the bystanders, "This man is one of them." ⁷⁰ But again he denied it. Then after a little while the bystanders again said to Peter, "Certainly you are one of them, for you are a Galilean, and you talk like one." ⁷¹ But he began to curse, and he swore an oath, "I do not know this man you are talking about." ⁷² At that moment the cock crowed for the second time. Then Peter remembered that Jesus had said to him, "Before the cock crows twice, you will deny me three times." And he broke down and wept.

CHAPTER 15

✤ Jesus before Pilate

s soon as it was morning, the chief priests held a consultation with the elders and scribes and the whole council. They bound Jesus, led him away, and handed him over to Pilate. ² Pilate asked him, "Are you the King of the Jews?" He answered him, "You say so." ³ Then the chief priests accused him of many things. ⁴ Pilate asked him again, "Have you no answer? See how many charges they bring against you." ⁵ But Jesus made no further reply, so that Pilate was amazed.

✤ Pilate Hands Jesus over to Be Crucified

⁶ Now at the festival he used to release a prisoner for them, anyone for whom they asked. ⁷ Now a man called Barabbas was in prison with the insurrectionists who had committed murder during the insurrection. ⁸ So the crowd came and began to ask Pilate to do for them according to his custom. ⁹ Then he answered them, "Do you want me to release for you the King of the Jews?" ¹⁰ For he realized that it was out of jealousy that the chief priests had handed him over. ¹¹ But the chief priests stirred up the crowd to have him release Barabbas for them instead. ¹² Pilate spoke to them again, "Then what do you wish me to do with the man you call the King of the Jews?" ¹³ They shouted back, "Crucify him!" ¹⁴ Pilate asked them, "Why, what evil has he done?" But they shouted all the more, "Crucify him!" ¹⁵ So Pilate, wishing to satisfy the crowd, released Barabbas for them, and after flogging Jesus, he handed him over to be crucified.

✤ The Soldiers Mock Jesus

¹⁶ Then the soldiers led him into the courtyard of the palace (that is, the governor's headquarters), and they called together the whole cohort. ¹⁷ And they clothed him in a purple cloak, and after twisting some thorns into a crown they put it on him. ¹⁸ And they began

saluting him, "Hail, King of the Jews!" **19** They struck his head with a reed, spat upon him, and knelt down in homage to him. **20** After mocking him, they stripped him of the purple cloak and put his own clothes on him. Then they led him out to crucify him.

✦ The Crucifixion of Jesus

21 They compelled a passer-by, who was coming in from the country, to carry his cross; it was Simon of Cyrene, the father of Alexander and Rufus. **22** Then they brought Jesus to the place called Golgotha (which means Place of a Skull). **23** And they offered him wine mixed with myrrh, but he did not take it. **24** And they crucified him and divided his clothes among them, casting lots to decide what each should take.

25 It was nine o'clock in the morning when they crucified him. **26** The inscription of the charge against him read, "The King of the Jews." **27** And with him they crucified two rebels, one on his right and one on his left. **29** Those who passed by derided him, shaking their heads and saying, "Aha! You who would destroy the temple and build it in three days, **30** save yourself, and come down from the cross!" **31** In the same way the chief priests, along with the scribes, were also mocking him among themselves and saying, "He saved others; he cannot save himself. **32** Let the Messiah, the King of Israel, come down from the cross now, so that we may see and believe." Those who were crucified with him also taunted him.

✦ The Death of Jesus

33 When it was noon, darkness came over the whole land until three in the afternoon. **34** At three o'clock Jesus cried out with a loud voice, "Eloi, Eloi, lema sabachthani?" which means, "My God, my God, why have you forsaken me?" **35** When some of the bystanders heard it, they said, "Listen, he is calling for Elijah." **36** And someone ran, filled a sponge with sour wine, put it on a stick, and gave it to him to drink, saying, "Wait, let us see whether Elijah will come to take him down." **37** Then Jesus gave a loud cry and breathed his last. **38** And the curtain of the temple was torn in two, from top to bottom. ³⁹ Now when the centurion who stood facing him saw that in this way he breathed his last, he said, "Truly this man was God's Son!"

⁴⁰ There were also women looking on from a distance. Among them were Mary Magdalene, and Mary the mother of James the younger and of Joses, and Salome, ⁴¹ who followed him when he was in Galilee and ministered to him, and there were many other women who had come up with him to Jerusalem.

✤ The Burial of Jesus

⁴² When evening had come, and since it was the day of Preparation, that is, the day before the Sabbath, ⁴³ Joseph of Arimathea, a respected member of the council who was also himself waiting expectantly for the kingdom of God, went boldly to Pilate and asked for the body of Jesus. ⁴⁴ Then Pilate wondered if he were already dead, and summoning the centurion he asked him whether he had been dead for some time. ⁴⁵ When he learned from the centurion that he was dead, he granted the body to Joseph. ⁴⁶ Then Joseph bought a linen cloth and, taking down the body, wrapped it in the linen cloth and laid it in a tomb that had been hewn out of the rock. He then rolled a stone against the door of the tomb. ⁴⁷ Mary Magdalene and Mary the mother of Joses saw where the body was laid.

CHAPTER 16

✤ The Resurrection of Jesus

 **hen the sabbath was over,** Mary Magdalene and Mary the mother of James and Salome bought spices, so that they might go and anoint him. ² And very early on the first day of the week, when the sun had risen, they went to the tomb. ³ They had been saying to one another, "Who will roll away the stone for us from the entrance to the tomb?" ⁴ When they looked up, they saw that

the stone, which was very large, had already been rolled back. ⁵ As they entered the tomb, they saw a young man, dressed in a white robe sitting on the right side, and they were alarmed. ⁶ But he said to them, "Do not be alarmed; you are looking for Jesus of Nazareth, who was crucified. He has been raised; he is not here. Look, there is the place they laid him. ⁷ But go, tell his disciples and Peter that he is going ahead of you to Galilee; there you will see him, just as he told you." ⁸ So they went out and fled from the tomb, for terror and amazement had seized them, and they said nothing to anyone, for they were afraid.

THE INTERMEDIATE ENDING OF MARK

[And all that had been commanded them they told briefly to those around Peter. And afterward Jesus himself sent out through them, from east to west, the sacred and imperishable proclamation of eternal salvation. Amen.]

THE LONG ENDING OF MARK
✦ Jesus Appears to Mary Magdalene

[⁹ Now after he rose early on the first day of the week, he appeared first to Mary Magdalene, from whom he had cast out seven demons. ¹⁰ She went out and told those who had been with him, while they were mourning and weeping. ¹¹ But when they heard that he was alive and had been seen by her, they would not believe it.

✦ Jesus Appears to Two Disciples

¹² After this he appeared in another form to two of them, as they were walking into the country. ¹³ And they went back and told the rest, but they did not believe them.

✦ Jesus Commissions the Disciples

¹⁴ Later he appeared to the eleven themselves as they were sitting at the table, and he upbraided them for their lack of faith and stubbornness, because they had not believed those who saw him after he had risen. ¹⁵ And he said to them, "Go into all the world and proclaim the good news to the whole creation. ¹⁶ The one who

believes and is baptized will be saved, but the one who does not believe will be condemned. **¹⁷** And these signs will accompany those who believe: by using my name they will cast out demons; they will speak in new tongues; **¹⁸** they will pick up snakes, and if they drink any deadly thing, it will not hurt them; they will lay their hands on the sick, and they will recover."

✢ The Ascension of Jesus

¹⁹ So then the Lord Jesus, after he had spoken to them, was taken up into heaven and sat down at the right hand of God. **²⁰** And they went out and proclaimed the good news everywhere, while the Lord worked with them and confirmed the message by the signs that accompanied it.]

✦ Gospel of Luke ✦

St. Luke focuses on how Jesus accomplishes God's promise of redemption of all people. Written between AD 70 and 85, Luke's Gospel is the first part of a two-volume work (the second being the Acts of the Apostles).

St. Paul calls Luke "the Beloved Physician." Luke shows a knowledge of illnesses and writes many descriptions of Jesus' miraculous healings.

What also distinguishes Luke's Gospel is how he describes Jesus' mother, Mary. The accounts of Mary's annunciation, her visit to Elizabeth, and the Magnificat are present only in this Gospel. Luke must have known Mary and heard about these events from her.

Luke writes this Gospel to encourage his friend Theophilus about this "good news" of Jesus Christ. Theophilus may have been a person of high social standing. The name means "friend of God" or "loved by God." We are also "friends of God," and we, too, can be encouraged about this Gospel and follow Jesus.

Luke accompanied Paul on his missionary journeys throughout the Roman Empire. Some historians say that Luke was martyred after Paul's death; others say he lived a long life, dying at the age of eighty-four "full of the Holy Spirit" after settling in present-day Greece to write his Gospel.

Luke is the patron saint of physicians, surgeons, and artists. His feast day is celebrated on October 18.

The winged ox represents St. Luke. In the time of Jesus, oxen were sacrificed in the temple. Luke begins with the announcement of the birth of John the Baptist to his father, the priest Zechariah, who was offering sacrifice in the temple. Luke also includes the parable of the Loving Father. In it, the fatted calf is slaughtered not only to celebrate the younger son's return, but also to foreshadow the joy of the parousia. The winged ox reminds us of Jesus, our high priest, and his sacrifice for our redemption.

CHAPTER 1

✧ Dedication to Theophilus

 **ince many have undertaken** to compile a narrative about the events that have been fulfilled among us, **²** just as they were handed on to us by those who from the beginning were eyewitnesses and servants of the word, **³** I, too, decided, as one having a grasp of everything from the start, to write a well-ordered account for you, most excellent Theophilus, **⁴** so that you may have a firm grasp of the words in which you have been instructed.

✧ The Birth of John the Baptist Foretold

⁵ In the days of King Herod of Judea, there was a priest named Zechariah, who belonged to the priestly order of Abijah. His wife was descended from the daughters of Aaron, and her name was Elizabeth. **⁶** Both of them were righteous before God, living blamelessly according to all the commandments and regulations of the Lord. **⁷** But they had no children because Elizabeth was barren, and both were getting on in years.

⁸ Once when he was serving as priest before God during his section's turn of duty, **⁹** he was chosen by lot, according to the custom of the priesthood, to enter the sanctuary of the Lord and offer incense. **¹⁰** Now at the time of the incense offering, the whole assembly of the people was praying outside. **¹¹** Then there appeared to him an angel of the Lord, standing at the right side of the altar of incense. **¹²** When Zechariah saw him, he was terrified, and fear overwhelmed him. **¹³** But the angel said to him, "Do not be afraid, Zechariah, for your prayer has been heard. Your wife Elizabeth will bear you a son, and you will name him John. **¹⁴** You will have joy and gladness, and many will rejoice at his birth, **¹⁵** for he will be great in the sight of the Lord. He must never drink wine or strong drink; even before his birth he will be filled with the Holy Spirit. **¹⁶** He will turn many of the people of Israel to the Lord their God. ¹⁷ With the spirit and power of Elijah he will go before him, to turn the hearts of parents to their children and the disobedient to the wisdom of the righteous, to make ready a people prepared for the Lord." ¹⁸ Zechariah said to the angel, "How can I know that this will happen? For I am an old man, and my wife is getting on in years." ¹⁹ The angel replied, "I am Gabriel. I stand in the presence of God, and I have been sent to speak to you and to bring you this good news. ²⁰ But now, because you did not believe my words, which will be fulfilled in their time, you will become mute, unable to speak, until the day these things occur."

²¹ Meanwhile the people were waiting for Zechariah and wondered at his delay in the sanctuary. ²² When he did come out, he could not speak to them, and they realized that he had seen a vision in the sanctuary. He kept motioning to them and remained unable to speak. ²³ When his time of service was ended, he went to his home.

²⁴ After those days his wife Elizabeth conceived, and for five months she remained in seclusion. She said, ²⁵ "This is what the Lord has done for me in this time, when he looked favorably on me and took away the disgrace I have endured among my people."

✦ The Annunciation of Mary

²⁶ In the sixth month the angel Gabriel was sent by God to a town in Galilee called Nazareth, ²⁷ to a virgin engaged to a man whose name was Joseph, of the house of David. The virgin's name was Mary. ²⁸ And he came to her and said, "Greetings, favored one! The Lord is with you." ²⁹ But she was much perplexed by his words and pondered what sort of greeting this might be. ³⁰ The angel said to her, "Do not be afraid, Mary, for you have found favor with God. ³¹ And now, you will conceive in your womb and bear a son, and you will name him Jesus. ³² He will be great and will be called the Son of the Most High, and the Lord God will give to him the throne of his ancestor David. ³³ He will reign over the house of Jacob forever, and of his kingdom there will be no end." ³⁴ Mary said to the angel, "How can this be, since I am a virgin?" ³⁵ The angel said to her, "The Holy Spirit will come upon you, and the power

of the Most High will overshadow you; therefore the child to be born will be holy; he will be called Son of God. ³⁶ And now, your relative Elizabeth in her old age has also conceived a son, and this is the sixth month for her who was said to be barren. ³⁷ For nothing will be impossible with God." ³⁸ Then Mary said, "Here am I, the servant of the Lord; let it be with me according to your word." Then the angel departed from her.

✤ The Visitation of Mary to Elizabeth

³⁹ In those days Mary set out and went with haste to a Judean town in the hill country, ⁴⁰ where she entered the house of Zechariah and greeted Elizabeth. ⁴¹ When Elizabeth heard Mary's greeting, the child leaped in her womb. And Elizabeth was filled with the Holy Spirit ⁴² and exclaimed with a loud cry, "Blessed are you among women, and blessed is the fruit of your womb. ⁴³ And why has this happened to me, that the mother of my Lord comes to me? ⁴⁴ For as soon as I heard the sound of your greeting, the child in my womb leaped for joy. ⁴⁵ And blessed is she who believed that there would be a fulfillment of what was spoken to her by the Lord."

✤ Mary's Song of Praise

⁴⁶ And Mary said,

"My soul magnifies the Lord,
    ⁴⁷ and my spirit rejoices in God my Savior,
⁴⁸ for he has looked with favor on the lowliness of
    his servant.
    Surely, from now on all generations will call me blessed;
⁴⁹ for the Mighty One has done great things for me,
    and holy is his name;
⁵⁰ indeed, his mercy is for those who fear him
    from generation to generation.
⁵¹ He has shown strength with his arm;
    he has scattered the proud in the imagination of
        their hearts.
⁵² He has brought down the powerful from their thrones
    and lifted up the lowly;

⁵³ he has filled the hungry with good things
　　and sent the rich away empty.
⁵⁴ He has come to the aid of his child Israel,
　　in remembrance of his mercy,
⁵⁵ according to the promise he made to our ancestors,
　　to Abraham and to his descendants forever."

⁵⁶ And Mary remained with her about three months and then returned to her home.

✧ The Birth of John

⁵⁷ Now the time came for Elizabeth to give birth, and she bore a son. ⁵⁸ Her neighbors and relatives heard that the Lord had shown his great mercy to her, and they rejoiced with her.

⁵⁹ On the eighth day they came to circumcise the child, and they were going to name him Zechariah after his father. ⁶⁰ But his mother said, "No; he is to be called John." ⁶¹ They said to her, "None of your relatives has this name." ⁶² Then they began motioning to his father to find out what name he wanted to give him. ⁶³ He asked for a writing tablet and wrote, "His name is John." And all of them were amazed. ⁶⁴ Immediately his mouth was opened and his tongue freed, and he began to speak, praising God. ⁶⁵ Fear came over all their neighbors, and all these things were talked about throughout the entire hill country of Judea. ⁶⁶ All who heard them pondered them and said, "What then will this child become?" For, indeed, the hand of the Lord was with him.

✧ Zechariah's Canticle

⁶⁷ Then his father Zechariah was filled with the Holy Spirit and prophesied:

⁶⁸ "Blessed be the Lord God of Israel,
　　for he has looked favorably on his people and
　　　redeemed them.
⁶⁹ He has raised up a mighty savior for us
　　in the house of his child David.

⁷⁰ as he spoke through the mouth of his holy prophets from
  of old,
> ⁷¹ that we would be saved from our enemies and from the
> hand of all who hate us.
⁷² Thus he has shown the mercy promised to our ancestors,
  and has remembered his holy covenant,
⁷³ the oath that he swore to our ancestor Abraham,
> to grant us ⁷⁴ that we, being rescued from the hands
>   of our enemies,
> might serve him without fear, ⁷⁵ in holiness
>   and righteousness
> in his presence all our days.
⁷⁶ And you, child, will be called the prophet of the
  Most High,
> for you will go before the Lord to prepare his ways,
⁷⁷ to give his people knowledge of salvation
> by the forgiveness of their sins.
⁷⁸ Because of the tender mercy of our God,
> the dawn from on high will break upon us,
⁷⁹ to shine upon those who sit in darkness and in the
  shadow of death,
> to guide our feet into the way of peace."

⁸⁰ The child grew and became strong in spirit, and he was in the wilderness until the day he appeared publicly to Israel.

CHAPTER 2

✦ The Birth of Jesus

 n those days a decree went out from Caesar Augustus that all the world should be registered. ² This was the first registration and was taken while Quirinius was governor of Syria. ³ All went to their own towns to be registered. ⁴ Joseph also went from the town of Nazareth in Galilee to Judea, to the city of David called Bethlehem, because he was descended from the house and family of David. [5] He went to be registered with Mary, to whom he was engaged and who was expecting a child. [6] While they were there, the time came for her to deliver her child. [7] And she gave birth to her first-born son and wrapped him in bands of cloth and laid him in a manger, because there was no place in the guest room.

✢ The Adoration of the Shepherds

[8] Now in that same region there were shepherds living in the fields, keeping watch over their flock by night. [9] Then an angel of the Lord stood before them, and the glory of the Lord shone around them, and they were terrified. [10] But the angel said to them, "Do not be afraid, for see, I am bringing you good news of great joy for all the people: [11] to you is born this day in the city of David a Savior, who is the Messiah, the Lord. [12] This will be a sign for you: you will find a child wrapped in bands of cloth and lying in a manger." [13] And suddenly there was with the angel a multitude of the heavenly host, praising God and saying,

[14] "Glory to God in the highest heaven,
    and on earth peace among those whom he favors!"

[15] When the angels had left them and gone into heaven, the shepherds said to one another, "Let us go now to Bethlehem and see this thing that has taken place, which the Lord has made known to us." [16] So they went with haste and found Mary and Joseph and the child lying in the manger. [17] When they saw this, they made known what had been told them about this child, [18] and all who heard it were amazed at what the shepherds told them, [19] and Mary treasured all these words and pondered them in her heart. [20] The shepherds returned, glorifying and praising God for all they had heard and seen, as it had been told them.

✢ Jesus Is Named

[21] When the eighth day came, it was time to circumcise the child, and he was called Jesus, the name given by the angel before he was conceived in the womb.

✧ The Presentation in the Temple

22 When the time came for their purification according to the law of Moses, they brought him up to Jerusalem to present him to the Lord **23** (as it is written in the law of the Lord, "Every firstborn male shall be designated as holy to the Lord"), **24** and they offered a sacrifice according to what is stated in the law of the Lord, "a pair of turtledoves or two young pigeons."

25 Now there was a man in Jerusalem whose name was Simeon; this man was righteous and devout, looking forward to the consolation of Israel, and the Holy Spirit rested on him. **26** It had been revealed to him by the Holy Spirit that he would not see death before he had seen the Lord's Messiah. **27** Guided by the Spirit, Simeon came into the temple; and when the parents brought in the child Jesus to do for him what was customary under the law, **28** Simeon took him in his arms and praised God, saying,

> **29** "Master, now you are dismissing your servant in peace,
>   according to your word,
> **30** for my eyes have seen your salvation,
>   **31** which you have prepared in the presence of all peoples,
> **32** a light for revelation to the gentiles
>   and for glory to your people Israel."

33 And the child's father and mother were amazed at what was being said about him. **34** Then Simeon blessed them and said to his mother Mary, "This child is destined for the falling and the rising of many in Israel and to be a sign that will be opposed **35** so that the inner thoughts of many will be revealed—and a sword will pierce your own soul, too."

36 There was also a prophet, Anna the daughter of Phanuel, of the tribe of Asher. She was of a great age, having lived with her husband seven years after her marriage, **37** then as a widow to the age of eighty-four. She never left the temple but worshiped there with fasting and prayer night and day. **38** At that moment she came, and began to praise God and to speak about the child to all who were looking for the redemption of Jerusalem.

✢ The Return to Nazareth

39 When they had finished everything required by the law of the Lord, they returned to Galilee, to their own town of Nazareth. **40** The child grew and became strong, filled with wisdom, and the favor of God was upon him.

✢ The Boy Jesus in the Temple

41 Now every year his parents went to Jerusalem for the festival of the Passover. **42** And when he was twelve years old, they went up as usual for the festival. **43** When the festival was ended and they started to return, the boy Jesus stayed behind in Jerusalem, but his parents were unaware of this. **44** Assuming that he was in the group of travelers, they went a day's journey. Then they started to look for him among their relatives and friends. **45** When they did not find him, they returned to Jerusalem to search for him. **46** After three days they found him in the temple, sitting among the teachers, listening to them and asking them questions. **47** And all who heard him were amazed at his understanding and his answers. **48** When his parents saw him they were astonished, and his mother said to him, "Child, why have you treated us like this? Your father and I have been anxiously looking for you." **49** He said to them, "Why were you searching for me? Did you not know that I must be in my Father's house?" **50** But they did not understand what he said to them. **51** Then he went down with them and came to Nazareth and was obedient to them, and his mother treasured all these things in her heart.

52 And Jesus increased in wisdom and in years and in divine and human favor.

CHAPTER 3

✦ **The Proclamation of John the Baptist**

**I**n the fifteenth year of the reign of Tiberius Caesar, when Pontius Pilate was governor of Judea, and Herod was ruler of Galilee, and his brother Philip ruler of the region of Ituraea and Trachonitis, and Lysanias ruler of Abilene, ² during the high priesthood of Annas and Caiaphas, the word of God came to John son of Zechariah in the wilderness. ³ He went into all the region around the Jordan, proclaiming a baptism of repentance for the forgiveness of sins, ⁴ as it is written in the book of the words of the prophet Isaiah,

> "The voice of one crying out in the wilderness:
> 'Prepare the way of the Lord,
>   make his paths straight.
> ⁵ Every valley shall be filled,
>   and every mountain and hill shall be made low,
> and the crooked shall be made straight,
>   and the rough ways made smooth,
> ⁶ and all flesh shall see the salvation of God.'"

⁷ John said to the crowds that came out to be baptized by him, "You brood of vipers! Who warned you to flee from the coming wrath? ⁸ Therefore, bear fruits worthy of repentance, and do not begin to say to yourselves, 'We have Abraham as our ancestor,' for I tell you, God is able from these stones to raise up children to Abraham. ⁹ Even now the ax is lying at the root of the trees; therefore every tree that does not bear good fruit will be cut down and thrown into the fire."

¹⁰ And the crowds asked him, "What, then, should we do?" ¹¹ In reply he said to them, "Whoever has two coats must share with anyone who has none, and whoever has food must do likewise." ¹² Even tax collectors came to be baptized, and they asked him, "Teacher, what should we do?" ¹³ He said to them, "Collect

no more than the amount prescribed for you." **14** Soldiers also asked him, "And we, what should we do?" He said to them, "Do not extort money from anyone by threats or false accusation, and be satisfied with your wages."

15 As the people were filled with expectation and all were questioning in their hearts concerning John, whether he might be the Messiah, **16** John answered all of them by saying, "I baptize you with water, but one who is more powerful than I is coming; I am not worthy to untie the strap of his sandals. He will baptize you with the Holy Spirit and fire. **17** His winnowing fork is in his hand to clear his threshing floor and to gather the wheat into his granary, but the chaff he will burn with unquenchable fire."

18 So, with many other exhortations he proclaimed the good news to the people. **19** But Herod the ruler, who had been rebuked by him because of Herodias, his brother's wife, and because of all the evil things that Herod had done, **20** added to them all by shutting up John in prison.

✢ The Baptism of Jesus

21 Now when all the people were baptized and when Jesus also had been baptized and was praying, the heaven was opened, **22** and the Holy Spirit descended upon him in bodily form like a dove. And a voice came from heaven, "You are my Son, the Beloved; with you I am well pleased."

✢ The Ancestors of Jesus

23 Jesus was about thirty years old when he began his work. He was the son (as was thought) of Joseph son of Heli, **24** son of Matthat, son of Levi, son of Melchi, son of Jannai, son of Joseph, **25** son of Mattathias, son of Amos, son of Nahum, son of Esli, son of Naggai, **26** son of Maath, son of Mattathias, son of Semein, son of Josech, son of Joda, **27** son of Joanan, son of Rhesa, son of Zerubbabel, son of Shealtiel, son of Neri, **28** son of Melchi, son of Addi, son of Cosam, son of Elmadam, son of Er, **29** son of Joshua, son of Eliezer, son of Jorim, son of Matthat, son of Levi, **30** son of Simeon, son of Judah, son of Joseph, son of Jonam, son of Eliakim, ³¹ son of Melea, son of Menna, son of Mattatha, son of Nathan, son of David, ³² son of Jesse, son of Obed, son of Boaz, son of Sala, son of Nahshon, ³³ son of Amminadab, son of Admin, son of Arni, son of Hezron, son of Perez, son of Judah, ³⁴ son of Jacob, son of Isaac, son of Abraham, son of Terah, son of Nahor, ³⁵ son of Serug, son of Reu, son of Peleg, son of Eber, son of Shelah, ³⁶ son of Cainan, son of Arphaxad, son of Shem, son of Noah, son of Lamech, ³⁷ son of Methuselah, son of Enoch, son of Jared, son of Mahalaleel, son of Cainan, ³⁸ son of Enos, son of Seth, son of Adam, son of God.

CHAPTER 4

✦ The Temptation of Jesus

 **esus, full of the Holy Spirit,** returned from the Jordan and was led by the Spirit in the wilderness, ² where for forty days he was tested by the devil. He ate nothing at all during those days, and when they were over, he was famished. ³ The devil said to him, "If you are the Son of God, command this stone to become a loaf of bread." ⁴ Jesus answered him, "It is written, 'One does not live by bread alone.'"

⁵ Then the devil led him up and showed him in an instant all the kingdoms of the world. ⁶ And the devil said to him, "To you I will give all this authority and their glory, for it has been given over to me, and I give it to anyone I please. ⁷ If you, then, will worship me, it will all be yours." ⁸ Jesus answered him, "It is written,

'Worship the Lord your God,
    and serve only him.'"

⁹ Then the devil led him to Jerusalem and placed him on the pinnacle of the temple and said to him, "If you are the Son of God, throw yourself down from here, ¹⁰ for it is written,

'He will command his angels concerning you,
    to protect you,'

11 and

> 'On their hands they will bear you up,
>> so that you will not dash your foot against a stone.'"

12 Jesus answered him, "It is said, 'Do not put the Lord your God to the test.'" **13** When the devil had finished every test, he departed from him until an opportune time.

✦ The Beginning of the Galilean Ministry

14 Then Jesus, in the power of the Spirit, returned to Galilee, and a report about him spread through all the surrounding region. **15** He began to teach in their synagogues and was praised by everyone.

✦ The Rejection of Jesus at Nazareth

16 When he came to Nazareth, where he had been brought up, he went to the synagogue on the Sabbath day, as was his custom. He stood up to read, **17** and the scroll of the prophet Isaiah was given to him. He unrolled the scroll and found the place where it was written:

> **18** "The Spirit of the Lord is upon me,
>> because he has anointed me
>> to bring good news to the poor.
> He has sent me to proclaim release to the captives
>> and recovery of sight to the blind,
>> to set free those who are oppressed,
> **19** to proclaim the year of the Lord's favor."

20 And he rolled up the scroll, gave it back to the attendant, and sat down. The eyes of all in the synagogue were fixed on him. **21** Then he began to say to them, "Today this scripture has been fulfilled in your hearing." **22** All spoke well of him and were amazed at the gracious words that came from his mouth. They said, "Is this not Joseph's son?" **23** He said to them, "Doubtless you will quote to me this proverb, 'Doctor, cure yourself!' And you will say, 'Do here also in your hometown the things that we have heard you did at Capernaum.'" **24** And he said, "Truly I tell you, no prophet is accepted in his hometown. **25** But the truth is, there were many widows in Israel in the time of Elijah, when the heaven was shut up three years and six months and there was a severe famine over all the land, **26** yet Elijah was sent to none of them except to a widow at Zarephath in Sidon. **27** There were also many with a skin disease in Israel in the time of the prophet Elisha, and none of them was cleansed except Naaman the Syrian." **28** When they heard this, all in the synagogue were filled with rage. **29** They got up, drove him out of the town, and led him to the brow of the hill on which their town was built, so that they might hurl him off the cliff. **30** But he passed through the midst of them and went on his way.

✢ Jesus Heals the Man with an Unclean Spirit

31 He went down to Capernaum, a city in Galilee, and was teaching them on the Sabbath. **32** They were astounded at his teaching because he spoke with authority. **33** In the synagogue there was a man who had the spirit of an unclean demon, and he cried out with a loud voice, **34** "Leave us alone! What have you to do with us, Jesus of Nazareth? Have you come to destroy us? I know who you are, the Holy One of God." **35** But Jesus rebuked him, saying, "Be quiet and come out of him!" Then the demon, throwing the man down before them, came out of him without doing him any harm. **36** They were all astounded and kept saying to one another, "What kind of word is this, that with authority and power he commands the unclean spirits and they come out?" **37** And news about him began to reach every place in the region.

✢ Healings at Simon's House

38 After leaving the synagogue he entered Simon's house. Now Simon's mother-in-law was suffering from a high fever, and they asked him about her. **39** Then he stood over her and rebuked the fever, and it left her. Immediately she got up and began to serve them.

40 As the sun was setting, all those caring for any who were sick with various kinds of diseases brought them to him, and he laid his hands on each of them and cured them. **⁴¹** Moreover, demons also came out of many, shouting, "You are the Son of God!" But he rebuked them and would not allow them to speak, because they knew that he was the Messiah.

✧ Jesus Preaches in the Synagogues

⁴² At daybreak he departed and went into a deserted place. And the crowds began looking for him, and when they reached him they tried to keep him from leaving them. **⁴³** But he said to them, "I must proclaim the good news of the kingdom of God to the other cities also, for I was sent for this purpose." **⁴⁴** So he continued proclaiming the message in the synagogues of Judea.

CHAPTER 5

✧ Jesus Calls the First Disciples

nce while Jesus was standing beside the Lake of Gennesaret and the crowd was pressing in on him to hear the word of God, **²** he saw two boats there at the shore of the lake; the fishermen had gotten out of them and were washing their nets. **³** He got into one of the boats, the one belonging to Simon, and asked him to put out a little way from the shore. Then he sat down and taught the crowds from the boat. **⁴** When he had finished speaking, he said to Simon, "Put out into the deep water and let down your nets for a catch." **⁵** Simon answered, "Master, we have worked all night long but have caught nothing. Yet if you say so, I will let down the nets." **⁶** When they had done this, they caught so many fish that their nets were beginning to burst. **⁷** So they signaled their partners in the other boat to come and help them. And they came and filled both boats, so that they began to sink. **⁸** But when Simon Peter saw it, he fell down at Jesus's knees, saying, "Go away from me, Lord, for I am a sinful man!" **⁹** For he and all who were with him were astounded at the catch of fish that they had taken, **¹⁰** and so also were James and John, sons of Zebedee, who were partners

with Simon. Then Jesus said to Simon, "Do not be afraid; from now on you will be catching people." [11] When they had brought their boats to shore, they left everything and followed him.

✤ Jesus Heals a Man with a Skin Disease

[12] Once, when he was in one of the cities, a man covered with a skin disease was there. When he saw Jesus, he bowed with his face to the ground and begged him, "Lord, if you are willing, you can make me clean." [13] Then Jesus stretched out his hand, touched him, and said, "I am willing. Be made clean." Immediately the skin disease left him. [14] And he ordered him to tell no one. "But go, show yourself to the priest, and, as Moses commanded, make an offering for your cleansing, as a testimony to them." [15] But now more than ever the word about Jesus spread abroad; many crowds were gathering to hear him and to be cured of their diseases. [16] Meanwhile, he would slip away to deserted places and pray.

✤ Jesus Heals a Paralytic

[17] One day while he was teaching, Pharisees and teachers of the law who had come from every village of Galilee and Judea and from Jerusalem were sitting nearby, and the power of the Lord was with him to heal. [18] Just then some men came carrying a paralyzed man on a stretcher. They were trying to bring him in and lay him before Jesus, [19] but, finding no way to bring him in because of the crowd, they went up on the roof and let him down on the stretcher through the tiles into the middle of the crowd in front of Jesus. [20] When he saw their faith, he said, "Friend, your sins are forgiven you." [21] Then the scribes and the Pharisees began to question, "Who is this who is speaking blasphemies? Who can forgive sins but God alone?" [22] When Jesus perceived their questionings, he answered them, "Why do you raise such questions in your hearts? [23] Which is easier: to say, 'Your sins are forgiven you,' or to say, 'Stand up and walk'? [24] But so that you may know that the Son of Man has authority on earth to forgive sins"—he said to the one who was paralyzed—"I say to you, stand up and take your stretcher and go to your home." [25] Immediately he stood up

before them, took what he had been lying on, and went to his home, glorifying God. **26** Amazement seized all of them, and they glorified God and were filled with fear, saying, "We have seen incredible things today."

✦ Jesus Calls Levi

27 After this he went out and saw a tax collector named Levi sitting at the tax-collection station, and he said to him, "Follow me." **28** And he got up, left everything, and followed him.

29 Then Levi gave a great banquet for him in his house, and there was a large crowd of tax collectors and others reclining at the table with them. **30** The Pharisees and their scribes were complaining to his disciples, saying, "Why do you eat and drink with tax collectors and sinners?" **31** Jesus answered them, "Those who are well have no need of a physician but those who are sick; **32** I have not come to call the righteous but sinners to repentance."

✦ The Question about Fasting

33 Then they said to him, "John's disciples, like the disciples of the Pharisees, frequently fast and pray, but your disciples eat and drink." **34** Jesus said to them, "You cannot make wedding attendants fast while the bridegroom is with them, can you? **35** The days will come when the bridegroom will be taken away from them, and then they will fast in those days." **36** He also told them a parable: "No one tears a piece from a new garment and sews it on an old garment; otherwise not only will one tear the new garment, but the piece from the new will not match the old garment. **37** Similarly, no one puts new wine into old wineskins; otherwise, the new wine will burst the skins and will spill out, and the skins will be ruined. **38** But new wine must be put into fresh wineskins. **39** And no one after drinking old wine desires new wine but says, 'The old is good.'"

CHAPTER 6

✤ Lord of the Sabbath

 **ne Sabbath while Jesus was going** through some grain fields, his disciples plucked some heads of grain, rubbed them in their hands, and ate them. ² But some of the Pharisees said, "Why are you doing what is not lawful on the Sabbath?" ³ Jesus answered, "Have you not read what David did when he and his companions were hungry? ⁴ How he entered the house of God and took and ate the bread of the Presence, which it is not lawful for any but the priests to eat, and gave some to his companions?" ⁵ Then he said to them, "The Son of Man is lord of the Sabbath."

✤ Jesus Heals the Man with a Withered Hand

⁶ On another Sabbath he entered the synagogue and taught, and there was a man there whose right hand was withered. ⁷ The scribes and the Pharisees were watching him to see whether he would cure on the Sabbath, so that they might find grounds to bring an accusation against him. ⁸ But he knew what they were thinking, he said to the man who had the withered hand, "Come and stand in the middle." He got up and stood there. ⁹ Then Jesus said to them, "I ask you, is it lawful to do good or to do harm on the Sabbath, to save life or to destroy it?" ¹⁰ After looking around at all of them, he said to him, "Stretch out your hand." He did so, and his hand was restored. ¹¹ But they were filled with fury and began discussing with one another what they might do to Jesus.

✤ Jesus Calls the Twelve Apostles

¹² Now during those days he went out to the mountain to pray, and he spent the night in prayer to God. ¹³ And when day came, he called his disciples and chose twelve of them, whom he also named apostles: ¹⁴ Simon, whom he named Peter, and his brother Andrew, and James, and John, and Philip, and Bartholomew, ¹⁵ and

Matthew, and Thomas, and James son of Alphaeus, and Simon, who was called the Zealot, ¹⁶ and Judas son of James, and Judas Iscariot, who became a traitor.

✤ Jesus Teaches and Heals

¹⁷ He came down with them and stood on a level place with a great crowd of his disciples and a great multitude of people from all Judea, Jerusalem, and the coast of Tyre and Sidon. ¹⁸ They had come to hear him and to be healed of their diseases, and those who were troubled with unclean spirits were cured. ¹⁹ And everyone in the crowd was trying to touch him, for power came out from him and healed all of them.

✤ Blessings and Woes

²⁰ Then he looked up at his disciples and said:

> "Blessed are you who are poor,
> for yours is the kingdom of God.
> ²¹ "Blessed are you who are hungry now,
> for you will be filled.
> "Blessed are you who weep now,
> for you will laugh.

²² "Blessed are you when people hate you and when they exclude you, revile you, and defame you on account of the Son of Man. ²³ Rejoice in that day and leap for joy, for surely your reward is great in heaven, for that is how their ancestors treated the prophets.

> ²⁴ "But woe to you who are rich,
> for you have received your consolation.
> ²⁵ "Woe to you who are full now,
> for you will be hungry.
> "Woe to you who are laughing now,
> for you will mourn and weep.

²⁶ "Woe to you when all speak well of you, for that is how their ancestors treated the false prophets.

✤ Love for Enemies

27 "But I say to you who are listening: Love your enemies; do good to those who hate you; **28** bless those who curse you; pray for those who mistreat you. **29** If anyone strikes you on the cheek, offer the other also, and from anyone who takes away your coat do not withhold even your shirt. **30** Give to everyone who asks of you; and if anyone takes away what is yours, do not ask for it back again. **31** Do to others as you would have them do to you.

32 "If you love those who love you, what credit is that to you? For even sinners love those who love them. **33** If you do good to those who do good to you, what credit is that to you? For even sinners do the same. **34** If you lend to those from whom you expect to receive payment, what credit is that to you? Even sinners lend to sinners, to receive as much again. **35** Instead love your enemies, do good, and lend, expecting nothing in return. Your reward will be great, and you will be children of the Most High, for he himself is kind to the ungrateful and the wicked. **36** Be merciful, just as your Father is merciful.

✤ Judging Others

37 "Do not judge, and you will not be judged; do not condemn, and you will not be condemned. Forgive, and you will be forgiven; **38** give, and it will be given to you. A good measure, pressed down, shaken together, running over, will be put into your lap, for the measure you give will be the measure you get back."

39 He also told them a parable: "Can a blind person guide a blind person? Will not both fall into a pit? **40** A disciple is not above the teacher, but every disciple who is fully qualified will be like the teacher. **41** Why do you see the speck in your neighbor's eye but do not notice the log in your own eye? **42** Or how can you say to your neighbor, 'Friend, let me take out the speck in your eye,' when you yourself do not see the log in your own eye? You hypocrite, first take the log out of your own eye, and then you will see clearly to take the speck out of your neighbor's eye.

✦ A Tree and Its Fruit

43 "No good tree bears bad fruit, nor again does a bad tree bear good fruit; **44** for each tree is known by its own fruit. For people do not gather figs from thorns, nor do they pick grapes from a bramble bush. **45** The good person out of the good treasure of the heart produces good, and the evil person out of evil treasure produces evil, for it is out of the abundance of the heart that the mouth speaks.

✦ The Two Foundations

46 "Why do you call me 'Lord, Lord,' and do not do what I tell you? **47** I will show you what someone is like who comes to me, hears my words, and acts on them. **48** That one is like a man building a house who dug deeply and laid the foundation on rock; when a flood arose, the river burst against that house but could not shake it because it had been well built. **49** But the one who hears and does not act is like a man who built a house on the ground without a foundation. When the river burst against it, it quickly collapsed, and great was the ruin of that house."

CHAPTER 7

✦ Jesus Heals a Centurion's Servant

fter Jesus had finished all his sayings in the hearing of the people, he entered Capernaum. **2** A centurion there had a slave whom he valued highly and who was ill and close to death. **3** When he heard about Jesus, he sent some Jewish elders to him, asking him to come and heal his slave. **4** When they came to Jesus, they appealed to him earnestly, saying, "He is worthy of having you do this for him, **5** for he loves our people, and it is he who built our synagogue for us." **6** And Jesus went with them, but when he was not far from the house, the centurion sent friends to say to him, "Lord, do not trouble yourself, for I am not worthy to have you come under my roof; **7** therefore I did not presume to come

to you. But only speak the word, and let my servant be healed. **8** For I also am a man set under authority, with soldiers under me, and I say to one, 'Go,' and he goes, and to another, 'Come,' and he comes, and to my slave, 'Do this,' and the slave does it." **9** When Jesus heard this he was amazed at him, and turning to the crowd following him, he said, "I tell you, not even in Israel have I found such faith." **10** When those who had been sent returned to the house, they found the slave in good health.

✛ Jesus Raises the Widow's Son at Nain

11 Soon afterward he went to a town called Nain, and his disciples and a large crowd went with him. **12** As he approached the gate of the town, a man who had died was being carried out. He was his mother's only son, and she was a widow, and with her was a large crowd from the town. **13** When the Lord saw her, he had compassion for her and said to her, "Do not cry." **14** Then he came forward and touched the bier, and the bearers stopped. And he said, "Young man, I say to you, rise!" **15** The dead man sat up and began to speak, and Jesus gave him to his mother. **16** Fear seized all of them, and they glorified God, saying, "A great prophet has risen among us!" and "God has visited his people!" **17** The word about him spread throughout the whole of Judea and all the surrounding region.

✛ Messengers from John the Baptist

18 The disciples of John reported all these things to him. So John summoned two of his disciples **19** and sent them to the Lord to ask, "Are you the one who is to come, or are we to expect someone else?" **20** When the men had come to him, they said, "John the Baptist has sent us to you to ask, 'Are you the one who is to come, or are we to expect someone else?'" **21** Jesus had just then cured many people of diseases, afflictions, and evil spirits and had given sight to many who were blind. **22** And he answered them, "Go and tell John what you have seen and heard: the blind receive their sight; the lame walk; those with a skin disease are cleansed; the deaf hear; the dead are raised, the poor have good news brought to them. ²³ And blessed is anyone who takes no offense at me."

²⁴ When John's messengers had gone, Jesus began to speak to the crowds about John: "What did you go out into the wilderness to look at? A reed shaken by the wind? ²⁵ What, then, did you go out to see? Someone dressed in soft robes? Look, those who put on fine clothing and live in luxury are in royal palaces. ²⁶ What, then, did you go out to see? A prophet? Yes, I tell you, and more than a prophet. ²⁷ This is the one about whom it is written,

'See, I am sending my messenger ahead of you,
who will prepare your way before you.'

²⁸ I tell you, among those born of women no one is greater than John, yet the least in the kingdom of God is greater than he." ²⁹ (And all the people who heard this, including the tax collectors, acknowledged the justice of God, having been baptized with John's baptism. ³⁰ But the Pharisees and the experts in the law, not having been baptized by him, rejected God's purpose for themselves.)

³¹ "To what then will I compare the people of this generation, and what are they like? ³² They are like children sitting in the marketplace and calling to one another,

'We played the flute for you, and you did not dance;
we wailed, and you did not weep.'

³³ For John the Baptist has come eating no bread and drinking no wine, and you say, 'He has a demon'; ³⁴ the Son of Man has come eating and drinking, and you say, 'Look, a glutton and a drunkard, a friend of tax collectors and sinners!' ³⁵ Nevertheless, wisdom is vindicated by all her children."

❖ Jesus Forgives a Sinful Woman

³⁶ One of the Pharisees asked Jesus to eat with him, and when he went into the Pharisee's house he reclined to dine. ³⁷ And a woman in the city who was a sinner, having learned that he was eating in the Pharisee's house, brought an alabaster jar of ointment.

³⁸ She stood behind him at his feet, weeping, and began to bathe his feet with her tears and to dry them with her hair, kissing his feet and anointing them with the ointment. ³⁹ Now when the Pharisee who had invited him saw it, he said to himself, "If this man were a prophet, he would have known who and what kind of woman this is who is touching him, that she is a sinner." ⁴⁰ Jesus spoke up and said to him, "Simon, I have something to say to you." "Teacher," he replied, "speak." ⁴¹ "A certain moneylender had two debtors; one owed five hundred denarii, and the other fifty. ⁴² When they could not pay, he canceled the debts for both of them. Now which of them will love him more?" ⁴³ Simon answered, "I suppose the one for whom he canceled the greater debt." And Jesus said to him, "You have judged rightly." ⁴⁴ Then turning toward the woman, he said to Simon, "Do you see this woman? I entered your house; you gave me no water for my feet, but she has bathed my feet with her tears and dried them with her hair. ⁴⁵ You gave me no kiss, but from the time I came in she has not stopped kissing my feet. ⁴⁶ You did not anoint my head with oil, but she has anointed my feet with ointment. ⁴⁷ Therefore, I tell you, her many sins have been forgiven; hence she has shown great love. But the one to whom little is forgiven loves little." ⁴⁸ Then he said to her, "Your sins are forgiven." ⁴⁹ But those who were at the table with him began to say among themselves, "Who is this who even forgives sins?" ⁵⁰ But he said to the woman, "Your faith has saved you; go in peace."

CHAPTER 8

✣ Some Women Accompany Jesus

 **oon afterward he went on** through one town and village after another, proclaiming and bringing the good news of the kingdom of God. The twelve were with him, ² as well as some women who had been cured of evil spirits and infirmities: Mary, called Magdalene, from whom seven demons had gone out, ³ and Joanna, the wife of

Herod's steward Chuza, and Susanna, and many others, who ministered to them out of their own resources.

✤ The Parable of the Sower

⁴ When a large crowd was gathering, as people were coming to him from town after town, he said in a parable: ⁵ "A sower went out to sow his seed, and as he sowed some fell on a path and was trampled on, and the birds of the air ate it up. ⁶ Some fell on rock, and as it grew up it withered for lack of moisture. ⁷ Some fell among thorns, and the thorns grew with it and choked it. ⁸ Some fell into good soil, and when it grew it produced a hundredfold." As he said this, he called out, "If you have ears to hear, then hear!"

✤ The Purpose of the Parables

⁹ Then his disciples asked him what this parable meant. ¹⁰ He said, "To you it has been given to know the secrets of the kingdom of God, but to others I speak in parables, so that

'looking they may not perceive
and hearing they may not understand.'

✤ The Parable of the Sower Revisited

¹¹ "Now the parable is this: The seed is the word of God. ¹² The ones on the path are those who have heard; then the devil comes and takes away the word from their hearts, so that they may not believe and be saved. ¹³ The ones on the rock are those who, when they hear the word, receive it with joy. But these have no root; they believe only for a while and in a time of testing fall away. ¹⁴ As for what fell among the thorns, these are the ones who hear, but as they go on their way they are choked by the cares and riches and pleasures of life, and their fruit does not mature. ¹⁵ But as for that in the good soil, these are the ones who, when they hear the word, hold it fast in an honest and good heart and bear fruit with endurance.

✤ See the Light

[16] "No one after lighting a lamp hides it under a jar or puts it under a bed; rather, one puts it on a lampstand, so that those who enter may see the light. [17] For nothing is hidden that will not be disclosed, nor is anything secret that will not become known and come to light. [18] So pay attention to how you listen, for to those who have, more will be given, and from those who do not have, even what they seem to have will be taken away."

✤ The True Family of Jesus

[19] Then his mother and his brothers came to him, but they could not reach him because of the crowd. [20] And he was told, "Your mother and your brothers are standing outside, wanting to see you." [21] But he said to them, "My mother and my brothers are those who hear the word of God and do it."

✤ Jesus Calms a Storm

[22] One day he got into a boat with his disciples, and he said to them, "Let us go across to the other side of the lake." So they put out, [23] and while they were sailing he fell asleep. A windstorm swept down on the lake, and the boat was filling with water, and they were in danger. [24] They went to him and woke him up, shouting, "Master, Master, we are perishing!" And waking up, he rebuked the wind and the raging waves; they ceased, and there was a calm. [25] Then he said to them, "Where is your faith?" They were terrified and amazed and said to one another, "Who then is this, that he commands even the winds and the water and they obey him?"

✤ Jesus Heals the Man with an Unclean Spirit

[26] Then they arrived at the country of the Gerasenes, which is opposite Galilee. [27] As he stepped out on shore, a man from the city who had demons met him. For a long time he had not worn any clothes, and he did not live in a house but in the tombs. [28] When he saw Jesus, he cried out fell down before him, shouting, "What have you to do with me, Jesus, Son of the Most High God? I beg you, do not torment me," [29] for Jesus had commanded

the unclean spirit to come out of the man. (For many times it had seized him; he was kept under guard and bound with chains and shackles, but he would break the bonds and be driven by the demon into the wilds.) 30 Jesus then asked him, "What is your name?" He said, "Legion," for many demons had entered him. 31 They begged him not to order them to go back into the abyss.

32 Now there on the hillside a large herd of swine was feeding, and the demons begged Jesus to let them enter these. So he gave them permission. 33 Then the demons came out of the man and entered the swine, and the herd stampeded down the steep bank into the lake and was drowned.

34 When the swineherds saw what had happened, they ran off and told it in the city and in the country. 35 Then people came out to see what had happened, and when they came to Jesus, they found the man from whom the demons had gone sitting at the feet of Jesus, clothed and in his right mind. And they became frightened. 36 Those who had seen it told them how the one who had been possessed by demons had been healed. 37 Then the whole throng of people of the surrounding region of the Gerasenes asked Jesus to leave them, for they were seized with great fear. So he got into the boat and returned. 38 The man from whom the demons had gone begged that he might be with him, but Jesus sent him away, saying, 39 "Return to your home, and declare how much God has done for you." So he went away, proclaiming throughout the city how much Jesus had done for him.

✤ A Girl Restored to Life and a Woman Healed

40 Now when Jesus returned, the crowd welcomed him, for they were all waiting for him. 41 Just then there came a man named Jairus, a leader of the synagogue. He fell at Jesus's feet and began pleading with him to come to his house, 42 for he had an only daughter, about twelve years old, who was dying.

As he went, the crowds pressed in on him. 43 Now there was a woman who had been suffering from a flow of blood for twelve years, and though she had spent all she had on physicians, no one could cure her. **44** She came up behind him and touched the fringe of his cloak, and immediately her flow of blood stopped. **45** Then Jesus asked, "Who touched me?" When all denied it, Peter said, "Master, the crowds are hemming you in and pressing against you." **46** But Jesus said, "Someone touched me, for I noticed that power had gone out from me." **47** When the woman saw that she could not remain hidden, she came trembling, and falling down before him, she declared in the presence of all the people why she had touched him and how she had been immediately healed. **48** He said to her, "Daughter, your faith has made you well; go in peace."

49 While he was still speaking, someone came from the synagogue leader's house to say, "Your daughter is dead; do not trouble the teacher any longer." **50** When Jesus heard this, he replied, "Do not be afraid. Only believe, and she will be saved." **51** When he came to the house, he did not allow anyone to enter with him, except Peter, John, and James and the child's father and mother. **52** Everyone was weeping and grieving for her, but he said, "Do not cry, for she is not dead but sleeping." **53** And they laughed at him, knowing that she was dead. **54** But taking her by the hand, he called out, "Child, get up!" **55** Her spirit returned, and she stood up at once, and he directed them to give her something to eat. **56** Her parents were astounded, but he ordered them to tell no one what had happened.

CHAPTER 9

✤ The Mission of the Twelve

 **hen Jesus called the twelve together** and gave them power and authority over all demons and to cure diseases, **2** and he sent them out to proclaim the kingdom of God and to heal the sick. **3** He said to them, "Take nothing for your journey: no staff, nor bag, nor bread, nor money—not even an extra tunic. **4** Whatever house you

enter, stay there, and leave from there. ⁵ Wherever they do not welcome you, as you are leaving that town shake the dust off your feet as a testimony against them." ⁶ So they departed and went through the villages, bringing the good news and curing diseases everywhere.

✦ Herod Hears of Jesus

⁷ Now Herod the ruler heard about all that had taken place, and he was perplexed because it was said by some that John had been raised from the dead, ⁸ by some that Elijah had appeared, and by others that one of the ancient prophets had arisen. ⁹ Herod said, "John I beheaded, but who is this about whom I hear such things?" And he tried to see him.

✦ Jesus Feeds the Five Thousand

¹⁰ On their return the apostles told Jesus all they had done. Then, taking them along, he slipped quietly into a city called Bethsaida. ¹¹ When the crowds found out about it, they followed him, and he welcomed them and spoke to them about the kingdom of God and healed those who needed to be cured.

¹² The day was drawing to a close, and the twelve came to him and said, "Send the crowd away, so that they may go into the surrounding villages and countryside to lodge and get provisions, for we are here in a deserted place." ¹³ But he said to them, "You give them something to eat." They said, "We have no more than five loaves and two fish—unless we are to go and buy food for all these people." ¹⁴ For there were about five thousand men. And he said to his disciples, "Have them sit down in groups of about fifty each." ¹⁵ They did so and had them all sit down. ¹⁶ And taking the five loaves and the two fish, he looked up to heaven and blessed and broke them and gave them to the disciples to set before the crowd. ¹⁷ And all ate and were filled, and what was left over was gathered up, twelve baskets of broken pieces.

✦ Peter's Declaration about Jesus

18 Once when Jesus was praying alone, with only the disciples near him, he asked them, "Who do the crowds say that I am?" **19** They answered, "John the Baptist; but others, Elijah; and still others, that one of the ancient prophets has arisen." **20** Then he said to them, "But who do you say that I am?" Peter answered, "The Messiah of God."

✦ Jesus Foretells His Death and Resurrection

21 He sternly ordered and commanded them not to tell anyone, **22** saying, "The Son of Man must undergo great suffering and be rejected by the elders, chief priests, and scribes and be killed and on the third day be raised."

23 Then he said to them all, "If any wish to come after me, let them deny themselves and take up their cross daily and follow me. **24** For those who want to save their life will lose it, and those who lose their life for my sake will save it. **25** For what does it profit them if they gain the whole world but lose or forfeit themselves? **26** Those who are ashamed of me and of my words, of them the Son of Man will be ashamed when he comes in his glory and the glory of the Father and of the holy angels. **27** Indeed, truly I tell you, there are some standing here who will not taste death before they see the kingdom of God."

✦ The Transfiguration

28 Now about eight days after these sayings Jesus took with him Peter and John and James and went up on the mountain to pray. **29** And while he was praying, the appearance of his face changed, and his clothes became as bright as a flash of lightning. **30** Suddenly they saw two men, Moses and Elijah, talking to him. **31** They appeared in glory and were speaking of his exodus, which he was about to fulfill in Jerusalem. **32** Now Peter and his companions were weighed down with sleep, but as they awoke they saw his glory and the two men who stood with him. **33** Just as they were leaving him, Peter said to Jesus, "Master, it is good for us to be here; let us set up three tents: one for you, one for Moses, and one for Elijah," not realizing what he was saying. ³⁴ While he was saying this, a cloud came and overshadowed them, and they were terrified as they entered the cloud. ³⁵ Then from the cloud came a voice that said, "This is my Son, my Chosen; listen to him!" ³⁶ When the voice had spoken, Jesus was found alone. And they kept silent and in those days told no one any of the things they had seen.

✧ Jesus Heals a Boy with a Demon

³⁷ On the next day, when they had come down from the mountain, a great crowd met him. ³⁸ Just then a man from the crowd shouted, "Teacher, I beg you to look at my son; he is my only child. ³⁹ Suddenly a spirit seizes him, and all at once he shrieks. It convulses him until he foams at the mouth; it mauls him and will scarcely leave him. ⁴⁰ I begged your disciples to cast it out, but they could not." ⁴¹ Jesus answered, "You faithless and perverse generation, how much longer must I be with you and put up with you? Bring your son here." ⁴² While he was being brought forward, the demon dashed him to the ground in convulsions. But Jesus rebuked the unclean spirit, healed the boy, and gave him back to his father. ⁴³ And all were astounded at the greatness of God.

✧ Jesus Again Foretells His Death

While everyone was amazed at all that he was doing, he said to his disciples, ⁴⁴ "Let these words sink into your ears: The Son of Man is going to be betrayed into human hands." ⁴⁵ But they did not understand this saying; its meaning remained concealed from them, so that they could not perceive it. And they were afraid to ask him about this saying.

✧ True Greatness

⁴⁶ An argument arose among them concerning which one of them was the greatest. ⁴⁷ But Jesus, aware of their inner thoughts, took a little child and put it by his side ⁴⁸ and said to them, "Whoever welcomes this child in my name welcomes me, and whoever

welcomes me welcomes the one who sent me, for the least among all of you is the greatest."

✤ For the Sake of the Name

[49] John answered, "Master, we saw someone casting out demons in your name, and we tried to stop him, because he does not follow with us." [50] But Jesus said to him, "Do not stop him, for whoever is not against you is for you."

✤ A Samaritan Village Refuses to Receive Jesus

[51] When the days drew near for him to be taken up, he set his face to go to Jerusalem. [52] And he sent messengers ahead of him. On their way they entered a village of the Samaritans to prepare for his arrival, [53] but they did not receive him because his face was set toward Jerusalem. [54] When his disciples James and John saw this, they said, "Lord, do you want us to command fire to come down from heaven and consume them?" [55] But he turned and rebuked them. [56] Then they went on to another village.

✤ Would-Be Followers of Jesus

[57] As they were going along the road, someone said to him, "I will follow you wherever you go." [58] And Jesus said to him, "Foxes have holes, and birds of the air have nests, but the Son of Man has nowhere to lay his head." [59] To another he said, "Follow me." But he said, "Lord, first let me go and bury my father." [60] And Jesus said to him, "Let the dead bury their own dead, but as for you, go and proclaim the kingdom of God." [61] Another said, "I will follow you, Lord, but let me first say farewell to those at my home." [62] And Jesus said to him, "No one who puts a hand to the plow and looks back is fit for the kingdom of God."

CHAPTER 10

✤ The Mission of the Seventy-Two

**fter this the Lord appointed** seventy-two others and sent them on ahead of him in pairs to every town and place where he himself intended to go. **2** He said to them, "The harvest is plentiful, but the laborers are few; therefore ask the Lord of the harvest to send out laborers into his harvest. **3** Go on your way; I am sending you out like lambs into the midst of wolves. **4** Carry no purse, no bag, no sandals, and greet no one on the road. **5** Whatever house you enter, first say, 'Peace to this house!' **6** And if a person of peace is there, your peace will rest on that person, but if not, it will return to you. **7** Remain in the same house, eating and drinking whatever they provide, for the laborer deserves to be paid. Do not move about from house to house. **8** Whenever you enter a town and its people welcome you, eat what is set before you; **9** cure the sick who are there, and say to them, 'The kingdom of God has come near to you.' **10** But whenever you enter a town and they do not welcome you, go out into its streets and say, **11** 'Even the dust of your town that clings to our feet, we wipe off in protest against you. Yet know this: the kingdom of God has come near.' **12** I tell you, on that day it will be more tolerable for Sodom than for that town.

✤ Woes to Unrepentant Cities

13 "Woe to you, Chorazin! Woe to you, Bethsaida! For if the deeds of power done in you had been done in Tyre and Sidon, they would have repented long ago, sitting in sackcloth and ashes. **14** Indeed, at the judgment it will be more tolerable for Tyre and Sidon than for you. **15** And you, Capernaum,

will you be exalted to heaven?

No, you will be brought down to Hades.

16 "Whoever listens to you listens to me, and whoever rejects you rejects me, and whoever rejects me rejects the one who sent me."

✦ The Return of the Seventy-Two

17 The seventy-two returned with joy, saying, "Lord, in your name even the demons submit to us!" **18** He said to them, "I watched Satan fall from heaven like a flash of lightning. **19** Indeed, I have given you authority to tread on snakes and scorpions and over all the power of the enemy, and nothing will hurt you. **20** Nevertheless, do not rejoice at this, that the spirits submit to you, but rejoice that your names are written in heaven."

✦ Jesus Rejoices

21 At that very hour Jesus rejoiced in the Holy Spirit and said, "I thank you, Father, Lord of heaven and earth, because you have hidden these things from the wise and the intelligent and have revealed them to infants; yes, Father, for such was your gracious will. **22** All things have been handed over to me by my Father, and no one knows who the Son is except the Father or who the Father is except the Son and anyone to whom the Son chooses to reveal him."

23 Then turning to the disciples, Jesus said to them privately, "Blessed are the eyes that see what you see! **24** For I tell you that many prophets and kings desired to see what you see but did not see it and to hear what you hear but did not hear it."

✦ The Parable of the Good Samaritan

25 An expert in the law stood up to test Jesus. "Teacher," he said, "what must I do to inherit eternal life?" **26** He said to him, "What is written in the law? What do you read there?" **27** He answered, "You shall love the Lord your God with all your heart and with all your soul and with all your strength and with all your mind and your neighbor as yourself." **28** And he said to him, "You have given the right answer; do this, and you will live."

29 But wanting to vindicate himself, he asked Jesus, "And who is my neighbor?" **30** Jesus replied, "A man was going down from Jerusalem to Jericho and fell into the hands of robbers, who stripped him, beat him, and took off, leaving him half dead. **31** Now by chance a priest was going down that road, and when he saw him he passed by on the other side. **32** So likewise a Levite, when he came to the place and saw him, passed by on the other side. **33** But a Samaritan while traveling came upon him, and when he saw him he was moved with compassion. **34** He went to him and bandaged his wounds, treating them with oil and wine. Then he put him on his own animal, brought him to an inn, and took care of him. **35** The next day he took out two denarii, gave them to the innkeeper, and said, 'Take care of him, and when I come back, I will repay you whatever more you spend.' **36** Which of these three, do you think, was a neighbor to the man who fell into the hands of the robbers?" **37** He said, "The one who showed him mercy." Jesus said to him, "Go and do likewise."

✦ Jesus Visits Martha and Mary

38 Now as they went on their way, he entered a certain village where a woman named Martha welcomed him. **39** She had a sister named Mary, who sat at Jesus's feet and listened to what he was saying. **40** But Martha was distracted by her many tasks, so she came to him and asked, "Lord, do you not care that my sister has left me to do all the work by myself? Tell her, then, to help me." **41** But the Lord answered her, "Martha, Martha, you are worried and distracted by many things, **42** but few things are needed— indeed only one. Mary has chosen the better part, which will not be taken away from her."

CHAPTER **11**

✣ The Lord's Prayer

**e was praying in a certain place,** and after he had finished, one of his disciples said to him, "Lord, teach us to pray, as John taught his disciples." **2** So he said to them, "When you pray, say:

Father, may your name be revered as holy.
> May your kingdom come.
> **3** Give us each day our daily bread.
> **4** And forgive us our sins,
>> for we ourselves forgive everyone indebted to us.
> And do not bring us to the time of trial.

✣ The Insistent Friend

5 And he said to them, "Suppose one of you has a friend, and you go to him at midnight and say to him, 'Friend, lend me three loaves of bread, **6** for a friend of mine has arrived, and I have nothing to set before him.' **7** And he answers from within, 'Do not bother me; the door has already been locked, and my children are with me in bed; I cannot get up and give you anything.' **8** I tell you, even though he will not get up and give him anything out of friendship, at least because of his persistence he will get up and give him whatever he needs.

9 "So I say to you, Ask, and it will be given to you; search, and you will find; knock, and the door will be opened for you. **10** For everyone who asks receives, and everyone who searches finds, and for everyone who knocks, the door will be opened. **11** Is there anyone among you who, if your child asks for a fish, will give a snake instead of a fish? **12** Or if the child asked for an egg, would give a scorpion? **13** If you, then, who are evil, know how to give good gifts to your children, how much more will the heavenly Father give the Holy Spirit to those who ask him!"

✤ Jesus and Beelzebul

14 Now he was casting out a demon that was mute; when the demon had gone out, the one who had been mute spoke, and the crowds were amazed. **15** But some of them said, "He casts out demons by Beelzebul, the ruler of the demons." **16** Others, to test him, kept demanding from him a sign from heaven. **17** But he knew what they were thinking and said to them, "Every kingdom divided against itself is laid waste, and a divided house falls. **18** If Satan also is divided against himself, how will his kingdom stand?—for you say that I cast out the demons by Beelzebul. **19** Now if I cast out the demons by Beelzebul, by whom do your exorcists cast them out? Therefore they will be your judges. **20** But if it is by the finger of God that I cast out the demons, then the kingdom of God has come upon you. **21** When a strong man, fully armed, guards his castle, his property is safe. **22** But when one stronger than he attacks him and overpowers him, he takes away his armor in which he trusted and divides his plunder. **23** Whoever is not with me is against me, and whoever does not gather with me scatters.

✤ The Return of the Unclean Spirit

24 "When the unclean spirit has gone out of a person, it wanders through waterless regions looking for a resting place, but not finding any it says, 'I will return to my house from which I came.' **25** When it returns, it finds it swept and put in order. **26** Then it goes and brings seven other spirits more evil than itself, and they enter and live there, and the last state of that person is worse than the first."

✤ True Blessedness

27 While he was saying this, a woman in the crowd raised her voice and said to him, "Blessed is the womb that bore you and the breasts that nursed you!" **28** But he said, "Blessed rather are those who hear the word of God and obey it!"

✦ The Sign of Jonah

29 When the crowds were increasing, he began to say, "This generation is an evil generation; it asks for a sign, but no sign will be given to it except the sign of Jonah. **30** For just as Jonah became a sign to the people of Nineveh, so the Son of Man will be to this generation. **31** The queen of the South will rise at the judgment with the people of this generation and condemn them, because she came from the ends of the earth to listen to the wisdom of Solomon, and indeed, something greater than Solomon is here! **32** The people of Nineveh will rise up at the judgment with this generation and condemn it, because they repented at the proclamation of Jonah, and indeed, something greater than Jonah is here!

✦ The Light of the Body

33 "No one after lighting a lamp puts it in a cellar or under a bushel basket; rather, one puts it on the lampstand so that those who enter may see the light. **34** Your eye is the lamp of your body. If your eye is healthy, your whole body is full of light, but if it is unhealthy, your body is full of darkness. **35** Therefore consider whether the light in you is not darkness. **36** But if your whole body is full of light, with no part of it in darkness, it will be as full of light as when a lamp gives you light with its rays."

✦ Jesus Denounces Pharisees and Experts in the Law

37 While he was speaking, a Pharisee invited him to dine with him, so he went in and took his place at the table. **38** The Pharisee was amazed to see that he did not first wash before dinner. **39** Then the Lord said to him, "Now you Pharisees clean the outside of the cup and of the dish, but inside you are full of greed and wickedness. **40** You fools! Did not the one who made the outside make the inside also? **41** So give for alms those things that are within and then everything will be clean for you.

42 "But woe to you Pharisees! For you tithe mint and rue and herbs of all kinds and neglect justice and the love of God; it is these you ought to have practiced, without neglecting the others.

43 Woe to you Pharisees! For you love to have the seat of honor in the synagogues and to be greeted with respect in the market-places. 44 Woe to you! For you are like unmarked graves on which people unknowingly walk."

45 One of the experts in the law answered him, "Teacher, when you say these things, you insult us, too." 46 And he said, "Woe also to you experts in the law! For you load people with burdens hard to bear, and you yourselves do not lift a finger to ease them. 47 Woe to you! For you build the tombs of the prophets whom your ancestors killed. 48 So you are witnesses and approve of the deeds of your ancestors, for they killed them, and you build their tombs. 49 For this reason the Wisdom of God said, 'I will send them prophets and apostles, some of whom they will kill and persecute,' 50 so that this generation may be charged with the blood of all the prophets shed since the foundation of the world, 51 from the blood of Abel to the blood of Zechariah, who perished between the altar and the sanctuary. Yes, I tell you, it will be charged against this generation. 52 Woe to you experts in the law! For you have taken away the key of knowledge; you did not enter yourselves, and you hindered those who were entering."

53 When he went outside, the scribes and the Pharisees became hostile to him and began to interrogate him about many things, 54 lying in wait for him, to catch him in something he might say.

CHAPTER 12

✦ A Warning against Hypocrisy

eanwhile, when the crowd had gathered by the thousands, so that they trampled on one another, he began to speak first to his disciples, "Beware of the yeast of the Pharisees, that is, their hypocrisy. 2 Nothing is covered up that will not be uncovered and nothing secret that will not become known. 3 Therefore whatever you have said in the dark will be heard in the light, and what you have whispered behind closed doors will be proclaimed from the housetops.

✤ Do Not Be Afraid

[4] "I tell you, my friends, do not fear those who kill the body and after that can do nothing more. [5] But I will show you whom to fear: fear the one who, after killing, has authority to cast into hell. Yes, I tell you, fear that one! [6] Are not five sparrows sold for two pennies? Yet not one of them is forgotten in God's sight. [7] But even the hairs of your head are all numbered. Do not be afraid; you are of more value than many sparrows.

[8] "And I tell you, everyone who acknowledges me before others, the Son of Man also will acknowledge before the angels of God, [9] but whoever denies me before others will be denied before the angels of God. [10] And everyone who speaks a word against the Son of Man will be forgiven, but whoever blasphemes against the Holy Spirit will not be forgiven. [11] When they bring you before the synagogues, the rulers, and the authorities, do not worry about how or what you will answer or what you are to say, [12] for the Holy Spirit will teach you at that very hour what you ought to say."

✤ The Parable of the Rich Fool

[13] Someone in the crowd said to him, "Teacher, tell my brother to divide the family inheritance with me." [14] But he said to him, "Friend, who set me to be a judge or arbitrator over you?" [15] And he said to them, "Take care! Be on your guard against all kinds of greed, for one's life does not consist in the abundance of possessions." [16] Then he told them a parable: "The land of a rich man produced abundantly. [17] And he thought to himself, 'What should I do, for I have no place to store my crops?' [18] Then he said, 'I will do this: I will pull down my barns and build larger ones, and there I will store all my grain and my goods. [19] And I will say to my soul, Soul, you have ample goods laid up for many years; relax, eat, drink, be merry.' [20] But God said to him, 'You fool! This very night your life is being demanded of you. And the things you have

prepared, whose will they be?' ²¹ So it is with those who store up treasures for themselves but are not rich toward God."

✤ Do Not Worry

²² He said to his disciples, "Therefore I tell you, do not worry about your life, what you will eat, or about your body, what you will wear. ²³ For life is more than food and the body more than clothing. ²⁴ Consider the ravens: they neither sow nor reap, they have neither storehouse nor barn, and yet God feeds them. Of how much more value are you than the birds! ²⁵ And which of you by worrying can add a single hour to your span of life? ²⁶ If then you are not able to do so small a thing as that, why do you worry about the rest? ²⁷ Consider the lilies, how they grow: they neither toil nor spin, yet I tell you, even Solomon in all his glory was not clothed like one of these. ²⁸ But if God so clothes the grass of the field, which is alive today and tomorrow is thrown into the oven, how much more will he clothe you, you of little faith! ²⁹ And do not keep seeking what you are to eat and what you are to drink, and do not keep worrying. ³⁰ For it is the nations of the world that seek after all these things, and your Father knows that you need them. ³¹ Instead, seek his kingdom, and these things will be given to you as well.

³² "Do not be afraid, little flock, for it is your Father's good pleasure to give you the kingdom. ³³ Sell your possessions and give alms. Make purses for yourselves that do not wear out, an unfailing treasure in heaven, where no thief comes near and no moth destroys. ³⁴ For where your treasure is, there your heart will be also.

✤ Be Ready

³⁵ "Be dressed for action and have your lamps lit; ³⁶ be like those who are waiting for their master to return from the wedding banquet, so that they may open the door for him as soon as he comes and knocks. ³⁷ Blessed are those slaves whom the master finds alert when he comes; truly I tell you, he will fasten his belt and have them sit down to eat, and he will come and serve them.

38 If he comes during the middle of the night or near dawn and finds them so, blessed are those slaves.

39 "But know this: if the owner of the house had known at what hour the thief was coming, he would not have let his house be broken into. **40** You also must be ready, for the Son of Man is coming at an hour you do not expect."

✦ Be Faithful

41 Peter said, "Lord, are you telling this parable for us or for everyone?" **42** And the Lord said, "Who, then, is the faithful and prudent manager whom his master will put in charge of his slaves, to give them their allowance of food at the proper time? **43** Blessed is that slave whom his master will find at work when he arrives. **44** Truly I tell you, he will put that one in charge of all his possessions. **45** But if that slave says to himself, 'My master is delayed in coming,' and if he begins to beat the other slaves, men and women, and to eat and drink and get drunk, **46** the master of that slave will come on a day when he does not expect him and at an hour that he does not know, and will cut him in pieces and put him with the unfaithful. **47** That slave who knew what his master wanted but did not prepare himself or do what was wanted will receive a severe beating. **48** But the one who did not know and did what deserved a beating will receive a light beating. From everyone to whom much has been given, much will be required, and from the one to whom much has been entrusted, even more will be demanded.

✦ Jesus the Cause of Division

49 "I have come to cast fire upon the earth, and how I wish it were already ablaze! **50** I have a baptism with which to be baptized, and what constraint I am under until it is completed! **51** Do you think that I have come to bring peace to the earth? No, I tell you, but rather division! **52** From now on five in one household will be divided, three against two and two against three; **53** they will be divided:

father against son
   and son against father,
mother against daughter
   and daughter against mother,
mother-in-law against her daughter-in-law
   and daughter-in-law against mother-in-law."

✧ Interpreting the Time

⁵⁴ He also said to the crowds, "When you see a cloud rising in the west, you immediately say, 'It is going to rain'; and so it happens. **⁵⁵** And when you see the south wind blowing, you say, 'There will be scorching heat'; and it happens. **⁵⁶** You hypocrites! You know how to interpret the appearance of earth and sky, but why do you not know how to interpret the present time?

✧ Settling with Your Opponent

⁵⁷ "And why do you not judge for yourselves what is right? **⁵⁸** Thus when you go with your accuser before a magistrate, on the way make an effort to reach a settlement, or you may be dragged before the judge, and the judge hand you over to the officer, and the officer throw you in prison. **⁵⁹** I tell you, you will never get out until you have paid the very last penny."

CHAPTER **13**

✧ Repent or Perish

 t that very time there were some present who told Jesus about the Galileans whose blood Pilate had mingled with their sacrifices. **²** He asked them, "Do you think that because these Galileans suffered in this way they were worse sinners than all other Galileans? **³** No, I tell you, but unless you repent, you will all perish as they did. **⁴** Or those eighteen who were killed when the tower of Siloam fell on them—do you think that they were worse offenders than

all the others living in Jerusalem? **⁵** No, I tell you; but unless you repent you will all perish just as they did."

✤ The Parable of the Barren Fig Tree

⁶ Then he told this parable: "A man had a fig tree planted in his vineyard, and he came looking for fruit on it and found none. **⁷** So he said to the man working the vineyard, 'See here! For three years I have come looking for fruit on this fig tree, and still I find none. Cut it down! Why should it be wasting the soil?' **⁸** He replied, 'Sir, let it alone for one more year, until I dig around it and put manure on it. **⁹** If it bears fruit next year, well and good, but if not, you can cut it down.'"

✤ Jesus Heals on the Sabbath

¹⁰ Now he was teaching in one of the synagogues on the Sabbath. **¹¹** And just then there appeared a woman with a spirit that had crippled her for eighteen years. She was bent over and was quite unable to stand up straight. **¹²** When Jesus saw her, he called her over and said, "Woman, you are set free from your ailment." **¹³** When he laid his hands on her, immediately she stood up straight and began praising God. **¹⁴** But the leader of the synagogue, indignant because Jesus had cured on the Sabbath, kept saying to the crowd, "There are six days on which work ought to be done; come on those days and be cured and not on the Sabbath day." **¹⁵** But the Lord answered him and said, "You hypocrites! Does not each of you on the Sabbath untie his ox or his donkey from the manger and lead it to water? **¹⁶** And ought not this woman, a daughter of Abraham whom Satan bound for eighteen long years, be set free from this bondage on the Sabbath day?" **¹⁷** When he said this, all his opponents were put to shame, and the entire crowd was rejoicing at all the wonderful things being done by him.

✤ The Parable of the Mustard Seed

¹⁸ He said therefore, "What is the kingdom of God like? And to what should I compare it? **¹⁹** It is like a mustard seed that someone took and sowed in the garden; it grew and became a tree, and the birds of the air made nests in its branches."

✧ The Parable of the Yeast

²⁰ And again he said, "To what should I compare the kingdom of God? ²¹ It is like yeast that a woman took and mixed in with three measures of flour until all of it was leavened."

✧ The Narrow Door

²² Jesus went through one town and village after another, teaching as he made his way to Jerusalem. ²³ Someone asked him, "Lord, will only a few be saved?" He said to them, ²⁴"Strive to enter through the narrow door, for many, I tell you, will try to enter and will not be able. ²⁵ Once the owner of the house has got up and shut the door, and you begin to stand outside and to knock at the door, saying, 'Lord, open to us,' then in reply he will say to you, 'I do not know where you come from.' ²⁶ Then you will begin to say, 'We ate and drank with you, and you taught in our streets.' ²⁷ But he will say to you, 'I do not know where you come from; go away from me, all you evildoers!' ²⁸ There will be weeping and gnashing of teeth when you see Abraham and Isaac and Jacob and all the prophets in the kingdom of God, and you yourselves thrown out. ²⁹ Then people will come from east and west, from north and south, and will take their places at the banquet in the kingdom of God. ³⁰ Indeed, some are last who will be first, and some are first who will be last."

✧ Jesus Laments over Jerusalem

³¹ At that very hour some Pharisees came and said to him, "Get away from here, for Herod wants to kill you." ³² He said to them, "Go and tell that fox for me, 'Listen, I am casting out demons and performing cures today and tomorrow, and on the third day I finish my work. ³³ Yet today, tomorrow, and the next day I must be on my way, because it is impossible for a prophet to be killed outside of Jerusalem.' ³⁴ Jerusalem, Jerusalem, the city that kills the prophets and stones those who are sent to it! How often have I desired

to gather your children together as a hen gathers her brood under her wings, and you were not willing! [35] See, your house is left to you. And I tell you, you will not see me until the time comes when you say, 'Blessed is the one who comes in the name of the Lord.'"

CHAPTER 14

✣ Jesus Heals the Man with Edema

n one occasion when Jesus was going to the house of a leader of the Pharisees to eat a meal on the Sabbath, they were watching him closely. [2] Just then, in front of him, there was a man who had edema. [3] And Jesus asked the experts in the law and Pharisees, "Is it lawful to cure people on the sabbath, or not?" [4] But they were silent. So Jesus took him and healed him and sent him away. [5] Then he said to them, "If one of you has a child or an ox that has fallen into a well, will you not immediately pull it out on a Sabbath day?" [6] And they could not reply to this.

✣ Humility and Hospitality

[7] When he noticed how the guests chose the places of honor, he told them a parable. [8] "When you are invited by someone to a wedding banquet, do not sit down at the place of honor, in case someone more distinguished than you has been invited by your host, [9] and the host who invited both of you may come and say to you, 'Give this person your place,' and then in disgrace you would start to take the lowest place. [10] But when you are invited, go and sit down at the lowest place, so that when your host comes, he may say to you, 'Friend, move up higher'; then you will be honored in the presence of all who sit at the table with you. [11] For all who exalt themselves will be humbled, and those who humble themselves will be exalted."

[12] He said also to the one who had invited him, "When you give a luncheon or a dinner, do not invite your friends or your brothers

and sisters or your relatives or rich neighbors, in case they may invite you in return, and you would be repaid. **13** But when you give a banquet, invite the poor, the crippled, the lame, and the blind. **14** And you will be blessed because they cannot repay you, for you will be repaid at the resurrection of the righteous."

✤ The Parable of the Great Dinner

15 One of the dinner guests, on hearing this, said to him, "Blessed is anyone who will eat bread in the kingdom of God!" **16** Then Jesus said to him, "Someone gave a great dinner and invited many. **17** At the time for the dinner he sent his slave to say to those who had been invited, 'Come; for everything is ready now.' **18** But they all alike began to make excuses. The first said to him, 'I have bought a piece of land, and I must go out and see it; please accept my regrets.' **19** Another said, 'I have bought five yoke of oxen, and I am going to try them out; please accept my regrets.' **20** Another said, 'I have just been married, and therefore I cannot come.' **21** So the slave returned and reported this to his master. Then the owner of the house became angry and said to his slave, 'Go out at once into the streets and lanes of the town and bring in the poor, the crippled, the blind, and the lame.' **22** And the slave said, 'Sir, what you ordered has been done, and there is still room.' **23** Then the master said to the slave, 'Go out into the roads and lanes, and compel people to come in, so that my house may be filled. **24** For I tell you, none of those who were invited will taste my dinner.'"

✤ The Cost of Discipleship

25 Now large crowds were traveling with him, and he turned and said to them, **26** "Whoever comes to me and does not hate father and mother, wife and children, brothers and sisters, yes, and even life itself, cannot be my disciple. **27** Whoever does not carry the cross and follow me cannot be my disciple. **28** For which of you, intending to build a tower, does not first sit down and estimate the cost, to see whether he has enough to complete it? **29** Otherwise, when he has laid a foundation and is not able to finish, all who see it will begin to ridicule him, **30** saying, 'This fellow began to build and was not able to finish.' **31** Or what king, going out to wage war against another king, will not sit down first and consider whether he is able with ten thousand to oppose the one who comes against him with twenty thousand? **32** If he cannot, then, while the other is still far away, he sends a delegation and asks for the terms of peace. **33** So therefore, none of you can become my disciple if you do not give up all your possessions.

✤ About Salt

34 "Salt is good, but if salt has lost its taste, how can its saltiness be restored? **35** It is useful neither for the soil nor for the manure pile; they throw it away. If you have ears to hear, then hear!"

CHAPTER **15**

✤ The Parable of the Found Sheep

ow all the tax collectors and sinners were coming near to listen to him. **2** And the Pharisees and the scribes were grumbling and saying, "This fellow welcomes sinners and eats with them."

3 So he told them this parable: **4** "Which one of you, having a hundred sheep and losing one of them, does not leave the ninety-nine in the wilderness and go after the one that is lost until he finds it? **5** And when he has found it, he lays it on his shoulders and rejoices. **6** And when he comes home, he calls together his friends and neighbors, saying to them, 'Rejoice with me, for I have found my lost sheep.' **7** Just so, I tell you, there will be more joy in heaven over one sinner who repents than over ninety-nine righteous persons who need no repentance.

✤ The Parable of the Found Coin

8 "Or what woman having ten silver coins, if she loses one of them, does not light a lamp, sweep the house, and search carefully until she finds it? **9** And when she has found it, she calls together her friends and neighbors, saying, 'Rejoice with me, for I have found the coin that I had lost.' **10** Just so, I tell you, there is joy in the presence of the angels of God over one sinner who repents."

✤ The Parable of the Loving Father

11 Then Jesus said, "There was a man who had two sons. **12** The younger of them said to his father, 'Father, give me the share of the wealth that will belong to me.' So he divided his assets between them. **13** A few days later the younger son gathered all he had and traveled to a distant region, and there he squandered his property in dissolute living. **14** When he had spent everything, a severe famine took place throughout that region, and he began to be in need. **15** So he went and hired himself out to one of the citizens of that region, who sent him to his fields to feed the pigs. **16** He would gladly have filled his stomach with the pods that the pigs were eating; and no one gave him anything. **17** But when he came to his senses he said, 'How many of my father's hired hands have bread enough and to spare, but here I am dying of hunger! **18** I will get up and go to my father, and I will say to him, "Father, I have sinned against heaven and before you; **19** I am no longer worthy to be called your son; treat me like one of your hired hands."' **20** So he set off and went to his father. But while he was still far off, his father saw him and was filled with compassion; he ran and put his arms around him and kissed him. **21** Then the son said to him, 'Father, I have sinned against heaven and before you; I am no longer worthy to be called your son.' **22** But the father said to his slaves, 'Quickly, bring out a robe—the best one—and put it on him; put a ring on his finger and sandals on his feet. **23** And get the fatted calf and kill it, and let us eat and celebrate, **24** for this son of mine was dead and is alive again; he was lost and is found!' And they began to celebrate.

25 "Now his elder son was in the field, and as he came and approached the house, he heard music and dancing. **26** He called one of the slaves and asked what was going on. **27** He replied, 'Your brother has come, and your father has killed the fatted calf because he has got him back safe and sound.' **28** Then he became angry and refused to go in. His father came out and began to plead with him. **29** But he answered his father, 'Listen! For all these years I have been working like a slave for you, and I have never disobeyed your command, yet you have never given me even a young goat so that I might celebrate with my friends. **30** But when this son of yours came back, who has devoured your assets with prostitutes, you killed the fatted calf for him!' **31** Then the father said to him, 'Son, you are always with me, and all that is mine is yours. **32** But we had to celebrate and rejoice, because this brother of yours was dead and has come to life; he was lost and has been found.'"

CHAPTER **16**

✢ The Parable of the Dishonest Manager

 **hen Jesus said to the disciples,** "There was a rich man who had a manager, and charges were brought to him that this man was squandering his property. **2** So he summoned him and said to him, 'What is this that I hear about you? Give me an accounting of your management, because you cannot be my manager any longer.' **3** Then the manager said to himself, 'What will I do, now that my master is taking the position away from me? I am not strong enough to dig, and I am ashamed to beg. **4** I have decided what to do so that, when I am dismissed as manager, people may welcome me into their homes.' **5** So, summoning his master's debtors one by one, he asked the first, 'How much do you owe my master?' **6** He answered, 'A hundred jugs of olive oil.' He said to him, 'Take your bill, sit down quickly, and make it fifty.' **7** Then he asked another, 'And how much do you owe?' He replied, 'A hundred containers of wheat.' He said to him, 'Take your bill and make it eighty.' **8** And his master commended the dishonest manager because he had acted shrewdly, for the children of this age are more shrewd in dealing with their own generation than are the

children of light. ⁹ And I tell you, make friends for yourselves by means of dishonest wealth so that when it is gone they may welcome you into the eternal homes.

¹⁰ "Whoever is faithful in a very little is faithful also in much; and whoever is dishonest in a very little is dishonest also in much. ¹¹ If, then, you have not been faithful with the dishonest wealth, who will entrust to you the true riches? ¹² And if you have not been faithful with what belongs to another, who will give you what is your own? ¹³ No slave can serve two masters; for a slave will either hate the one and love the other or be devoted to the one and despise the other. You cannot serve God and wealth."

✦ The Law and the Kingdom of God

¹⁴ The Pharisees, who were lovers of money, heard all this, and they ridiculed him. ¹⁵ So he said to them, "You are those who justify yourselves in the sight of others, but God knows your hearts, for what is prized by human beings is an abomination in the sight of God.

¹⁶ "The Law and the Prophets were until John came; since then the good news of the kingdom of God is being proclaimed, and everyone tries to enter it by force. ¹⁷ But it is easier for heaven and earth to pass away than for one stroke of a letter in the law to be dropped.

¹⁸ "Anyone who divorces his wife and marries another commits adultery, and whoever marries a woman divorced from her husband commits adultery.

✦ The Rich Man and Lazarus

¹⁹ "There was a rich man who was dressed in purple and fine linen and who feasted sumptuously every day. ²⁰ And at his gate lay a poor man named Lazarus, covered with sores, ²¹ who longed to satisfy his hunger with what fell from the rich man's table; even the dogs would come and lick his sores. ²² The poor man died and was carried away by the angels to be with Abraham. The rich man also died and was buried. ²³ In Hades, where he was being tormented, he lifted up his eyes and saw Abraham far away with

Lazarus by his side. ²⁴ He called out, 'Father Abraham, have mercy on me, and send Lazarus to dip the tip of his finger in water and cool my tongue; for I am in agony in these flames.' ²⁵ But Abraham said, 'Child, remember that during your lifetime you received your good things, and Lazarus in like manner evil things; but now he is comforted here, and you are in agony. ²⁶ Besides all this, between you and us a great chasm has been fixed, so that those who might want to pass from here to you cannot do so, and no one can cross from there to us.' ²⁷ He said, 'Then I beg you, father, to send him to my father's house— ²⁸ for I have five brothers—that he may warn them, so that they will not also come into this place of torment.' ²⁹ Abraham replied, 'They have Moses and the prophets; they should listen to them.' ³⁰ He said, 'No, father Abraham, but if someone from the dead goes to them, they will repent.' ³¹ He said to him, 'If they do not listen to Moses and the prophets, neither will they be convinced even if someone rises from the dead.'"

CHAPTER 17

✢ Some Sayings of Jesus

esus said to his disciples, "Occasions for sin are bound to come, but woe to anyone by whom they come! ² It would be better for you if a millstone were hung around your neck and you were thrown into the sea than for you to cause one of these little ones to sin. ³ Be on your guard! If a brother or sister sins, you must rebuke the offender, and if there is repentance, you must forgive. ⁴ And if the same person sins against you seven times a day, and turns back to you seven times and says, 'I repent,' you must forgive."

⁵ The apostles said to the Lord, "Increase our faith!" ⁶ The Lord replied, "If you had faith the size of a mustard seed, you could say to this mulberry tree, 'Be uprooted and planted in the sea,' and it would obey you.

✤ The Unprofitable Servant

⁷ "Who among you would say to your slave who has just come in from plowing or tending sheep in the field, 'Come here at once and take your place at the table'? ⁸ Would you not rather say to him, 'Prepare supper for me; put on your apron and serve me while I eat and drink; later you may eat and drink'? ⁹ Do you thank the slave for doing what was commanded? ¹⁰ So you also, when you have done all that you were ordered to do, say, 'We are worthless slaves; we have done only what we ought to have done.'"

✤ Jesus Heals Ten Men with a Skin Disease

¹¹ On the way to Jerusalem Jesus was going through the region between Samaria and Galilee. ¹² As he entered a village, ten men with a skin disease approached him. Keeping their distance, ¹³ they called out, saying, "Jesus, Master, have mercy on us!" ¹⁴ When he saw them, he said to them, "Go and show yourselves to the priests." And as they went, they were made clean. ¹⁵ Then one of them, when he saw that he was healed, turned back, praising God with a loud voice. ¹⁶ He prostrated himself at Jesus's feet and thanked him. And he was a Samaritan. ¹⁷ Then Jesus asked, "Were not ten made clean? So where are the other nine? ¹⁸ Did none of them return to give glory to God except this foreigner?" ¹⁹ Then he said to him, "Get up and go on your way; your faith has made you well."

✤ The Coming of the Kingdom

²⁰ Once Jesus was asked by the Pharisees when the kingdom of God was coming, and he answered, "The kingdom of God is not coming with things that can be observed, ²¹ nor will they say, 'Look, here it is!' or 'There it is!' For, in fact, the kingdom of God is among you."

²² Then he said to the disciples, "The days are coming when you will long to see one of the days of the Son of Man, and you will not see it. ²³ They will say to you, 'Look there!' or 'Look here!' Do not go; do not set off in pursuit. ²⁴ For as the lightning flashes and lights up the sky from one side to the other, so will the Son

of Man be in his day. ²⁵ But first he must endure much suffering and be rejected by this generation. ²⁶ Just as it was in the days of Noah, so, too, it will be in the days of the Son of Man. ²⁷ They were eating and drinking and marrying and being given in marriage until the day Noah entered the ark, and the flood came and destroyed all of them. ²⁸ Likewise, just as it was in the days of Lot, they were eating and drinking, buying and selling, planting and building, ²⁹ but on the day that Lot left Sodom it rained fire and sulfur from heaven and destroyed all of them; ³⁰ it will be like that on the day that the Son of Man is revealed. ³¹ On that day, anyone on the housetop who has belongings in the house must not come down to take them away, and likewise anyone in the field must not turn back. ³² Remember Lot's wife. ³³ Those who try to make their life secure will lose it, but those who lose their life will keep it. ³⁴ I tell you, on that night there will be two in one bed; one will be taken and the other left. ³⁵ There will be two women grinding meal together; one will be taken and the other left." ³⁷ Then they asked him, "Where, Lord?" He said to them, "Where the corpse is, there the eagles will gather."

CHAPTER 18

✤ The Parable of the Widow and the Unjust Judge

 **hen Jesus told them a parable** about their need to pray always and not to lose heart. ² He said, "In a certain city there was a judge who feared neither God nor had respect for people. ³ In that city there was a widow who kept coming to him and saying, 'Grant me justice against my accuser.' ⁴ For a while he refused, but later he said to himself, 'Though I have no fear of God and no respect for anyone, ⁵ yet because this widow keeps bothering me, I will grant her justice, so that she may not wear me out by continually coming.'" ⁶ And the Lord said, "Listen to what the unjust judge says. ⁷ And will not God grant justice to his chosen ones who cry

to him day and night? Will he delay long in helping them? **8** I tell you, he will quickly grant justice to them. And yet, when the Son of Man comes, will he find faith on earth?"

✣ The Parable of the Pharisee and the Tax Collector

9 He also told this parable to some who trusted in themselves that they were righteous and regarded others with contempt: **10** "Two men went up to the temple to pray, one a Pharisee and the other a tax collector. **11** The Pharisee, standing by himself, was praying thus, 'God, I thank you that I am not like other people: thieves, rogues, adulterers, or even like this tax collector. **12** I fast twice a week; I give a tenth of all my income.' **13** But the tax collector, standing far off, would not even lift up his eyes to heaven but was beating his breast and saying, 'God, be merciful to me, a sinner!' **14** I tell you, this man went down to his home justified rather than the other, for all who exalt themselves will be humbled, but all who humble themselves will be exalted."

✣ Let the Children Come to Me

15 People were bringing even infants to him that he might touch them, and when the disciples saw it, they sternly ordered them not to do it. **16** But Jesus called for them and said, "Let the children come to me, and do not stop them, for it is to such as these that the kingdom of God belongs. **17** Truly I tell you, whoever does not receive the kingdom of God as a little child will never enter it."

✣ The Rich Ruler

18 A certain ruler asked him, "Good Teacher, what must I do to inherit eternal life?" **19** Jesus said to him, "Why do you call me good? No one is good but God alone. **20** You know the commandments: 'You shall not commit adultery. You shall not murder. You shall not steal. You shall not bear false witness. Honor your father and mother.'" **21** He replied, "I have kept all these since my youth." **22** When Jesus heard this, he said to him, "There is still one thing lacking. Sell all that you own and distribute the money to the poor, and you will have treasure in heaven; then come, follow me."

²³ But when he heard this, he became sad, for he was very rich. ²⁴ Jesus looked at him and said, "How hard it is for those who have wealth to enter the kingdom of God! ²⁵ Indeed, it is easier for a camel to go through the eye of a needle than for someone who is rich to enter the kingdom of God.

²⁶ Those who heard it said, "Then who can be saved?" ²⁷ He replied, "What is impossible for mortals is possible for God."

²⁸ Then Peter said, "Look, we have left our homes and followed you." ²⁹ And he said to them, "Truly I tell you, there is no one who has left house or wife or brothers or parents or children for the sake of the kingdom of God, ³⁰ who will not get back very much more in this age and in the age to come eternal life."

✦ A Third Time Jesus Foretells His Death and Resurrection

³¹ Then he took the twelve aside and said to them, "Look, we are going up to Jerusalem, and everything that is written about the Son of Man by the prophets will be accomplished. ³² For he will be handed over to the gentiles; and he will be mocked and insulted and spat upon. ³³ After they have flogged him, they will kill him, and on the third day he will rise again." ³⁴ But they understood nothing about all these things; in fact, what he said was hidden from them, and they did not grasp what was said.

✦ Jesus Heals a Blind Beggar Near Jericho

³⁵ As he approached Jericho, a blind man was sitting by the road-side begging. ³⁶ When he heard a crowd going by, he asked what was happening. ³⁷ They told him, "Jesus of Nazareth is passing by." ³⁸ Then he shouted, "Jesus, Son of David, have mercy on me!" ³⁹ Those who were in front sternly ordered him to be quiet, but he shouted even more loudly, "Son of David, have mercy on me!" ⁴⁰ Jesus stood still and ordered the man to be brought to him; and when he came near, he asked him, ⁴¹ "What do you want me to do for you?" He said, "Lord, let me see again." ⁴² Jesus said to him, "Receive your sight; your faith has saved you." ⁴³ Immediately he

regained his sight and followed him, glorifying God, and all the people, when they saw it, praised God.

CHAPTER 19

✦ Jesus and Zacchaeus

He entered Jericho and was passing through it. ² A man was there named Zacchaeus; he was a chief tax collector and was rich. ³ He was trying to see who Jesus was, but on account of the crowd he could not, because he was short in stature. ⁴ So he ran ahead and climbed a sycamore tree to see him, because he was going to pass that way. ⁵ When Jesus came to the place, he looked up and said to him, "Zacchaeus, hurry and come down, for I must stay at your house today." ⁶ So he hurried down and was happy to welcome him. ⁷ All who saw it began to grumble and said, "He has gone to be the guest of one who is a sinner." ⁸ Zacchaeus stood there and said to the Lord, "Look, half of my possessions, Lord, I will give to the poor, and if I have defrauded anyone of anything, I will pay back four times as much." ⁹ Then Jesus said to him, "Today salvation has come to this house, because he, too, is a son of Abraham. ¹⁰ For the Son of Man came to seek out and to save the lost."

✦ The Parable of the Ten Pounds

¹¹ As they were listening to this, he went on to tell a parable, because he was near Jerusalem and because they supposed that the kingdom of God was to appear immediately. ¹² So he said, "A nobleman went to a distant region to receive royal power for himself and then return. ¹³ He summoned ten of his slaves and gave them ten pounds and said to them, 'Do business with these until I come back.' ¹⁴ But the citizens of his country hated him and sent a delegation after him, saying, 'We do not want this man to rule over us.' ¹⁵ When he returned, having received royal power, he ordered these slaves, to whom he had given the money to be

summoned so that he might find out what they had gained by doing business. **16** The first came forward and said, 'Lord, your pound has made ten more pounds.' **17** He said to him, 'Well done, good slave! Because you have been trustworthy in a very small thing, take charge of ten cities.' **18** Then the second came, saying, 'Lord, your pound has made five pounds.' **19** He said to him, 'And you, rule over five cities.' **20** Then the other came, saying, 'Lord, here is your pound. I wrapped it up in a piece of cloth, **21** for I was afraid of you, because you are a harsh man; you take what you did not deposit and reap what you did not sow.' **22** He said to him, 'I will judge you by your own words, you wicked slave! You knew, did you, that I was a harsh man, taking what I did not deposit and reaping what I did not sow? **23** Why, then, did you not put my money into the bank? Then when I returned, I could have collected it with interest.' **24** He said to the bystanders, 'Take the pound from him and give it to the one who has ten pounds.' **25** (And they said to him, 'Lord, he has ten pounds!') **26** 'I tell you, to all those who have, more will be given, but from those who have nothing, even what they have will be taken away. **27** But as for these enemies of mine who did not want me to be king over them—bring them here and slaughter them in my presence.'"

✦ Jesus' Triumphal Entry into Jerusalem

28 After he had said this, he went on ahead, going up to Jerusalem.

29 When he had come near Bethphage and Bethany, at the place called the Mount of Olives, he sent two of the disciples, **30** saying, "Go into the village ahead of you, and as you enter it you will find tied there a colt that has never been ridden. Untie it and bring it here. **31** If anyone asks you, 'Why are you untying it?' just say this, 'The Lord needs it.'" **32** So those who were sent departed and found it as he had told them. **33** As they were untying the colt, its owners asked them, "Why are you untying the colt?" **34** They said, "The Lord needs it." **35** Then they brought it to Jesus, and after throwing their cloaks on the colt, they set Jesus on it. **36** As he rode along, people kept spreading their cloaks on the road. **37** Now as he was approaching the path down from the Mount of Olives, the whole multitude of the disciples began to praise God joyfully with a loud voice for all the deeds of power that they had seen, **38** saying,

> "Blessed is the king
>> who comes in the name of the Lord!
> Peace in heaven,
>> and glory in the highest heaven!"

39 Some of the Pharisees in the crowd said to him, "Teacher, order your disciples to stop." **40** He answered, "I tell you, if these were silent, the stones would shout out."

✦ Jesus Weeps over Jerusalem

41 As he came near and saw the city, he wept over it, **42** saying, "If you, even you, had only recognized on this day the things that make for peace! But now they are hidden from your eyes. **43** Indeed, the days will come upon you when your enemies will set up ramparts around you and surround you and hem you in on every side. **44** They will crush you to the ground, you and your children within you, and they will not leave within you one stone upon another, because you did not recognize the time of your visitation from God."

✦ Jesus Cleanses the Temple

45 Then he entered the temple and began to drive out those who were selling things there, **46** and he said, "It is written,

> 'My house shall be a house of prayer,'
>> but you have made it a den of robbers."

47 Every day he was teaching in the temple. The chief priests, the scribes, and the leaders of the people kept looking for a way to kill him, **48** but they did not find anything they could do, for all the people were spellbound by what they heard.

CHAPTER 20

✤ The Authority of Jesus Questioned

**ne day as he was teaching** the people in the temple and proclaiming the good news, the chief priests and the scribes came with the elders ² and said to him, "Tell us, by what authority are you doing these things? Who is it who gave you this authority?" ³ He answered them, "I will also ask you a question, and you tell me: ⁴ Did the baptism of John come from heaven, or was it of human origin?" ⁵ They discussed it with one another, saying, "If we say, 'From heaven,' he will say, 'Why did you not believe him?' ⁶ But if we say, 'Of human origin,' all the people will stone us, for they are convinced that John was a prophet." ⁷ So they answered that they did not know where it came from. ⁸ Then Jesus said to them, "Neither will I tell you by what authority I am doing these things."

✤ The Parable of the Wicked Tenants

⁹ He began to tell the people this parable: "A man planted a vineyard and leased it to tenants, and went away for a long time. ¹⁰ When the season came, he sent a slave to the tenants in order that they might give him his share of the produce of the vineyard, but the tenants beat him and sent him away empty-handed. ¹¹ Next he sent another slave; that one also they beat and insulted and sent away empty-handed. ¹² And he sent still a third; this one also they wounded and threw out. ¹³ Then the owner of the vineyard said, 'What shall I do? I will send my beloved son; perhaps they will respect him.' ¹⁴ But when the tenants saw him, they discussed it among themselves and said, 'This is the heir; let us kill him so that the inheritance may be ours.' ¹⁵ So they threw him out of the vineyard and killed him. What then will the owner of the vineyard do to them? ¹⁶ He will come and destroy those tenants and give the vineyard to others." When they heard this, they said,

"Heaven forbid!" **17** But he looked at them and said, "What then does this text mean:

'The stone that the builders rejected
has become the cornerstone'?

18 Everyone who falls on that stone will be broken to pieces, and it will crush anyone on whom it falls." **19** When the scribes and chief priests realized that he had told this parable against them, they wanted to lay hands on him at that very hour, but they feared the people.

✣ The Question about Paying Taxes

20 So they watched him and sent spies who pretended to be honest, in order to trap him by what he said and then hand him over to the jurisdiction and authority of the governor. **21** So they asked him, "Teacher, we know that you are right in what you say and teach, and you show deference to no one but teach the way of God in accordance with truth. **22** Is it lawful for us to pay tribute to Caesar or not?" **23** But he perceived their craftiness and said to them, **24** "Show me a denarius. Whose head and whose title does it bear?" They said, "Caesar's." **25** He said to them, "Then give to Caesar the things that are Caesar's and to God the things that are God's." **26** And they were not able in the presence of the people to trap him by what he said, and being amazed by his answer they became silent.

✣ The Question about the Resurrection

27 Some Sadducees, those who say there is no resurrection, came to him **28** and asked him a question: "Teacher, Moses wrote for us that if a man's brother dies leaving a wife but no children, the man shall marry the widow and raise up children for his brother. **29** Now there were seven brothers; the first married a woman and died childless; **30** then the second **31** and the third married her, and so in the same way all seven died childless. **32** Finally the woman also died. **33** In the resurrection, therefore, whose wife will the woman be? For the seven had married her."

34 Jesus said to them, "Those who belong to this age marry and are given in marriage, **35** but those who are considered worthy of a place in that age and in the resurrection from the dead neither marry nor are given in marriage. **36** Indeed they cannot die anymore, because they are like angels and are children of God, being children of the resurrection. **37** And the fact that the dead are raised Moses himself showed, in the story about the bush, where he speaks of the Lord as the God of Abraham, the God of Isaac, and the God of Jacob. **38** Now he is God not of the dead but of the living, for to him all of them are alive." **39** Then some of the scribes answered, "Teacher, you have spoken well." **40** For they no longer dared to ask him another question.

✤ The Question about David's Son

41 Then he said to them, "How can they say that the Messiah is David's son? **42** For David himself says in the book of Psalms,

'The Lord said to my Lord,
"Sit at my right hand
43 until I make your enemies a footstool for your feet."'

44 David thus calls him Lord, so how can he be his son?"

✤ Jesus Denounces the Scribes

45 In the hearing of all the people he said to the disciples, **46** "Beware of the scribes who like to walk around in long robes and who love respectful greetings in the marketplaces and the best seats in the synagogues and places of honor at banquets. **47** They devour widows' houses and for the sake of appearance say long prayers. They will receive the greater condemnation."

CHAPTER 21

✦ The Widow's Offering

**e looked up and saw** rich people putting their gifts into the treasury; ² he also saw a poor widow put in two small copper coins. ³ He said, "Truly I tell you, this poor widow has put in more than all of them, ⁴ for all of them have contributed out of their abundance, but she out of her poverty has put in all she had to live on."

✦ The Destruction of the Temple Foretold

⁵ When some were speaking about the temple, how it was adorned with beautiful stones and gifts dedicated to God, he said, ⁶ "As for these things that you see, the days will come when not one stone will be left upon another; all will be thrown down."

✦ Signs and Persecutions

⁷ They asked him, "Teacher, when will this be, and what will be the sign that this is about to take place?" ⁸ And he said, "Beware that you are not led astray, for many will come in my name and say, 'I am he!' and, 'The time is near!' Do not go after them.

⁹ "When you hear of wars and insurrections, do not be terrified, for these things must take place first, but the end will not follow immediately." ¹⁰ Then he said to them, "Nation will rise against nation and kingdom against kingdom; ¹¹ there will be great earthquakes and in various places famines and plagues, and there will be dreadful portents and great signs from heaven.

¹² "But before all this occurs, they will arrest you and persecute you; they will hand you over to synagogues and prisons, and you will be brought before kings and governors because of my name. ¹³ This will give you an opportunity to testify. ¹⁴ So make up your minds not to prepare your defense in advance, ¹⁵ for I will give you words and a wisdom that none of your opponents will be able to withstand or contradict. ¹⁶ You will be betrayed even by parents

and siblings, by relatives and friends, and they will put some of you to death. **17** You will be hated by all because of my name. **18** But not a hair of your head will perish. **19** By your endurance you will gain your souls.

✤ The Destruction of Jerusalem Foretold

20 "When you see Jerusalem surrounded by armies, then know that its desolation has come near. **21** Then those in Judea must flee to the mountains, and those inside the city must leave it, and those out in the country must not enter it, **22** for these are days of vengeance, as a fulfillment of all that is written. **23** Woe to those who are pregnant and to those who are nursing infants in those days! For there will be great distress on the earth and wrath against this people; **24** they will fall by the edge of the sword and be taken away as captives among all nations, and Jerusalem will be trampled on by the nations, until the times of the nations are fulfilled.

✤ The Coming of the Son of Man

25 "There will be signs in the sun, the moon, and the stars and on the earth distress among nations confused by the roaring of the sea and the waves. **26** People will faint from fear and foreboding of what is coming upon the world, for the powers of the heavens will be shaken. **27** Then they will see 'the Son of Man coming in a cloud' with power and great glory. **28** Now when these things begin to take place, stand up and raise your heads, because your redemption is drawing near."

✤ The Lesson of the Fig Tree

29 Then he told them a parable: "Look at the fig tree and all the trees; **30** as soon as they sprout leaves you can see for yourselves and know that summer is already near. **31** So also, when you see these things taking place, you know that the kingdom of God is near. **32** Truly I tell you, this generation will not pass away until all things have taken place. **33** Heaven and earth will pass away, but my words will not pass away.

✤ Be Ready

34 "Be on guard so that your hearts are not weighed down with dissipation and drunkenness and the worries of this life and that day does not catch you unexpectedly, **35** like a trap. For it will come upon all who live on the face of the whole earth. **36** Be alert at all times, praying that you may have the strength to escape all these things that will take place and to stand before the Son of Man."

37 Every day he was teaching in the temple, and at night he would go out and spend the night on the Mount of Olives, as it was called. **38** And all the people would get up early in the morning to listen to him in the temple.

CHAPTER 22

✤ The Plot to Kill Jesus

ow the Festival of Unleavened Bread, which is called the Passover, was near. **2** The chief priests and the scribes were looking for a way to put Jesus to death, for they were afraid of the people.

3 Then Satan entered into Judas called Iscariot, who was one of the twelve; **4** he went away and conferred with the chief priests and officers of the temple police about how he might betray him to them. **5** They were greatly pleased and agreed to give him money. **6** So he consented and began to look for an opportunity to betray him to them when no crowd was present.

✤ The Preparation of the Passover

7 Then came the day of Unleavened Bread, on which the Passover lamb had to be sacrificed. **8** So Jesus sent Peter and John, saying, "Go and prepare the Passover meal for us that we may eat it." **9** They asked him, "Where do you want us to make preparations for it?" **10** "Listen," he said to them, "when you have entered the city, a man carrying a jar of water will meet you; follow him into the house he enters **11** and say to the owner of the house, 'The teacher asks you, "Where is the guest room, where I may eat the Passover with my disciples?"' ¹² He will show you a large room upstairs, already furnished. Make preparations for us there." ¹³ So they went and found everything as he had told them, and they prepared the Passover meal.

✦ The Institution of the Lord's Supper

¹⁴ When the hour came, he took his place at the table, and the apostles with him. ¹⁵ He said to them, "I have eagerly desired to eat this Passover with you before I suffer, ¹⁶ for I tell you, I will not eat it until it is fulfilled in the kingdom of God." ¹⁷ Then he took a cup, and after giving thanks he said, "Take this and divide it among yourselves, ¹⁸ for I tell you that from now on I will not drink of the fruit of the vine until the kingdom of God comes." ¹⁹ Then he took a loaf of bread, and when he had given thanks he broke it and gave it to them, saying, "This is my body, which is given for you. Do this in remembrance of me." ²⁰ And he did the same with the cup after supper, saying, "This cup that is poured out for you is the new covenant in my blood. ²¹ But see, the one who betrays me is with me, and his hand is on the table. ²² For the Son of Man is going as it has been determined, but woe to that one by whom he is betrayed!" ²³ Then they began to ask one another which one of them it could be who would do this.

✦ The Dispute about Greatness

²⁴ A dispute also arose among them as to which one of them was to be regarded as the greatest. ²⁵ But he said to them, "The kings of the gentiles lord it over them, and those in authority over them are called benefactors. ²⁶ But not so with you; rather the greatest among you must become like the youngest and the leader like one who serves. ²⁷ For who is greater, the one who is at the table or the one who serves? Is it not the one at the table? But I am among you as one who serves.

²⁸ "You are those who have stood by me in my trials, ²⁹ and I confer on you, just as my Father has conferred on me, a kingdom,

³⁰ so that you may eat and drink at my table in my kingdom, and you will sit on thrones judging the twelve tribes of Israel.

✦ Jesus Predicts Peter's Denial

³¹ "Simon, Simon, listen! Satan has demanded to sift all of you like wheat, ³² but I have prayed for you that your own faith may not fail, and you, when once you have turned back, strengthen your brothers." ³³ And he said to him, "Lord, I am ready to go with you to prison and to death!" ³⁴ Jesus said, "I tell you, Peter, the cock will not crow this day until you have denied three times that you know me."

✦ Purse, Bag, and Sword

³⁵ He said to them, "When I sent you out without a purse, bag, or sandals, did you lack anything?" They said, "No, not a thing." ³⁶ He said to them, "But now, the one who has a purse must take it, and likewise a bag. And the one who has no sword must sell his cloak and buy one. ³⁷ For I tell you, this scripture must be fulfilled in me, 'And he was counted among the lawless,' and indeed what is written about me is being fulfilled." ³⁸ They said, "Lord, look, here are two swords." He replied, "It is enough."

✦ Jesus Prays on the Mount of Olives

³⁹ He came out and went, as was his custom, to the Mount of Olives, and the disciples followed him. ⁴⁰ When he reached the place, he said to them, "Pray that you may not come into the time of trial." ⁴¹ Then he withdrew from them about a stone's throw, knelt down, and prayed, ⁴² "Father, if you are willing, remove this cup from me, yet not my will but yours be done." ⁴³ Then an angel from heaven appeared to him and gave him strength. ⁴⁴ In his anguish he prayed more earnestly, and his sweat became like great drops of blood falling down on the ground. ⁴⁵ When he got up from prayer, he came to the disciples and found them sleeping because of grief, ⁴⁶ and he said to them, "Why are you sleeping? Get up and pray that you may not come into the time of trial."

✦ The Betrayal and Arrest of Jesus

⁴⁷ While he was still speaking, suddenly a crowd came, and the one called Judas, one of the twelve, was leading them. He approached Jesus to kiss him, ⁴⁸ but Jesus said to him, "Judas, is it with a kiss that you are betraying the Son of Man?" ⁴⁹ When those who were around him saw what was coming, they asked, "Lord, should we strike with the sword?" ⁵⁰ Then one of them struck the slave of the high priest and cut off his right ear. ⁵¹ But Jesus said, "No more of this!" And he touched his ear and healed him. ⁵² Then Jesus said to the chief priests, the officers of the temple police, and the elders who had come for him, "Have you come out with swords and clubs as if I were a rebel? ⁵³ When I was with you day after day in the temple, you did not lay hands on me. But this is your hour and the power of darkness!"

✦ Peter Denies Jesus

⁵⁴ Then they seized him and led him away, bringing him into the high priest's house. But Peter was following at a distance. ⁵⁵ When they had kindled a fire in the middle of the courtyard and sat down together, Peter sat among them. ⁵⁶ Then a female servant, seeing him in the firelight, stared at him and said, "This man also was with him." ⁵⁷ But he denied it, saying, "Woman, I do not know him." ⁵⁸ A little later someone else, on seeing him, said, "You also are one of them." But Peter said, "Man, I am not!" ⁵⁹ Then about an hour later still another kept insisting, "Surely this man also was with him, for he is a Galilean." ⁶⁰ But Peter said, "Man, I do not know what you are talking about!" At that moment, while he was still speaking, the cock crowed. ⁶¹ The Lord turned and looked at Peter. Then Peter remembered the word of the Lord, how he had said to him, "Before the cock crows today, you will deny me three times." ⁶² And he went out and wept bitterly.

✦ The Mocking and Beating of Jesus

⁶³ Now the men who were holding Jesus began to mock him and beat him; ⁶⁴ they also blindfolded him and kept asking him,

"Prophesy! Who is it that struck you?" **65** They kept heaping many other insults on him.

✤ Jesus before the Council

66 When day came, the assembly of the elders of the people, both chief priests and scribes, gathered together, and they brought him to their council. **67** They said, "If you are the Messiah, tell us." He replied, "If I tell you, you will not believe, **68** and if I question you, you will not answer. **69** But from now on the Son of Man will be seated at the right hand of the power of God." **70** All of them asked, "Are you, then, the Son of God?" He said to them, "You say that I am." **71** Then they said, "What further testimony do we need? We have heard it ourselves from his own lips!"

CHAPTER 23

✤ Jesus before Pilate

 hen the assembly rose as a body and brought Jesus before Pilate. **2** They began to accuse him, saying, "We found this man inciting our nation, forbidding us to pay taxes to Caesar, and saying that he himself is the Messiah, a king." **3** Then Pilate asked him, "Are you the king of the Jews?" He answered, "You say so." **4** Then Pilate said to the chief priests and the crowds, "I find no basis for an accusation against this man." **5** But they were insistent and said, "He stirs up the people by teaching throughout all Judea, from Galilee where he began even to this place."

✤ Jesus before Herod

6 When Pilate heard this, he asked whether the man was a Galilean. **7** And when he learned that he was under Herod's jurisdiction, he sent him off to Herod, who was himself in Jerusalem at that time. **8** When Herod saw Jesus, he was very glad, for he had been wanting to see him for a long time because he had heard about him and was hoping to see him perform some sign. **9** He questioned him at some length, but Jesus gave him no answer. **10** The chief priests and the scribes stood by vehemently accusing him. **11** Even Herod with his soldiers treated him with contempt and mocked him; then he put an elegant robe on him and sent him back to Pilate. **12** That same day Herod and Pilate became friends with each other; before this they had been enemies.

✤ Jesus Sentenced to Death

13 Pilate then called together the chief priests, the leaders, and the people **14** and said to them, "You brought me this man as one who was inciting the people, and here I have examined him in your presence and have not found this man guilty of any of your charges against him. **15** Neither has Herod, for he sent him back to us. Indeed, he has done nothing to deserve death. **16** I will therefore have him flogged and release him."

18 Then they all shouted out together, "Away with this fellow! Release Barabbas for us!" **19** (This was a man who had been put in prison for an insurrection that had taken place in the city and for murder.) **20** Pilate, wanting to release Jesus, addressed them again, **21** but they kept shouting, "Crucify, crucify him!" **22** A third time he said to them, "Why, what evil has he done? I have found in him no ground for the sentence of death; I will therefore have him flogged and then release him." **23** But they kept urgently demanding with loud shouts that he should be crucified, and their voices prevailed. **24** So Pilate gave his verdict that their demand should be granted. **25** He released the man they asked for, the one who had been put in prison for insurrection and murder, and he handed Jesus over as they wished.

✤ The Crucifixion of Jesus

26 As they led him away, they seized a man, Simon of Cyrene, who was coming from the country, and they laid the cross on him, and made him carry it behind Jesus. **27** A great number of the people followed him, and among them were women who were beating their breasts and wailing for him. **28** But Jesus turned to them and said, "Daughters of Jerusalem, do not weep for me, but weep for yourselves and for your children. ²⁹ For the days are surely coming when they will say, 'Blessed are the barren, and the wombs that never bore, and the breasts that never nursed.' ³⁰ Then they will begin to say to the mountains, 'Fall on us'; and to the hills, 'Cover us.' ³¹ For if they do this when the wood is green, what will happen when it is dry?"

³² Two others also, who were criminals, were led away to be put to death with him. ³³ When they came to the place that is called The Skull, they crucified Jesus there with the criminals, one on his right and one on his left. ³⁴ Then Jesus said, "Father, forgive them, for they do not know what they are doing." And they cast lots to divide his clothing. ³⁵ And the people stood by watching, but the leaders scoffed at him, saying, "He saved others; let him save himself if he is the Messiah of God, his chosen one!" ³⁶ The soldiers also mocked him, coming up and offering him sour wine ³⁷ and saying, "If you are the King of the Jews, save yourself!" ³⁸ There was also an inscription over him, "This is the King of the Jews."

³⁹ One of the criminals who were hanged there kept deriding him and saying, "Are you not the Messiah? Save yourself and us!" ⁴⁰ But the other rebuked him, saying, "Do you not fear God, since you are under the same sentence of condemnation? ⁴¹ And we indeed have been condemned justly, for we are getting what we deserve for our deeds, but this man has done nothing wrong." ⁴² Then he said, "Jesus, remember me when you come into your kingdom." ⁴³ He replied, "Truly I tell you, today you will be with me in paradise."

✤ The Death of Jesus

⁴⁴ It was now about noon, and darkness came over the whole land until three in the afternoon, ⁴⁵ while the sun's light failed, and the curtain of the temple was torn in two. ⁴⁶ Then Jesus, crying with a loud voice, said, "Father, into your hands I commend my spirit." Having said this, he breathed his last. ⁴⁷ When the centurion saw what had taken place, he praised God and said, "Certainly

this man was innocent." **48** And when all the crowds who had gathered there for this spectacle saw what had taken place, they returned home, beating their breasts. **49** But all his acquaintances, including the women who had followed him from Galilee, stood at a distance watching these things.

✢ The Burial of Jesus

50 Now there was a good and righteous man named Joseph who, though a member of the council, **51** had not agreed to their plan and action. He came from the Jewish town of Arimathea, and he was waiting expectantly for the kingdom of God. **52** This man went to Pilate and asked for the body of Jesus. **53** Then he took it down, wrapped it in a linen cloth, and laid it in a rock-hewn tomb where no one had ever been laid. **54** It was the day of Preparation, and the Sabbath was beginning. **55** The women who had come with him from Galilee followed, and they saw the tomb and how his body was laid. **56** Then they returned and prepared spices and ointments.

On the Sabbath they rested according to the commandment.

CHAPTER 24

✢ The Resurrection of Jesus

 **ut on the first day of the week,** at early dawn, they went to the tomb, taking the spices that they had prepared. **2** They found the stone rolled away from the tomb, **3** but when they went in they did not find the body. **4** While they were perplexed about this, suddenly two men in dazzling clothes stood beside them. **5** The women were terrified and bowed their faces to the ground, but the men said to them, "Why do you look for the living among the dead? He is not here but has risen. **6** Remember how he told you, while he was still in Galilee, **7** that the Son of Man must be handed over to the hands of sinners and be crucified and on the third day rise

again." **8** Then they remembered his words, **9** and returning from the tomb they told all this to the eleven and to all the rest. **10** Now it was Mary Magdalene, Joanna, Mary the mother of James, and the other women with them who told this to the apostles. **11** But these words seemed to them an idle tale, and they did not believe them. **12** But Peter got up and ran to the tomb; stooping and looking in, he saw the linen cloths by themselves; then he went home, amazed at what had happened.

✤ On the Road to Emmaus

13 Now on that same day two of them were going to a village called Emmaus, about seven miles from Jerusalem, **14** and talking with each other about all these things that had happened. **15** While they were talking and discussing, Jesus himself came near and went with them, **16** but their eyes were kept from recognizing him. **17** And he said to them, "What are you discussing with each other while you walk along?" They stood still, looking sad. **18** Then one of them, whose name was Cleopas, answered him, "Are you the only stranger in Jerusalem who does not know the things that have taken place there in these days?" **19** He asked them, "What things?" They replied, "The things about Jesus of Nazareth, who was a prophet mighty in deed and word before God and all the people, **20** and how our chief priests and leaders handed him over to be condemned to death and crucified him. **21** But we had hoped that he was the one to redeem Israel. Yes, and besides all this, it is now the third day since these things took place. **22** Moreover, some women of our group astounded us. They were at the tomb early this morning, **23** and when they did not find his body there they came back and told us that they had indeed seen a vision of angels who said that he was alive. **24** Some of those who were with us went to the tomb and found it just as the women had said, but they did not see him." **25** Then he said to them, "Oh, how foolish you are and how slow of heart to believe all that the prophets have declared! **26** Was it not necessary that the Messiah should suffer these things and then enter into his glory?" **27** Then beginning with Moses and all the prophets, he interpreted to them the things about himself in all the scriptures.

28 As they came near the village to which they were going, he walked ahead as if he were going on. **29** But they urged him strongly, saying, "Stay with us, because it is almost evening and the day is now nearly over." So he went in to stay with them. **30** When he was at the table with them, he took bread, blessed and broke it, and gave it to them. **31** Then their eyes were opened, and they recognized him, and he vanished from their sight. **32** They said to each other, "Were not our hearts burning within us while he was talking to us on the road, while he was opening the scriptures to us?" **33** That same hour they got up and returned to Jerusalem, and they found the eleven and their companions gathered together. **34** They were saying, "The Lord has risen indeed, and he has appeared to Simon!" **35** Then they told what had happened on the road and how he had been made known to them in the breaking of the bread.

✢ Jesus Appears to His Disciples

36 While they were talking about this, Jesus himself stood among them and said to them, "Peace be with you." **37** They were startled and terrified and thought that they were seeing a ghost. **38** He said to them, "Why are you frightened, and why do doubts arise in your hearts? **39** Look at my hands and my feet; see that it is I myself. Touch me and see, for a ghost does not have flesh and bones as you see that I have." **40** And when he had said this, he showed them his hands and his feet. **41** Yet for all their joy they were disbelieving and still wondering, and he said to them, "Have you anything here to eat?" **42** They gave him a piece of broiled fish, **43** and he took it and ate in their presence.

44 Then he said to them, "These are my words that I spoke to you while I was still with you—that everything written about me in the law of Moses, the prophets, and the psalms must be fulfilled." **45** Then he opened their minds to understand the scriptures, **46** and he said to them, "Thus it is written, that the Messiah is to suffer and to rise from the dead on the third day **47** and that repentance and forgiveness of sins is to be proclaimed in his name to all nations, beginning from Jerusalem. **48** You are witnesses of these things. **49** And see, I am sending upon you what my Father promised, so stay here in the city until you have been clothed with power from on high."

✦ The Ascension of Jesus

50 Then he led them out as far as Bethany, and, lifting up his hands, he blessed them. **51** While he was blessing them, he withdrew from them and was carried up into heaven. **52** And they worshiped him and returned to Jerusalem with great joy, **53** and they were continually in the temple blessing God.

✦ Gospel of John ✦

St. John was born in Galilee to Zebedee, a fisherman, and Salome, a relative of Mary, Jesus' mother. John and his brother, James, helped their father fish in the Sea of Galilee. John was a disciple of John the Baptist until Jesus called him—along with James, Peter, and Andrew—to follow him. Jesus referred to John and James as "sons of thunder" because of their enthusiasm and zeal.

John is often known as "the Beloved Disciple." He sat next to Jesus at the Last Supper. Along with Peter, John followed Jesus into the palace of the high priest after Jesus' arrest and was present when Jesus died at Calvary. Before he died, Jesus entrusted John to take care of his mother. When Mary Magdalene announced Christ's resurrection to the apostles, John was among the first to run to the tomb.

John not only wrote the fourth Gospel, but he also wrote three epistles (or letters) and the Book of Revelation. The last to be written, sometime between AD 90 and 100, his Gospel is the fruit of a long meditation on the mystery of Jesus Christ and gives us the beautiful teachings on the Bread of Life, the Good Shepherd, and the True Vine. John gives us five chapters on Jesus at the Last Supper. Many believe John wrote this Gospel in Ephesus, while others think it may have been in Syria, perhaps the city of Antioch.

Along with Peter and James, John helped to build and encourage the workings of the early Churches in Ephesus and Jerusalem. In his old age, John was carried into the community, and his announcement to them was simply: "Little children, love one another." He died around AD 100 in Ephesus, in what is now Turkey.

John is the patron saint of love, loyalty, friendships, and authors. His feast day is celebrated on December 27.

John's symbol is an eagle, a bird that soars to the heavens and is believed to be able to look straight into the sun. John begins his Gospel by proclaiming Jesus as the incarnate Word of God who has revealed the Father to us.

Chapter 1

✦ The Word Became Flesh

**I**n the beginning was the Word,** and the Word was with God, and the Word was God. ² He was in the beginning with God. ³ All things came into being through him, and without him not one thing came into being. What has come into being ⁴ in him was life, and the life was the light of all people. ⁵ The light shines in the darkness, and the darkness did not overtake it.

⁶ There was a man sent from God, whose name was John. ⁷ He came as a witness to testify to the light, so that all might believe through him. ⁸ He himself was not the light, but he came to testify to the light. ⁹ The true light, which enlightens everyone, was coming into the world.

¹⁰ He was in the world, and the world came into being through him, yet the world did not know him. ¹¹ He came to what was his own, and his own people did not accept him. ¹² But to all who received him, who believed in his name, he gave power to become children of God, ¹³ who were born, not of blood or of the will of the flesh or of the will of man, but of God.

¹⁴ And the Word became flesh and lived among us, and we have seen his glory, the glory as of a father's only son, full of grace and truth. ¹⁵ (John testified to him and cried out, "This was he of whom I said, 'He who comes after me ranks ahead of me because he was before me.'") ¹⁶ From his fullness we have all received, grace upon grace. ¹⁷ The law indeed was given through Moses; grace and truth came through Jesus Christ. ¹⁸ No one has ever seen God. It the only Son, himself God, who is close to the Father's heart, who has made him known.

✦ The Testimony of John the Baptist

¹⁹ This is the testimony given by John when the Jews sent priests and Levites from Jerusalem to ask him, "Who are you?" ²⁰ He confessed and did not deny it, but he confessed, "I am not the Messiah." ²¹ And they asked him, "What then? Are you Elijah?" He said, "I am not." "Are you the prophet?" He answered, "No." ²² Then they said to him, "Who are you? Let us have an answer for those who sent us. What do you say about yourself?" ²³ He said,

"I am the voice of one crying out in the wilderness,
'Make straight the way of the Lord,'"

as the prophet Isaiah said.

²⁴ Now they had been sent from the Pharisees. ²⁵ They asked him, "Why, then, are you baptizing if you are neither the Messiah, nor Elijah, nor the prophet?" ²⁶ John answered them, "I baptize with water. Among you stands one whom you do not know, ²⁷ the one who is coming after me; I am not worthy to untie the strap of his sandal." ²⁸ This took place in Bethany across the Jordan where John was baptizing.

✦ The Lamb of God

²⁹ The next day he saw Jesus coming toward him and declared, "Here is the Lamb of God who takes away the sin of the world! ³⁰ This is he of whom I said, 'After me comes a man who ranks ahead of me because he was before me.' ³¹ I myself did not know him, but I came baptizing with water for this reason, that he might be revealed to Israel." ³² And John testified, "I saw the Spirit descending from heaven like a dove, and it remained on him. ³³ I myself did not know him, but the one who sent me to baptize with water said to me, 'He on whom you see the Spirit descend and remain is the one who baptizes with the Holy Spirit.' ³⁴ And I myself have seen and have testified that this is the Chosen One."

✧ The First Disciples of Jesus

35 The next day John again was standing with two of his disciples, **36** and as he watched Jesus walk by he exclaimed, "Look, here is the Lamb of God!" **37** The two disciples heard him say this, and they followed Jesus. **38** When Jesus turned and saw them following, he said to them, "What are you looking for?" They said to him, "Rabbi" (which translated means Teacher), "where are you staying?" **39** He said to them, "Come and see." They came and saw where he was staying, and they remained with him that day. It was about four o'clock in the afternoon. **40** One of the two who heard John speak and followed him was Andrew, Simon Peter's brother. **41** He first found his brother Simon and said to him, "We have found the Messiah" (which is translated Anointed). **42** He brought Simon to Jesus, who looked at him and said, "You are Simon son of John. You are to be called Cephas" (which is translated Peter).

✧ Jesus Calls Philip and Nathanael

43 The next day Jesus decided to go to Galilee. He found Philip and said to him, "Follow me." **44** Now Philip was from Bethsaida, the city of Andrew and Peter. **45** Philip found Nathanael and said to him, "We have found him about whom Moses in the Law and also the Prophets wrote, Jesus son of Joseph from Nazareth." **46** Nathanael said to him, "Can anything good come out of Nazareth?" Philip said to him, "Come and see." **47** When Jesus saw Nathanael coming toward him, he said of him, "Here is truly an Israelite in whom there is no deceit!" **48** Nathanael asked him, "Where did you get to know me?" Jesus answered, "I saw you under the fig tree before Philip called you." **49** Nathanael replied, "Rabbi, you are the Son of God! You are the King of Israel!" **50** Jesus answered, "Do you believe because I told you that I saw you under the fig tree? You will see greater things than these." **51** And he said to him, "Very truly, I tell you, you will see heaven opened and the angels of God ascending and descending upon the Son of Man."

CHAPTER 2

✦ The Wedding at Cana

**O**n the third day there was a wedding** in Cana of Galilee, and the mother of Jesus was there. **2** Jesus and his disciples had also been invited to the wedding. **3** When the wine gave out, the mother of Jesus said to him, "They have no wine." **4** And Jesus said to her, "Woman, what concern is that to me and to you? My hour has not yet come." **5** His mother said to the servants, "Do whatever he tells you." **6** Now standing there were six stone water jars for the Jewish rites of purification, each holding twenty or thirty gallons. **7** Jesus said to them, "Fill the jars with water." And they filled them up to the brim. **8** He said to them, "Now draw some out, and take it to the person in charge of the banquet." So they took it. **9** When the person in charge tasted the water that had become wine and did not know where it came from (though the servants who had drawn the water knew), that person called the bridegroom **10** and said to him, "Everyone serves the good wine first and then the inferior wine after the guests have become drunk. But you have kept the good wine until now." **11** Jesus did this, the first of his signs, in Cana of Galilee and revealed his glory, and his disciples believed in him.

12 After this he went down to Capernaum with his mother, his brothers, and his disciples, and they remained there a few days.

✦ Jesus Cleanses the Temple

13 The Passover of the Jews was near, and Jesus went up to Jerusalem. **14** In the temple he found people selling cattle, sheep, and doves and the money changers seated at their tables. **15** Making a whip of cords, he drove all of them out of the temple, with the sheep and the cattle. He also poured out the coins of the money changers and overturned their tables. **16** He told those who were selling the doves, "Take these things out of here! Stop making my Father's house a marketplace!" **17** His disciples remembered that it was written, "Zeal for your house will consume me." **18** The Jews then said to him, "What sign can you show us for doing this?" **19** Jesus answered them, "Destroy this temple, and in three days I will raise it up." **20** The Jews then said, "This temple has been under construction for forty-six years, and will you raise it up in three days?" **21** But he was speaking of the temple of his body. **22** After he was raised from the dead, his disciples remembered that he had said this, and they believed the scripture and the word that Jesus had spoken.

23 When he was in Jerusalem during the Passover festival, many believed in his name because they saw the signs that he was doing. **24** But Jesus on his part would not entrust himself to them, because he knew all people **25** and needed no one to testify about anyone, for he himself knew what was in everyone.

CHAPTER 3

✦ Nicodemus Visits Jesus

 **ow there was a Pharisee** named Nicodemus, a leader of the Jews. **2** He came to Jesus by night and said to him, "Rabbi, we know that you are a teacher who has come from God, for no one can do these signs that you do unless God is with that person." **3** Jesus answered him, "Very truly, I tell you, no one can see the kingdom of God without being born from above." **4** Nicodemus said to him, "How can anyone be born after having grown old? Can one enter a second time into the mother's womb and be born?" **5** Jesus answered, "Very truly, I tell you, no one can enter the kingdom of God without being born of water and Spirit. **6** What is born of the flesh is flesh, and what is born of the Spirit is spirit. **7** Do not be astonished that I said to you, 'You must be born from above.' **8** The wind blows where it chooses, and you hear the sound of it, but you do not know where it comes from or where it goes. So it

is with everyone who is born of the Spirit." ⁹ Nicodemus said to him, "How can these things be?" ¹⁰ Jesus answered him, "Are you a teacher of Israel, and yet you do not understand these things?

¹¹ "Very truly, I tell you, we speak of what we know and testify to what we have seen yet you do not receive our testimony. ¹² If I have told you about earthly things and you do not believe, how can you believe if I tell you about heavenly things? ¹³ No one has ascended into heaven except the one who descended from heaven, the Son of Man. ¹⁴ And just as Moses lifted up the serpent in the wilderness, so must the Son of Man be lifted up, ¹⁵ that whoever believes in him may have eternal life.

¹⁶ "For God so loved the world that he gave his only Son, so that everyone who believes in him may not perish but may have eternal life.

¹⁷ "Indeed, God did not send the Son into the world to condemn the world but in order that the world might be saved through him. ¹⁸ Those who believe in him are not condemned, but those who do not believe are condemned already because they have not believed in the name of the only Son of God. ¹⁹ And this is the judgment, that the light has come into the world, and people loved darkness rather than light because their deeds were evil. ²⁰ For all who do evil hate the light and do not come to the light, so that their deeds may not be exposed. ²¹ But those who do what is true come to the light, so that it may be clearly seen that their deeds have been done in God."

✣ Jesus and John the Baptist

²² After this Jesus and his disciples went into the region of Judea, and he spent some time there with them and baptized. ²³ John also was baptizing at Aenon near Salim because water was abundant there, and people kept coming and were being baptized. ²⁴ (John, of course, had not yet been thrown into prison.)

²⁵ Now a discussion about purification arose between John's disciples and a Jew. ²⁶ They came to John and said to him, "Rabbi,

the one who was with you across the Jordan, to whom you testified, here he is baptizing, and all are going to him." **²⁷** John answered, "No one can receive anything except what has been given from heaven. **²⁸** You yourselves are my witnesses that I said, 'I am not the Messiah, but I have been sent ahead of him.' **²⁹** He who has the bride is the bridegroom. The friend of the bridegroom who stands and hears him rejoices greatly at the bridegroom's voice. For this reason my joy has been fulfilled. **³⁰** He must increase, but I must decrease."

✤ The One Who Comes from Heaven

³¹ The one who comes from above is above all; the one who is of the earth belongs to the earth and speaks about earthly things. The one who comes from heaven is above all. **³²** He testifies to what he has seen and heard, yet no one accepts his testimony. **³³** Whoever has accepted his testimony has certified this, that God is true. **³⁴** He whom God has sent speaks the words of God, for he gives the Spirit without measure. **³⁵** The Father loves the Son and has placed all things in his hands. **³⁶** Whoever believes in the Son has eternal life; whoever disobeys the Son will not see life but must endure God's wrath.

CHAPTER 4

✤ Jesus and the Woman of Samaria

**ow when Jesus** learned that the Pharisees had heard, "Jesus is making and baptizing more disciples than John" **²** (although it was not Jesus himself but his disciples who baptized) **³** he left Judea and started back to Galilee. **⁴** But he had to go through Samaria. **⁵** So he came to a Samaritan city called Sychar, near the plot of ground that Jacob had given to his son Joseph. **⁶** Jacob's well was there, and Jesus, tired out by his journey, was sitting by the well. It was about noon.

7 A Samaritan woman came to draw water, and Jesus said to her, "Give me a drink." 8 (His disciples had gone to the city to buy food.) 9 The Samaritan woman said to him, "How is it that you, a Jew, ask a drink of me, a woman of Samaria?" (Jews do not share things in common with Samaritans.) 10 Jesus answered her, "If you knew the gift of God and who it is that is saying to you, 'Give me a drink,' you would have asked him, and he would have given you living water." 11 The woman said to him, "Sir, you have no bucket, and the well is deep. Where do you get that living water? 12 Are you greater than our ancestor Jacob, who gave us the well and with his sons and his flocks drank from it?" 13 Jesus said to her, "Everyone who drinks of this water will be thirsty again, 14 but those who drink of the water that I will give them will never be thirsty. The water that I will give will become in them a spring of water gushing up to eternal life." 15 The woman said to him, "Sir, give me this water, so that I may never be thirsty or have to keep coming here to draw water."

16 Jesus said to her, "Go, call your husband, and come back." 17 The woman answered him, "I have no husband." Jesus said to her, "You are right in saying, 'I have no husband,' 18 for you have had five husbands, and the one you have now is not your husband. What you have said is true!" 19 The woman said to him, "Sir, I see that you are a prophet. 20 Our ancestors worshiped on this mountain, but you say that the place where people must worship is in Jerusalem." 21 Jesus said to her, "Woman, believe me, the hour is coming when you will worship the Father neither on this mountain nor in Jerusalem. 22 You worship what you do not know; we worship what we know, for salvation is from the Jews. 23 But the hour is coming and is now here when the true worshipers will worship the Father in spirit and truth, for the Father seeks such as these to worship him. 24 God is spirit, and those who worship him must worship in spirit and truth." 25 The woman said to him, "I know that Messiah is coming" (who is called Christ). "When he comes, he will proclaim all things to us." 26 Jesus said to her, "I am he, the one who is speaking to you."

²⁷ Just then his disciples came. They were astonished that he was speaking with a woman, but no one said, "What do you want?" or, "Why are you speaking with her?" ²⁸ Then the woman left her water jar and went back to the city. She said to the people, ²⁹ "Come and see a man who told me everything I have ever done! He cannot be the Messiah, can he?" ³⁰ They left the city and were on their way to him.

³¹ Meanwhile the disciples were urging him, "Rabbi, eat something." ³² But he said to them, "I have food to eat that you do not know about." ³³ So the disciples said to one another, "Surely no one has brought him something to eat?" ³⁴ Jesus said to them, "My food is to do the will of him who sent me and to complete his work. ³⁵ Do you not say, 'Four months more, then comes the harvest'? But I tell you, look around you, and see how the fields are ripe for harvesting. ³⁶ The reaper is already receiving wages and is gathering fruit for eternal life, so that sower and reaper may rejoice together. ³⁷ For here the saying holds true, 'One sows and another reaps.' ³⁸ I sent you to reap that for which you did not labor. Others have labored, and you have entered into their labor."

³⁹ Many Samaritans from that city believed in him because of the woman's testimony, "He told me everything I have ever done." ⁴⁰ So when the Samaritans came to him, they asked him to stay with them, and he stayed there two days. ⁴¹ And many more believed because of his word. ⁴² They said to the woman, "It is no longer because of what you said that we believe, for we have heard for ourselves, and we know that this is truly the Savior of the world."

✤ Jesus Returns to Galilee

⁴³ When the two days were over, he went from that place to Galilee ⁴⁴ (for Jesus himself had testified that a prophet has no honor in the prophet's own country). ⁴⁵ When he came to Galilee, the Galileans welcomed him, since they had seen all that he had done in Jerusalem at the festival, for they, too, had gone to the festival.

✦ Jesus Heals an Official's Son

⁴⁶ Then he came again to Cana in Galilee, where he had changed the water into wine. Now there was a royal official whose son lay ill in Capernaum. ⁴⁷ When he heard that Jesus had come from Judea to Galilee, he went and begged him to come down and heal his son, for he was at the point of death. ⁴⁸ Then Jesus said to him, "Unless you see signs and wonders you will not believe." ⁴⁹ The official said to him, "Sir, come down before my little boy dies." ⁵⁰ Jesus said to him, "Go; your son will live." The man believed the word that Jesus spoke to him and started on his way. ⁵¹ As he was going down, his slaves met him and told him that his child was alive. ⁵² So he asked them the hour when he began to recover, and they said to him, "Yesterday at one in the afternoon the fever left him." ⁵³ The father realized that this was the hour when Jesus had said to him, "Your son will live." So he himself believed, along with his whole household. ⁵⁴ Now this was the second sign that Jesus did after coming from Judea to Galilee.

CHAPTER 5

✦ Jesus Heals on the Sabbath

fter this there was a festival of the Jews, and Jesus went up to Jerusalem.

² Now in Jerusalem by the Sheep Gate there is a pool, called in Hebrew Beth-zatha, which has five porticoes. ³ In these lay many ill, blind, lame, and paralyzed people. ⁵ One man was there who had been ill for thirty-eight years. ⁶ When Jesus saw him lying there and knew that he had been there a long time, he said to him, "Do you want to be made well?" ⁷ The ill man answered him, "Sir, I have no one to put me into the pool when the water is stirred up, and while I am making my way someone else steps down ahead of me." ⁸ Jesus said to him, "Stand up, take your mat and walk." ⁹ At once the man was made well, and he took up his mat and began to walk.

Now that day was a Sabbath. **¹⁰** So the Jews said to the man who had been cured, "It is the Sabbath; it is not lawful for you to carry your mat." **¹¹** But he answered them, "The man who made me well said to me, 'Take up your mat and walk.'" **¹²** They asked him, "Who is the man who said to you, 'Take it up and walk'?" **¹³** Now the man who had been healed did not know who it was, for Jesus had disappeared in the crowd that was there. **¹⁴** Later Jesus found him in the temple and said to him, "See, you have been made well! Do not sin any more, so that nothing worse happens to you." **¹⁵** The man went away and told the Jews that it was Jesus who had made him well. **¹⁶** Therefore the Jews started persecuting Jesus, because he was doing such things on the Sabbath. **¹⁷** But Jesus answered them, "My Father is still working, and I also am working." **¹⁸** For this reason the Jews were seeking all the more to kill him, because he was not only breaking the Sabbath, but was also calling God his own Father, thereby making himself equal to God.

✦ The Authority of the Son

¹⁹ Jesus said to them, "Very truly, I tell you, the Son can do nothing on his own but only what he sees the Father doing, for whatever the Father does, the Son does likewise. **²⁰** The Father loves the Son and shows him all that he himself is doing, and he will show him greater works than these, so that you will be astonished. **²¹** Indeed, just as the Father raises the dead and gives them life, so also the Son gives life to whomever he wishes. **²²** The Father judges no one but has given all judgment to the Son, **²³** so that all may honor the Son just as they honor the Father. Anyone who does not honor the Son does not honor the Father who sent him. **²⁴** Very truly, I tell you, anyone who hears my word and believes him who sent me has eternal life and does not come under judgment but has passed from death to life.

²⁵ "Very truly, I tell you, the hour is coming, and is now here when the dead will hear the voice of the Son of God, and those who hear will live. **²⁶** For just as the Father has life in himself, so he has granted the Son also to have life in himself, **²⁷** and he has given him authority to execute judgment because he is the Son of Man. 28 Do not be astonished at this, for the hour is coming when all who are in their graves will hear his voice 29 and will come out: those who have done good to the resurrection of life, and those who have done evil to the resurrection of condemnation.

✦ Witnesses to Jesus

30 "I can do nothing on my own. As I hear, I judge, and my judgment is just because I seek to do not my own will but the will of him who sent me.

31 "If I testify about myself, my testimony is not true. 32 There is another who testifies on my behalf, and I know that his testimony to me is true. 33 You sent messengers to John, and he testified to the truth. 34 Not that I accept such human testimony, but I say these things so that you may be saved. 35 He was a burning and shining lamp, and you were willing to rejoice for a while in his light. 36 But I have a testimony greater than John's. The works that the Father has given me to complete, the very works that I am doing, testify on my behalf that the Father has sent me. 37 And the Father who sent me has himself testified on my behalf. You have never heard his voice or seen his form, 38 and you do not have his word abiding in you, because you do not believe him whom he has sent.

39 "You search the scriptures because you think that in them you have eternal life, and it is they that testify on my behalf. 40 Yet you refuse to come to me to have life. 41 I do not accept glory from humans. 42 But I know that you do not have the love of God in you. 43 I have come in my Father's name, and you do not accept me; if another comes in his own name, you will accept him. 44 How can you believe when you accept glory from one another and do not seek the glory that comes from the one who alone is God? 45 Do not think that I will accuse you before the Father; your accuser is Moses, on whom you have set your hope. 46 If you believed Moses, you would believe me, for he wrote about me. 47 But if you do not believe what he wrote, how will you believe what I say?"

CHAPTER 6

✣ Jesus Feeds the Five Thousand

 **fter this Jesus went** to the other side of the Sea of Galilee, also called the Sea of Tiberias. ² A large crowd kept following him because they saw the signs that he was doing for the sick. ³ Jesus went up the mountain and sat down there with his disciples. ⁴ Now the Passover, the festival of the Jews, was near. ⁵ When he looked up and saw a large crowd coming toward him, Jesus said to Philip, "Where are we to buy bread for these people to eat?" ⁶ He said this to test him, for he himself knew what he was going to do. ⁷ Philip answered him, "Two hundred denarii would not buy enough bread for each of them to get a little." ⁸ One of his disciples, Andrew, Simon Peter's brother, said to him, ⁹ "There is a boy here who has five barley loaves and two fish. But what are they among so many people?" ¹⁰ Jesus said, "Make the people sit down." Now there was a great deal of grass in the place, so they sat down, about five thousand in all. ¹¹ Then Jesus took the loaves, and when he had given thanks he distributed them to those who were seated; so also the fish, as much as they wanted. ¹² When they were satisfied, he told his disciples, "Gather up the fragments left over, so that nothing may be lost." ¹³ So they gathered them up, and from the fragments of the five barley loaves, left by those who had eaten, they filled twelve baskets. ¹⁴ When the people saw the sign that he had done, they began to say, "This is indeed the prophet who is to come into the world."

¹⁵ When Jesus realized that they were about to come and take him by force to make him king, he withdrew again to the mountain by himself.

✦ Jesus Walks on the Water

16 When evening came, his disciples went down to the sea, **17** got into a boat, and started across the sea to Capernaum. It was now dark, and Jesus had not yet come to them. **18** The sea became rough because a strong wind was blowing. **19** When they had rowed about three or four miles, they saw Jesus walking on the sea and coming near the boat, and they were terrified. **20** But he said to them, "It is I; do not be afraid." **21** Then they wanted to take him into the boat, and immediately the boat reached the land toward which they were going.

✦ I Am the Bread of Life

22 The next day the crowd that had stayed on the other side of the sea saw that there had been only one boat there. They also saw that Jesus had not got into the boat with his disciples but that his disciples had gone away alone. **23** But some boats from Tiberias came near the place where they had eaten the bread after the Lord had given thanks. **24** So when the crowd saw that neither Jesus nor his disciples were there, they themselves got into the boats and went to Capernaum looking for Jesus.

25 When they found him on the other side of the sea, they said to him, "Rabbi, when did you come here?" **26** Jesus answered them, "Very truly, I tell you, you are looking for me not because you saw signs but because you ate your fill of the loaves. **27** Do not work for the food that perishes but for the food that endures for eternal life, which the Son of Man will give you. For it is on him that God the Father has set his seal." **28** Then they said to him, "What must we do to perform the works of God?" **29** Jesus answered them, "This is the work of God, that you believe in him whom he has sent." **30** So they said to him, "What sign are you going to give us, then, so that we may see it and believe you? What work are you performing? **31** Our ancestors ate the manna in the wilderness, as it is written, 'He gave them bread from heaven to eat.'" **32** Then Jesus said to them, "Very truly, I tell you, it was not Moses who gave you the bread from heaven, but it is my Father who gives you the true bread from heaven. **33** For the bread of God is that which comes down from heaven and gives life to the world." **34** They said to him, "Sir, give us this bread always."

35 Jesus said to them, "I am the bread of life. Whoever comes to me will never be hungry, and whoever believes in me will never be thirsty. **36** But I said to you that you have seen me and yet do not believe. **37** Everything that the Father gives me will come to me, and anyone who comes to me I will never drive away, **38** for I have come down from heaven not to do my own will but the will of him who sent me. **39** And this is the will of him who sent me, that I should lose nothing of all that he has given me but raise it up on the last day. **40** This is indeed the will of my Father, that all who see the Son and believe in him may have eternal life, and I will raise them up on the last day."

41 Then the Jews began to complain about him because he said, "I am the bread that came down from heaven." **42** They were saying, "Is not this Jesus, the son of Joseph, whose father and mother we know? How can he now say, 'I have come down from heaven'?" **43** Jesus answered them, "Do not complain among yourselves. **44** No one can come to me unless drawn by the Father who sent me, and I will raise that person up on the last day. **45** It is written in the prophets, 'And they shall all be taught by God.' Everyone who has heard and learned from the Father comes to me. **46** Not that anyone has seen the Father except the one who is from God; he has seen the Father. **47** Very truly, I tell you, whoever believes has eternal life. **48** I am the bread of life. **49** Your ancestors ate the manna in the wilderness, and they died. **50** This is the bread that comes down from heaven, so that one may eat of it and not die. **51** I am the living bread that came down from heaven. Whoever eats of this bread will live forever, and the bread that I will give for the life of the world is my flesh."

52 The Jews then disputed among themselves, saying, "How can this man give us his flesh to eat?" **53** So Jesus said to them, "Very truly, I tell you, unless you eat the flesh of the Son of Man and drink his blood, you have no life in you. ⁵⁴ Those who eat my flesh and drink my blood have eternal life, and I will raise them up on the last day, ⁵⁵ for my flesh is true food and my blood is true drink. ⁵⁶ Those who eat my flesh and drink my blood abide in me, and I in them. ⁵⁷ Just as the living Father sent me and I live because of the Father, so whoever eats me will live because of me. ⁵⁸ This is the bread that came down from heaven, not like that which your ancestors ate, and they died. But the one who eats this bread will live forever." ⁵⁹ He said these things while he was teaching in the synagogue at Capernaum.

✣ The Words of Eternal Life

⁶⁰ When many of his disciples heard it, they said, "This teaching is difficult; who can accept it?" ⁶¹ But Jesus, being aware that his disciples were complaining about it, said to them, "Does this offend you? ⁶² Then what if you were to see the Son of Man ascending to where he was before? ⁶³ It is the spirit that gives life; the flesh is useless. The words that I have spoken to you are spirit and life. ⁶⁴ But among you there are some who do not believe." For Jesus knew from the beginning who were the ones who did not believe and who was the one that would betray him. ⁶⁵ And he said, "For this reason I have told you that no one can come to me unless it is granted by the Father."

⁶⁶ Because of this many of his disciples turned back and no longer went about with him. ⁶⁷ So Jesus asked the twelve, "Do you also wish to go away?" ⁶⁸ Simon Peter answered him, "Lord, to whom can we go? You have the words of eternal life. ⁶⁹ We have come to believe and know that you are the Holy One of God." ⁷⁰ Jesus answered them, "Did I not choose you, the twelve? Yet one of you is a devil." ⁷¹ He was speaking of Judas son of Simon Iscariot, for he, though one of the twelve, was going to betray him.

CHAPTER 7

✤ Jesus in Galilee

**fter this Jesus went** about in Galilee. He did not wish to go about in Judea because the Jews were looking for an opportunity to kill him. **²** Now the Jewish Festival of Booths was near. **³** So his brothers said to him, "Leave here and go to Judea so that your disciples also may see the works you are doing, **⁴** for no one who wants to be widely known acts in secret. If you do these things, show yourself to the world." **⁵** (For not even his brothers believed in him.) **⁶** Jesus said to them, "My time has not yet come, but your time is always here. **⁷** The world cannot hate you, but it hates me because I testify against it that its works are evil. **⁸** Go to the festival yourselves. I am not going to this festival, for my time has not yet fully come." **⁹** After saying this, he remained in Galilee.

✤ Jesus at the Festival of Booths

¹⁰ But after his brothers had gone to the festival, then he also went, not publicly but, as it were, in secret. **¹¹** The Jews were looking for him at the festival and saying, "Where is he?" **¹²** And there was considerable complaining about him among the crowds. While some were saying, "He is a good man," others were saying, "No, he is deceiving the crowd." **¹³** Yet no one would speak openly about him for fear of the Jews.

¹⁴ About the middle of the festival Jesus went up into the temple and began to teach. **¹⁵** The Jews were astonished at it, saying, "How does this man have such learning, when he has never been taught?" **¹⁶** Then Jesus answered them, "My teaching is not mine but his who sent me. **¹⁷** Anyone who resolves to do the will of God will know whether the teaching is from God or whether I am speaking on my own. **¹⁸** Those who speak on their own seek their own glory, but the one who seeks the glory of him who sent him is true, and there is nothing unjust in him.

19 "Did not Moses give you the law? Yet none of you keeps the law. Why are you looking for an opportunity to kill me?" 20 The crowd answered, "You have a demon! Who is trying to kill you?" 21 Jesus answered them, "I performed one work, and all of you are astonished. 22 Because of this Moses gave you circumcision (it is, of course, not from Moses, but from the patriarchs), and you circumcise a man on the Sabbath. 23 If a man receives circumcision on the Sabbath in order that the law of Moses may not be broken, are you angry with me because I healed a man's whole body on the Sabbath? 24 Do not judge by appearances, but judge with right judgment."

✦ Is This the Messiah?

25 Now some of the people of Jerusalem were saying, "Is not this the man whom they are trying to kill? 26 And here he is, speaking openly, but they say nothing to him! Can it be that the authorities really know that this is the Messiah? 27 Yet we know where this man is from, but when the Messiah comes no one will know where he is from." 28 Then Jesus cried out as he was teaching in the temple, "You know me, and you know where I am from. I have not come on my own. But the one who sent me is true, and you do not know him. 29 I know him, because I am from him, and he sent me." 30 Then they tried to arrest him, but no one laid hands on him because his hour had not yet come. 31 Yet many in the crowd believed in him and were saying, "When the Messiah comes, will he do more signs than this man has done?"

✦ Officers Are Sent to Arrest Jesus

32 The Pharisees heard the crowd muttering such things about him, and the chief priests and Pharisees sent temple police to arrest him. 33 Jesus then said, "I will be with you a little while longer, and then I am going to him who sent me. 34 You will search for me, but you will not find me, and where I am, you cannot come." 35 The Jews said to one another, "Where does this man intend to go that we will not find him? Does he intend to go to the dispersion among the Greeks and teach the Greeks? 36 What does he

mean by saying, 'You will search for me, but you will not find me' and 'Where I am, you cannot come'?"

✤ Rivers of Living Water

[37] On the last day of the festival, the great day, while Jesus was standing there, he cried out, "Let anyone who is thirsty come to me, [38] and let the one who believes in me drink. As the scripture has said, 'Out of the believer's heart shall flow rivers of living water.'" [39] Now he said this about the Spirit, which believers in him were to receive, for as yet there was no Spirit because Jesus was not yet glorified.

✤ Division among the People

[40] When they heard these words, some in the crowd said, "This is really the prophet." [41] Others said, "This is the Messiah." But some asked, "Surely the Messiah does not come from Galilee, does he? [42] Has not the scripture said that the Messiah is descended from David and comes from Bethlehem, the village where David lived?" [43] So there was a division in the crowd because of him. [44] Some of them wanted to arrest him, but no one laid hands on him.

✤ The Unbelief of Those in Authority

[45] Then the temple police went back to the chief priests and Pharisees, who asked them, "Why did you not arrest him?" [46] The police answered, "Never has anyone spoken like this!" [47] Then the Pharisees replied, "Surely you have not been deceived, too, have you? [48] Has any one of the authorities or of the Pharisees believed in him? [49] But this crowd, which does not know the law, they are accursed." [50] Nicodemus, who had gone to Jesus before and who was one of them, asked, [51] "Our law does not judge people without first giving them a hearing to find out what they are doing, does it?" [52] They replied, "Surely you are not also from Galilee, are you? Search and you will see that no prophet is to arise from Galilee."

✦ The Woman Caught in Adultery

⁵³ Then each of them went home,

CHAPTER 8

hile Jesus went to the Mount of Olives. ² Early in the morning he came again to the temple. All the people came to him, and he sat down and began to teach them. ³ The scribes and the Pharisees brought a woman who had been caught in adultery, and, making her stand before all of them, ⁴ they said to him, "Teacher, this woman was caught in the very act of committing adultery. ⁵ Now in the law Moses commanded us to stone such women. Now what do you say?" ⁶ They said this to test him, so that they might have some charge to bring against him. Jesus bent down and wrote with his finger on the ground. ⁷ When they kept on questioning him, he straightened up and said to them, "Let anyone among you who is without sin be the first to throw a stone at her." ⁸ And once again he bent down and wrote on the ground. ⁹ When they heard it, they went away, one by one, beginning with the elders, and Jesus was left alone with the woman standing before him. ¹⁰ Jesus straightened up and said to her, "Woman, where are they? Has no one condemned you?" ¹¹ She said, "No one, sir." And Jesus said, "Neither do I condemn you. Go your way, and from now on do not sin again."

✦ I Am the Light of the World

¹² Again Jesus spoke to them, saying, "I am the light of the world. Whoever follows me will never walk in darkness but will have the light of life." ¹³ Then the Pharisees said to him, "You are testifying on your own behalf; your testimony is not valid." ¹⁴ Jesus answered, "Even if I testify on my own behalf, my testimony is valid because I know where I have come from and where I am going, but you do not know where I come from or where I am going.

¹⁵ You judge by human standards; I judge no one. ¹⁶ Yet even if I do judge, my judgment is valid, for it is not I alone who judge but I and the Father who sent me. ¹⁷ In your law it is written that the testimony of two witnesses is valid. ¹⁸ I testify on my own behalf, and the Father who sent me testifies on my behalf." ¹⁹ Then they said to him, "Where is your Father?" Jesus answered, "You know neither me nor my Father. If you knew me, you would know my Father also." ²⁰ He spoke these words while he was teaching in the treasury of the temple, but no one arrested him, because his hour had not yet come.

✧ Jesus Foretells His Death

²¹ Again he said to them, "I am going away, and you will search for me, but you will die in your sin. Where I am going, you cannot come." ²² Then the Jews said, "Is he going to kill himself? Is that what he means by saying, 'Where I am going, you cannot come'?" ²³ He said to them, "You are from below, I am from above; you are from this world, I am not from this world. ²⁴ I told you that you would die in your sins, for you will die in your sins unless you believe that I am he." ²⁵ They said to him, "Who are you?" Jesus said to them, "Why do I speak to you at all? ²⁶ I have much to say about you and much to condemn, but the one who sent me is true, and I declare to the world what I have heard from him." ²⁷ They did not understand that he was speaking to them about the Father. ²⁸ So Jesus said, "When you have lifted up the Son of Man, then you will realize that I am he, and that I do nothing on my own, but I speak these things as the Father instructed me. ²⁹ And the one who sent me is with me; he has not left me alone, for I always do what is pleasing to him." ³⁰ As he was saying these things, many believed in him.

✧ True Disciples

³¹ Then Jesus said to the Jews who had believed in him, "If you continue in my word, you are truly my disciples, ³² and you will know the truth, and the truth will make you free." ³³ They answered

him, "We are descendants of Abraham and have never been slaves to anyone. What do you mean by saying, 'You will be made free'?"

34 Jesus answered them, "Very truly, I tell you, everyone who commits sin is a slave to sin. 35 The slave does not have a permanent place in the household; the son has a place there forever. 36 So if the Son makes you free, you will be free indeed. 37 I know that you are descendants of Abraham, yet you look for an opportunity to kill me because there is no place in you for my word. 38 I declare what I have seen in the Father's presence; as for you, you should do what you have heard from the Father."

✦ Jesus and Abraham

39 They answered him, "Abraham is our father." Jesus said to them, "If you were Abraham's children, you would be doing what Abraham did, 40 but now you are trying to kill me, a man who has told you the truth that I heard from God. This is not what Abraham did. 41 You are indeed doing what your father does." They said to him, "We are not illegitimate children; we have one father, God himself." 42 Jesus said to them, "If God were your Father, you would love me, for I came from God, and now I am here. I did not come on my own, but he sent me. 43 Why do you not understand what I say? It is because you cannot accept my word. 44 You are from your father the devil, and you choose to do your father's desires. He was a murderer from the beginning and does not stand in the truth, because there is no truth in him. When he lies, he speaks according to his own nature, for he is a liar and the father of lies. 45 But because I tell the truth, you do not believe me. 46 Which of you convicts me of sin? If I tell the truth, why do you not believe me? 47 Whoever is from God hears the words of God. The reason you do not hear them is that you are not from God."

48 The Jews answered him, "Are we not right in saying that you are a Samaritan and have a demon?" 49 Jesus answered, "I do not have a demon, but I honor my Father, and you dishonor me. 50 Yet I do not seek my own glory; there is one who seeks it, and he is the judge. 51 Very truly, I tell you, whoever keeps my word will never

see death." **52** The Jews said to him, "Now we know that you have a demon. Abraham died, and so did the prophets, yet you say, 'Whoever keeps my word will never taste death.' **53** Are you greater than our father Abraham, who died? The prophets also died. Who do you claim to be?" **54** Jesus answered, "If I glorify myself, my glory is nothing. It is my Father who glorifies me, he of whom you say, 'He is our God,' **55** though you do not know him. But I know him; if I would say that I do not know him, I would be a liar like you. But I do know him and I keep his word. **56** Your ancestor Abraham rejoiced that he would see my day; he saw it and was glad." **57** Then the Jews said to him, "You are not yet fifty years old, and have you seen Abraham?" **58** Jesus said to them, "Very truly, I tell you, before Abraham was, I am." **59** So they picked up stones to throw at him, but Jesus hid himself and went out of the temple.

CHAPTER 9

✦ Jesus Heals the Man Born Blind

 **A**s he walked along, he saw a man blind from birth. **2** His disciples asked him, "Rabbi, who sinned, this man or his parents, that he was born blind?" **3** Jesus answered, "Neither this man nor his parents sinned; he was born blind so that God's works might be revealed in him. **4** We must work the works of him who sent me while it is day; night is coming, when no one can work. **5** As long as I am in the world, I am the light of the world." **6** When he had said this, he spat on the ground and made mud with the saliva and spread the mud on the man's eyes, **7** saying to him, "Go, wash in the pool of Siloam" (which means Sent). Then he went and washed and came back able to see. **8** The neighbors and those who had seen him before as a beggar began to ask, "Is this not the man who used to sit and beg?" **9** Some were saying, "It is he." Others were saying, "No, but it is someone like him." He kept

saying, "I am he." **10** But they kept asking him, "Then how were your eyes opened?" **11** He answered, "The man called Jesus made mud, spread it on my eyes, and said to me, 'Go to Siloam and wash.' Then I went and washed and received my sight." **12** They said to him, "Where is he?" He said, "I do not know."

✢ The Pharisees Investigate the Healing

13 They brought to the Pharisees the man who had formerly been blind. **14** Now it was a Sabbath day when Jesus made the mud and opened his eyes. **15** Then the Pharisees also began to ask him how he had received his sight. He said to them, "He put mud on my eyes. Then I washed, and now I see." **16** Some of the Pharisees said, "This man is not from God, for he does not observe the Sabbath." Others said, "How can a man who is a sinner perform such signs?" And they were divided. **17** So they said again to the blind man, "What do you say about him? It was your eyes he opened." He said, "He is a prophet."

18 The Jews did not believe that he had been blind and had received his sight until they called the parents of the man who had received his sight **19** and asked them, "Is this your son, who you say was born blind? How then does he now see?" **20** His parents answered, "We know that this is our son and that he was born blind, **21** but we do not know how it is that now he sees, nor do we know who opened his eyes. Ask him; he is of age. He will speak for himself." **22** His parents said this because they were afraid of the Jews, for the Jews had already agreed that anyone who confessed Jesus to be the Messiah would be put out of the synagogue. **23** Therefore his parents said, "He is of age; ask him."

24 So for the second time they called the man who had been blind, and they said to him, "Give glory to God! We know that this man is a sinner." **25** He answered, "I do not know whether he is a sinner. One thing I do know, that though I was blind, now I see." **26** They said to him, "What did he do to you? How did he open your eyes?" **27** He answered them, "I have told you already, and you would not listen. Why do you want to hear it again? Do you also want to become his disciples?" **28** Then they reviled him, saying, "You are his disciple, but we are disciples of Moses. **29** We know that God has spoken to Moses, but as for this man, we do not know where he comes from." **30** The man answered, "Here is an astonishing thing! You do not know where he comes from, yet he opened my eyes. **31** We know that God does not listen to sinners, but he does listen to one who worships him and obeys his will. **32** Never since the world began has it been heard that anyone opened the eyes of a person born blind. **33** If this man were not from God, he could do nothing." **34** They answered him, "You were born entirely in sins, and are you trying to teach us?" And they drove him out.

✢ Spiritual Blindness

35 Jesus heard that they had driven him out, and when he found him, he said, "Do you believe in the Son of Man?" **36** He answered, "And who is he, sir? Tell me, so that I may believe in him." **37** Jesus said to him, "You have seen him, and the one speaking with you is he." **38** He said, "Lord, I believe." And he worshiped him. **39** Jesus said, "I came into this world for judgment, so that those who do not see may see, and those who do see may become blind." **40** Some of the Pharisees near him heard this and said to him, "Surely we are not blind, are we?" **41** Jesus said to them, "If you were blind, you would not have sin. But now that you say, 'We see,' your sin remains.

CHAPTER 10

✦ I Am the Good Shepherd

**ery truly, I tell you,** anyone who does not enter the sheepfold by the gate but climbs in by another way is a thief and a bandit. **2** The one who enters by the gate is the shepherd of the sheep. **3** The gatekeeper opens the gate for him, and the sheep hear his voice. He calls his own sheep by name and leads them out. **4** When he has brought out all his own, he goes ahead of them, and the sheep follow him because they know his voice. **5** They will not follow a stranger, but they will run from him because they do not know the voice of strangers." **6** Jesus used this figure of speech with them, but they did not understand what he was saying to them.

7 So again Jesus said to them, "Very truly, I tell you, I am the gate for the sheep. **8** All who came before me are thieves and bandits, but the sheep did not listen to them. **9** I am the gate. Whoever enters by me will be saved and will come in and go out and find pasture. **10** The thief comes only to steal and kill and destroy. I came that they may have life and have it abundantly.

11 "I am the good shepherd. The good shepherd lays down his life for the sheep. **12** The hired hand, who is not the shepherd and does not own the sheep, sees the wolf coming and leaves the sheep and runs away, and the wolf snatches them and scatters them. **13** The hired hand runs away because a hired hand does not care for the sheep. **14** I am the good shepherd. I know my own, and my own know me, **15** just as the Father knows me, and I know the Father. And I lay down my life for the sheep. **16** I have other sheep that do not belong to this fold. I must bring them also, and they will listen to my voice. So there will be one flock, one shepherd. **17** For this reason the Father loves me, because I lay down my life in order to take it up again. **18** No one takes it from me, but I lay it down of my own accord. I have power to lay it down, and I have power to take it up again. I have received this command from my Father."

[19] Again the Jews were divided because of these words. [20] Many of them were saying, "He has a demon and is out of his mind. Why listen to him?" [21] Others were saying, "These are not the words of one who has a demon. Can a demon open the eyes of the blind?"

✦ The Father and I Are One

[22] At that time the Festival of the Dedication took place in Jerusalem. It was winter, [23] and Jesus was walking in the temple, in the portico of Solomon. [24] So the Jews gathered around him and said to him, "How long will you keep us in suspense? If you are the Messiah, tell us plainly." [25] Jesus answered, "I have told you, and you do not believe. The works that I do in my Father's name testify to me, [26] but you do not believe because you do not belong to my sheep. [27] My sheep hear my voice. I know them, and they follow me. [28] I give them eternal life, and they will never perish. No one will snatch them out of my hand. [29] My Father, in regard to what he has given me, is greater than all, and no one can snatch them out of the Father's hand. [30] The Father and I are one."

[31] The Jews took up stones again to stone him. [32] Jesus replied, "I have shown you many good works from the Father. For which of these are you going to stone me?" [33] The Jews answered, "It is not for a good work that we are going to stone you but for blasphemy, because you, though only a human, are making yourself God." [34] Jesus answered, "Is it not written in your law, 'I said, you are gods'? [35] If those to whom the word of God came were called 'gods'—and the scripture cannot be annulled—[36] can you say that the one whom the Father has sanctified and sent into the world is blaspheming because I said, 'I am God's Son'? [37] If I am not doing the works of my Father, then do not believe me. [38] But if I do them, even though you do not believe me, believe the works, so that you may know and understand that the Father is in me and I am in the Father." [39] Then they tried to arrest him again, but he escaped from their hands.

40 He went away again across the Jordan to the place where John had been baptizing earlier, and he remained there. **41** Many came to him, and they were saying, "John performed no sign, but everything that John said about this man was true." **42** And many believed in him there.

CHAPTER **11**

✢ The Death of Lazarus

**ow a certain man was ill,** Lazarus of Bethany, the village of Mary and her sister Martha. **2** Mary was the one who anointed the Lord with perfume and wiped his feet with her hair; her brother Lazarus was ill. **3** So the sisters sent a message to Jesus, "Lord, he whom you love is ill." **4** But when Jesus heard it, he said, "This illness does not lead to death; rather, it is for God's glory, so that the Son of God may be glorified through it." **5** Accordingly, though Jesus loved Martha and her sister and Lazarus, **6** after having heard that Lazarus was ill, he stayed two days longer in the place where he was.

7 Then after this he said to the disciples, "Let us go to Judea again." **8** The disciples said to him, "Rabbi, the Jews were just now trying to stone you, and are you going there again?" **9** Jesus answered, "Are there not twelve hours of daylight? Those who walk during the day do not stumble because they see the light of this world. **10** But those who walk at night stumble because the light is not in them." **11** After saying this, he told them, "Our friend Lazarus has fallen asleep, but I am going there to awaken him." **12** The disciples said to him, "Lord, if he has fallen asleep, he will be all right." **13** Jesus, however, had been speaking about his death, but they thought that he was referring merely to sleep. **14** Then Jesus told them plainly, "Lazarus is dead. **15** For your sake I am glad I was not there, so that you may believe. But let us go to him."

16 Thomas, who was called the Twin, said to his fellow disciples, "Let us also go, that we may die with him."

✤ I Am the Resurrection and the Life

17 When Jesus arrived, he found that Lazarus had already been in the tomb four days. **18** Now Bethany was near Jerusalem, some two miles away, **19** and many of the Jews had come to Martha and Mary to console them about their brother. **20** When Martha heard that Jesus was coming, she went and met him, while Mary stayed at home. **21** Martha said to Jesus, "Lord, if you had been here, my brother would not have died. **22** But even now I know that God will give you whatever you ask of him." **23** Jesus said to her, "Your brother will rise again." **24** Martha said to him, "I know that he will rise again in the resurrection on the last day." **25** Jesus said to her, "I am the resurrection and the life. Those who believe in me, even though they die, will live, **26** and everyone who lives and believes in me will never die. Do you believe this?" **27** She said to him, "Yes, Lord, I believe that you are the Messiah, the Son of God, the one coming into the world."

✤ Jesus Weeps

28 When she had said this, she went back and called her sister Mary and told her privately, "The Teacher is here and is calling for you." **29** And when she heard it, she got up quickly and went to him. **30** Now Jesus had not yet come to the village but was still at the place where Martha had met him. **31** The Jews who were with her in the house consoling her saw Mary get up quickly and go out. They followed her because they thought that she was going to the tomb to weep there. **32** When Mary came where Jesus was and saw him, she knelt at his feet and said to him, "Lord, if you had been here, my brother would not have died." **33** When Jesus saw her weeping, and the Jews who came with her also weeping, he was greatly disturbed in spirit and deeply moved. **34** He said, "Where have you laid him?" They said to him, "Lord, come and see." **35** Jesus began to weep. **36** So the Jews said, "See how he loved him!" **37** But some of them said, "Could not he who opened the eyes of the blind man have kept this man from dying?"

✦ Jesus Raises Lazarus to Life

38 Then Jesus, again greatly disturbed, came to the tomb. It was a cave, and a stone was lying against it. **39** Jesus said, "Take away the stone." Martha, the sister of the dead man, said to him, "Lord, already there is a stench because he has been dead four days." **40** Jesus said to her, "Did I not tell you that if you believed you would see the glory of God?" **41** So they took away the stone. And Jesus looked upward and said, "Father, I thank you for having heard me. **42** I knew that you always hear me, but I have said this for the sake of the crowd standing here, so that they may believe that you sent me." **43** When he had said this, he cried with a loud voice, "Lazarus, come out!" **44** The dead man came out, his hands and feet bound with strips of cloth and his face wrapped in a cloth. Jesus said to them, "Unbind him, and let him go."

✦ The Plot to Kill Jesus

45 Many of the Jews therefore, who had come with Mary and had seen what Jesus did believed in him. **46** But some of them went to the Pharisees and told them what Jesus had done. **47** So the chief priests and the Pharisees called a meeting of the council and said, "What are we to do? This man is performing many signs. **48** If we let him go on like this, everyone will believe in him, and the Romans will come and destroy both our holy place and our nation." **49** But one of them, Caiaphas, who was high priest that year, said to them, "You know nothing at all! **50** You do not understand that it is better for you to have one man die for the people than to have the whole nation destroyed." **51** He did not say this on his own, but being high priest that year he prophesied that Jesus was about to die for the nation, **52** and not for the nation only, but to gather into one the dispersed children of God. **53** So from that day on they planned to put him to death.

54 Jesus therefore no longer walked about openly among the Jews but went from there to a town called Ephraim in the region near the wilderness, and he remained there with the disciples.

55 Now the Passover of the Jews was near, and many went up from the country to Jerusalem before the Passover to purify themselves. **56** They were looking for Jesus and were asking one another as they stood in the temple, "What do you think? Surely he will not come to the festival, will he?" **57** Now the chief priests and the Pharisees had given orders that anyone who knew where Jesus was should let them know, so that they might arrest him.

CHAPTER 12

✣ Mary Anoints Jesus

 **ix days before the Passover** Jesus came to Bethany, the home of Lazarus, whom he had raised from the dead. **2** There they gave a dinner for him. Martha served, and Lazarus was one of those reclining with him. **3** Mary took a pound of costly perfume made of pure nard, anointed Jesus's feet, and wiped them with her hair. The house was filled with the fragrance of the perfume. **4** But Judas Iscariot, one of his disciples (the one who was about to betray him), said, **5** "Why was this perfume not sold for three hundred denarii and the money given to the poor?" **6** (He said this not because he cared about the poor but because he was a thief; he kept the common purse and used to steal what was put into it.) **7** Jesus said, "Leave her alone. She bought it so that she might keep it for the day of my burial. **8** You always have the poor with you, but you do not always have me."

✣ The Plot to Kill Lazarus

9 When the great crowd of the Jews learned that he was there, they came not only because of Jesus but also to see Lazarus, whom he had raised from the dead. **10** So the chief priests planned to put

Lazarus to death as well, **11** since it was on account of him that many of the Jews were deserting and were believing in Jesus.

✤ Jesus' Triumphal Entry into Jerusalem

12 The next day the great crowd that had come to the festival heard that Jesus was coming to Jerusalem. **13** So they took branches of palm trees and went out to meet him, shouting,

> "Hosanna!
> Blessed is the one who comes in the name of the Lord—
>   the King of Israel!"

14 Jesus found a young donkey and sat on it, as it is written:

> **15** "Do not be afraid, daughter of Zion.
> Look, your king is coming,
>   sitting on a donkey's colt!"

16 His disciples did not understand these things at first, but when Jesus was glorified, then they remembered that these things had been written of him and had been done to him. **17** So the crowd that had been with him when he called Lazarus out of the tomb and raised him from the dead continued to testify. **18** It was also because they heard that he had performed this sign that the crowd went to meet him. **19** The Pharisees then said to one another, "You see, you can do nothing. Look, the world has gone after him!"

✤ The Mystery of Life and Death

20 Now among those who went up to worship at the festival were some Greeks. **21** They came to Philip, who was from Bethsaida in Galilee, and said to him, "Sir, we wish to see Jesus." **22** Philip went and told Andrew, then Andrew and Philip went and told Jesus. **23** Jesus answered them, "The hour has come for the Son of Man to be glorified. **24** Very truly, I tell you, unless a grain of wheat falls into the earth and dies, it remains just a single grain, but if it dies it bears much fruit. **25** Those who love their life lose it, and those who hate their life in this world will keep it for eternal life.

26 Whoever serves me must follow me, and where I am, there will my servant be also. Whoever serves me, the Father will honor.

✧ Jesus Speaks about His Death

27 "Now my soul is troubled. And what should I say: 'Father, save me from this hour'? No, it is for this reason that I have come to this hour. **28** Father, glorify your name." Then a voice came from heaven, "I have glorified it, and I will glorify it again." **29** The crowd standing there heard it and said that it was thunder. Others said, "An angel has spoken to him." **30** Jesus answered, "This voice has come for your sake, not for mine. **31** Now is the judgment of this world; now the ruler of this world will be driven out. **32** And I, when I am lifted up from the earth, will draw all people to myself." **33** He said this to indicate the kind of death he was to die. **34** The crowd answered him, "We have heard from the law that the Messiah remains forever. How can you say that the Son of Man must be lifted up? Who is this Son of Man?" **35** Jesus said to them, "The light is with you for a little longer. Walk while you have the light, so that the darkness may not overtake you. If you walk in the darkness, you do not know where you are going. **36** While you have the light, believe in the light, so that you may become children of light."

✧ The Unbelief of the People

After Jesus had said this, he departed and hid from them. **37** Although he had performed so many signs in their presence, they did not believe in him. **38** This was to fulfill the word spoken by the prophet Isaiah:

> "Lord, who has believed our message,
>   and to whom has the arm of the Lord been revealed?"

39 And so they could not believe, because Isaiah also said,

> **40** "He has blinded their eyes
>   and hardened their heart,
> so that they might not look with their eyes
>   and understand with their heart and turn —
>   and I would heal them."

⁴¹ Isaiah said this because he saw his glory and spoke about him.
⁴² Nevertheless many, even of the authorities, believed in him.
But because of the Pharisees they did not confess it, for fear that
they would be put out of the synagogue, ⁴³ for they loved human
glory more than the glory that comes from God.

✦ The Father

⁴⁴ Then Jesus cried aloud: "Whoever believes in me believes not
in me but in him who sent me. ⁴⁵ And whoever sees me sees him
who sent me. ⁴⁶ I have come as light into the world, so that everyone who believes in me should not remain in the darkness. ⁴⁷ I do
not judge anyone who hears my words and does not keep them,
for I came not to judge the world, but to save the world. ⁴⁸ The
one who rejects me and does not receive my words has a judge;
on the last day the word that I have spoken will serve as judge,
⁴⁹ for I have not spoken on my own, but the Father who sent me
has himself given me a commandment about what to say and what
to speak. ⁵⁰ And I know that his commandment is eternal life.
What I speak, therefore, I speak just as the Father has told me."

CHAPTER 13

✦ Jesus Washes the Disciples' Feet

 **ow before the festival** of the Passover, Jesus knew
that his hour had come to depart from this world
and go to the Father. Having loved his own who
were in the world, he loved them to the end. ² The
devil had already decided that Judas son of Simon Iscariot would
betray Jesus. And during supper ³ Jesus, knowing that the Father
had given all things into his hands and that he had come from
God and was going to God, ⁴ got up from supper, took off his outer
robe, and tied a towel around himself. ⁵ Then he poured water
into a basin and began to wash the disciples' feet and to wipe
them with the towel that was tied around him. ⁶ He came to Simon
Peter, who said to him, "Lord, are you going to wash my feet?"

⁷ Jesus answered, "You do not know now what I am doing, but later you will understand." ⁸ Peter said to him, "You will never wash my feet." Jesus answered, "Unless I wash you, you have no share with me." ⁹ Simon Peter said to him, "Lord, not my feet only but also my hands and my head!" ¹⁰ Jesus said to him, "One who has bathed does not need to wash, except for the feet, but is entirely clean. And you are clean, though not all of you." ¹¹ For he knew who was to betray him; for this reason he said, "Not all of you are clean."

¹² After he had washed their feet, had put on his robe, and had reclined again, he said to them, "Do you know what I have done to you? ¹³ You call me Teacher and Lord, and you are right, for that is what I am. ¹⁴ So if I, your Lord and Teacher, have washed your feet, you also ought to wash one another's feet. ¹⁵ For I have set you an example, that you also should do as I have done to you. ¹⁶ Very truly, I tell you, servants are not greater than their master, nor are messengers greater than the one who sent them. ¹⁷ If you know these things, you are blessed if you do them. ¹⁸ I am not speaking of all of you; I know whom I have chosen. But it is to fulfill the scripture, 'The one who ate my bread has lifted his heel against me.' ¹⁹ I tell you this now, before it occurs, so that when it does occur you may believe that I am he. ²⁰ Very truly, I tell you, whoever receives one whom I send receives me, and whoever receives me receives him who sent me."

✤ Jesus Foretells His Betrayal

²¹ After saying this Jesus was troubled in spirit and declared, "Very truly, I tell you, one of you will betray me." ²² The disciples looked at one another, uncertain of whom he was speaking. ²³ One of his disciples—the one whom Jesus loved—was reclining close to his heart; ²⁴ Simon Peter therefore motioned to him to ask Jesus of whom he was speaking. ²⁵ So while reclining next to Jesus, he asked him, "Lord, who is it?" ²⁶ Jesus answered, "It is the one to whom I give this piece of bread when I have dipped it in the dish." So when he had dipped the piece of bread, he gave it to Judas son

of Simon Iscariot. **27** After he received the piece of bread, Satan entered into him. Jesus said to him, "Do quickly what you are going to do." **28** Now no one knew why he said this to him. **29** Some thought that, because Judas had the common purse, Jesus was telling him, "Buy what we need for the festival," or, that he should give something to the poor. **30** So, after receiving the piece of bread, he immediately went out. And it was night.

✤ The New Commandment

31 When he had gone out, Jesus said, "Now the Son of Man has been glorified, and God has been glorified in him. **32** If God has been glorified in him, God will also glorify him in himself and will glorify him at once. **33** Little children, I am with you only a little longer. You will look for me; and as I said to the Jews so now I say to you, 'Where I am going, you cannot come.' **34** I give you a new commandment, that you love one another. Just as I have loved you, you also should love one another. **35** By this everyone will know that you are my disciples, if you have love for one another."

✤ Jesus Foretells Peter's Denial

36 Simon Peter said to him, "Lord, where are you going?" Jesus answered, "Where I am going, you cannot follow me now, but you will follow afterward." **37** Peter said to him, "Lord, why can I not follow you now? I will lay down my life for you." **38** Jesus answered, "Will you lay down your life for me? Very truly, I tell you, before the cock crows, you will have denied me three times.

CHAPTER **14**

✦ I am the Way, the Truth, and the Light

**o not let your hearts be troubled.** Believe in God; believe also in me. **2** In my Father's house there are many dwelling places. If it were not so, would I have told you that I go to prepare a place for you? **3** And if I go and prepare a place for you, I will come again and will take you to myself, so that where I am, there you may be also. **4** And you know the way to the place where I am going." **5** Thomas said to him, "Lord, we do not know where you are going. How can we know the way?" **6** Jesus said to him, "I am the way, and the truth, and the life. No one comes to the Father except through me. **7** If you know me, you will know my Father also. From now on you do know him and have seen him."

8 Philip said to him, "Lord, show us the Father, and we will be satisfied." **9** Jesus said to him, "Have I been with you all this time, Philip, and you still do not know me? Whoever has seen me has seen the Father. How can you say, 'Show us the Father'? **10** Do you not believe that I am in the Father and the Father is in me? The words that I say to you I do not speak on my own, but the Father who dwells in me does his works. **11** Believe me that I am in the Father and the Father is in me, but if you do not, then believe me because of the works themselves. **12** Very truly, I tell you, the one who believes in me will also do the works that I do and, in fact, will do greater works than these, because I am going to the Father. **13** I will do whatever you ask in my name, so that the Father may be glorified in the Son. **14** If in my name you ask me for anything, I will do it.

✦ The Promise of the Holy Spirit

15 "If you love me, you will keep my commandments. **16** And I will ask the Father, and he will give you another Advocate, to be with you forever. **17** This is the Spirit of truth, whom the world cannot receive because it neither sees him nor knows him. You know him because he abides with you, and he will be in you.

18 "I will not leave you orphaned; I am coming to you. 19 In a little while the world will no longer see me, but you will see me; because I live, you also will live. 20 On that day you will know that I am in my Father, and you in me, and I in you. 21 They who have my commandments and keep them are those who love me, and those who love me will be loved by my Father, and I will love them and reveal myself to them." 22 Judas (not Iscariot) said to him, "Lord, how is it that you will reveal yourself to us and not to the world?" 23 Jesus answered him, "Those who love me will keep my word, and my Father will love them, and we will come to them and make our home with them. 24 Whoever does not love me does not keep my words, and the word that you hear is not mine but is from the Father who sent me.

25 "I have said these things to you while I am still with you. 26 But the Advocate, the Holy Spirit, whom the Father will send in my name, will teach you everything, and remind you of all that I have said to you. 27 Peace I leave with you; my peace I give to you. I do not give to you as the world gives. Do not let your hearts be troubled, and do not let them be afraid. 28 You heard me say to you, 'I am going away, and I am coming to you.' If you loved me, you would rejoice that I am going to the Father, because the Father is greater than I. 29 And now I have told you this before it occurs, so that when it does occur you may believe. 30 I will no longer talk much with you, for the ruler of this world is coming. He has no power over me, 31 but I do as the Father has commanded me, so that the world may know that I love the Father. Rise, let us be on our way.

CHAPTER 15

✤ I Am the True Vine

I am the true vine, and my Father is the vinegrower. **2** He removes every branch in me that bears no fruit. Every branch that bears fruit he prunes to make it bear more fruit. **3** You have already been cleansed by the word that I have spoken to you. **4** Abide in me as I abide in you. Just as the branch cannot bear fruit by itself unless it abides in the vine, neither can you unless you abide in me. **5** I am the vine; you are the branches. Those who abide in me and I in them bear much fruit, because apart from me you can do nothing. **6** Whoever does not abide in me is thrown away like a branch and withers; such branches are gathered, thrown into the fire, and burned. **7** If you abide in me and my words abide in you, ask for whatever you wish, and it will be done for you. **8** My Father is glorified by this, that you bear much fruit and become my disciples. **9** As the Father has loved me, so I have loved you; abide in my love. **10** If you keep my commandments, you will abide in my love, just as I have kept my Father's commandments and abide in his love. **11** I have said these things to you so that my joy may be in you, and that your joy may be complete.

12 "This is my commandment, that you love one another as I have loved you. **13** No one has greater love than this, to lay down one's life for one's friends. **14** You are my friends if you do what I command you. **15** I do not call you servants any longer, because the servant does not know what the master is doing, but I have called you friends, because I have made known to you everything that I have heard from my Father. **16** You did not choose me, but I chose you. And I appointed you to go and bear fruit, fruit that will last, so that the Father will give you whatever you ask him in my name. **17** I am giving you these commands so that you may love one another.

✦ The World's Hatred

18 "If the world hates you, be aware that it hated me before it hated you. **19** If you belonged to the world, the world would love you as its own. Because you do not belong to the world, but I have chosen you out of the world, therefore the world hates you. **20** Remember the word that I said to you, 'Slaves are not greater than their master.' If they persecuted me, they will persecute you; if they kept my word, they will keep yours also. **21** But they will do all these things to you on account of my name, because they do not know him who sent me. **22** If I had not come and spoken to them, they would not have sin; but now they have no excuse for their sin. **23** Whoever hates me hates my Father also. **24** If I had not done among them the works that no one else did, they would not have sin. But now they have seen and hated both me and my Father. **25** It was to fulfill the word that is written in their law, 'They hated me without a cause.'

26 "When the Advocate comes, whom I will send to you from the Father, the Spirit of truth who comes from the Father, he will testify on my behalf. **27** You also are to testify because you have been with me from the beginning.

CHAPTER 16

 **have said these things** to you to keep you from falling away. **2** They will put you out of the synagogues. Indeed, an hour is coming when those who kill you will think that by doing so they are offering worship to God. **3** And they will do this because they have not known the Father or me. **4** But I have said these things to you so that when their hour comes you may remember that I told you about them.

✦ The Work of the Holy Spirit

"I did not say these things to you from the beginning, because I was with you. **5** But now I am going to him who sent me, yet none of you asks me, 'Where are you going?' **6** But because I have said these things to you, sorrow has filled your hearts. [7] Nevertheless, I tell you the truth: it is to your advantage that I go away, for if I do not go away, the Advocate will not come to you, but if I go, I will send him to you. [8] And when he comes, he will prove the world wrong about sin and righteousness and judgment: [9] about sin, because they do not believe in me; [10] about righteousness, because I am going to the Father, and you will see me no longer; [11] about judgment, because the ruler of this world has been condemned.

[12] "I still have many things to say to you, but you cannot bear them now. [13] When the Spirit of truth comes, he will guide you into all the truth, for he will not speak on his own but will speak whatever he hears, and he will declare to you the things that are to come. [14] He will glorify me because he will take what is mine and declare it to you. [15] All that the Father has is mine. For this reason I said that he will take what is mine and declare it to you.

✦ Sorrow Will Turn into Joy

[16] "A little while, and you will no longer see me, and again a little while, and you will see me." [17] Then some of his disciples said to one another, "What does he mean by saying to us, 'A little while, and you will no longer see me, and again a little while, and you will see me,' and 'because I am going to the Father'?" [18] They said, "What does he mean by this 'a little while'? We do not know what he is talking about." [19] Jesus knew that they wanted to ask him, so he said to them, "Are you discussing among yourselves what I meant when I said, 'A little while, and you will no longer see me, and again a little while, and you will see me'? [20] Very truly, I tell you, you will weep and mourn, but the world will rejoice; you will have pain, but your pain will turn into joy. [21] When a woman is in labor, she has pain because her hour has come. But when her child is born, she no longer remembers the anguish because of the joy of having brought a human being into the world. [22] So you have pain now, but I will see you again, and your hearts will rejoice, and no one will take your joy from you. [23] On that day you will ask nothing of me. Very truly, I tell you, if you ask anything

of the Father in my name, he will give it to you. **24** Until now you have not asked for anything in my name. Ask and you will receive, so that your joy may be complete.

✤ Peace for the Disciples

25 "I have said these things to you in figures of speech. The hour is coming when I will no longer speak to you in figures but will tell you plainly of the Father. **26** On that day you will ask in my name. I do not say to you that I will ask the Father on your behalf, **27** for the Father himself loves you because you have loved me and have believed that I came from God. **28** I came from the Father and have come into the world; again, I am leaving the world and am going to the Father."

29 His disciples said, "Yes, now you are speaking plainly, not in any figure of speech! **30** Now we know that you know all things and do not need to have anyone question you; by this we believe that you came from God." **31** Jesus answered them, "Do you now believe? **32** The hour is coming, indeed it has come, when you will be scattered, each one to his home, and you will leave me alone. Yet I am not alone because the Father is with me. **33** I have said this to you so that in me you may have peace. In the world you face persecution, but take courage: I have conquered the world!"

CHAPTER **17**

✤ Jesus Prays for His Disciples

 **fter Jesus had spoken** these words, he looked up to heaven and said, "Father, the hour has come; glorify your Son so that the Son may glorify you, **2** since you have given him authority over all people, to give eternal life to all whom you have given him. **3** And this is eternal life, that they may know you, the only true God, and Jesus Christ, whom you have sent. **4** I glorified you on earth by finishing the work that you gave me to do. **5** So now, Father, glorify

me in your own presence with the glory that I had in your presence before the world existed.

6 "I have made your name known to those whom you gave me from the world. They were yours, and you gave them to me, and they have kept your word. **7** Now they know that everything you have given me is from you, **8** for the words that you gave to me I have given to them, and they have received them and know in truth that I came from you; and they have believed that you sent me. **9** I am asking on their behalf; I am not asking on behalf of the world but on behalf of those whom you gave me, because they are yours. **10** All mine are yours, and yours are mine, and I have been glorified in them. **11** And now I am no longer in the world, but they are in the world, and I am coming to you. Holy Father, protect them in your name that you have given me, so that they may be one, as we are one. **12** While I was with them, I protected them in your name that you have given me. I guarded them, and not one of them was lost except the one destined to be lost, so that the scripture might be fulfilled. **13** But now I am coming to you, and I speak these things in the world so that they may have my joy made complete in themselves. **14** I have given them your word, and the world has hated them because they do not belong to the world, just as I do not belong to the world. **15** I am not asking you to take them out of the world, but I ask you to protect them from the evil one. **16** They do not belong to the world, just as I do not belong to the world. **17** Sanctify them in the truth; your word is truth. **18** As you have sent me into the world, so I have sent them into the world. **19** And for their sakes I sanctify myself, so that they also may be sanctified in truth.

20 "I ask not only on behalf of these but also on behalf of those who will believe in me through their word, **21** that they may all be one. As you, Father, are in me and I am in you, may they also be in us, so that the world may believe that you have sent me. **22** The glory that you have given me I have given them, so that they may be one, as we are one, **23** I in them and you in me, that they may become completely one, so that the world may know that you have sent me and have loved them even as you have loved me. ²⁴ Father, I desire that those also, whom you have given me, may be with me where I am, to see my glory, which you have given me because you loved me before the foundation of the world.

²⁵ "Righteous Father, the world does not know you, but I know you, and these know that you have sent me. ²⁶ I made your name known to them, and I will make it known, so that the love with which you have loved me may be in them and I in them."

CHAPTER 18

✤ The Betrayal and Arrest of Jesus

 **fter Jesus had spoken** these words, he went out with his disciples across the Kidron Valley to a place where there was a garden, which he and his disciples entered. ² Now Judas, who betrayed him, also knew the place because Jesus often met there with his disciples. ³ So Judas brought a detachment of soldiers together with police from the chief priests and the Pharisees, and they came there with lanterns and torches and weapons. ⁴ Then Jesus, knowing all that was to happen to him, came forward and asked them, "Whom are you looking for?" ⁵ They answered, "Jesus of Nazareth." Jesus replied, "I am he." Judas, who betrayed him, was standing with them. ⁶ When Jesus said to them, "I am he," they stepped back and fell to the ground. ⁷ Again he asked them, "Whom are you looking for?" And they said, "Jesus of Nazareth." ⁸ Jesus answered, "I told you that I am he. So if you are looking for me, let these men go." ⁹ This was to fulfill the word that he had spoken, "I did not lose a single one of those whom you gave me." ¹⁰ Then Simon Peter, who had a sword, drew it, struck the high priest's slave, and cut off his right ear. The slave's name was Malchus. ¹¹ Jesus said to Peter, "Put your sword back into its sheath. Am I not to drink the cup that the Father has given me?"

✥ Jesus before Caiaphas

¹² So the soldiers, their officer, and the Jewish police arrested Jesus and bound him. ¹³ First they took him to Annas, who was the father-in-law of Caiaphas, the high priest that year. ¹⁴ Caiaphas was the one who had advised the Jews that it was better to have one person die for the people.

✥ Peter Denies Jesus

¹⁵ Simon Peter and another disciple followed Jesus. Since that disciple was known to the high priest, he went with Jesus into the courtyard of the high priest, ¹⁶ but Peter was standing outside at the gate. So the other disciple, who was known to the high priest, went out, spoke to the woman who guarded the gate, and brought Peter in. ¹⁷ The woman said to Peter, "You are not also one of this man's disciples, are you?" He said, "I am not." ¹⁸ Now the slaves and the police had made a charcoal fire because it was cold, and they were standing around it and warming themselves. Peter also was standing with them and warming himself.

✥ Caiaphas Questions Jesus

¹⁹ Then the high priest questioned Jesus about his disciples and about his teaching. ²⁰ Jesus answered, "I have spoken openly to the world; I have always taught in synagogues and in the temple, where all the Jews come together. I have said nothing in secret. ²¹ Why do you ask me? Ask those who heard what I said to them; they know what I said." ²² When he had said this, one of the police standing nearby struck Jesus on the face, saying, "Is that how you answer the high priest?" ²³ Jesus answered, "If I have spoken wrongly, testify to the wrong. But if I have spoken rightly, why do you strike me?" ²⁴ Then Annas sent him bound to Caiaphas the high priest.

✥ Peter Denies Jesus Again

²⁵ Now Simon Peter was standing and warming himself. They asked him, "You are not also one of his disciples, are you?" He denied it and said, "I am not." ²⁶ One of the slaves of the high

priest, a relative of the man whose ear Peter had cut off, asked, "Did I not see you in the garden with him?" **²⁷** Again Peter denied it, and at that moment the cock crowed.

✤ Jesus before Pilate

²⁸ Then they took Jesus from Caiaphas to Pilate's headquarters. It was early in the morning. They themselves did not enter the headquarters, so as to avoid ritual defilement and to be able to eat the Passover. **²⁹** So Pilate went out to them and said, "What accusation do you bring against this man?" **³⁰** They answered, "If this man were not a criminal, we would not have handed him over to you." **³¹** Pilate said to them, "Take him yourselves and judge him according to your law." The Jews replied, "We are not permitted to put anyone to death." **³²** (This was to fulfill what Jesus had said when he indicated the kind of death he was to die.)

³³ Then Pilate entered the headquarters again, summoned Jesus, and asked him, "Are you the King of the Jews?" **³⁴** Jesus answered, "Do you ask this on your own, or did others tell you about me?" **³⁵** Pilate replied, "I am not a Jew, am I? Your own nation and the chief priests have handed you over to me. What have you done?" **³⁶** Jesus answered, "My kingdom does not belong to this world. If my kingdom belonged to this world, my followers would be fighting to keep me from being handed over to the Jews. But as it is, my kingdom is not from here." **³⁷** Pilate asked him, "So you are a king?" Jesus answered, "You say that I am a king. For this I was born, and for this I came into the world, to testify to the truth. Everyone who belongs to the truth listens to my voice." **³⁸** Pilate asked him, "What is truth?"

✤ Jesus Sentenced to Death

After he had said this, he went out to the Jews again and told them, "I find no case against him. **³⁹** But you have a custom that I release someone for you at the Passover. Do you want me to release for you the King of the Jews?" **⁴⁰** They shouted in reply, "Not this man but Barabbas!" Now Barabbas was a rebel.

CHAPTER 19

Then Pilate took Jesus and had him flogged. ² And the soldiers wove a crown of thorns and put it on his head, and they dressed him in a purple robe. ³ They kept coming up to him, saying, "Hail, King of the Jews!" and striking him on the face. ⁴ Pilate went out again and said to them, "Look, I am bringing him out to you to let you know that I find no case against him." ⁵ So Jesus came out wearing the crown of thorns and the purple robe. Pilate said to them, "Behold the man!" ⁶ When the chief priests and the police saw him, they shouted, "Crucify him! Crucify him!" Pilate said to them, "Take him yourselves and crucify him; I find no case against him." ⁷ The Jews answered him, "We have a law, and according to that law he ought to die because he has claimed to be the Son of God."

⁸ Now when Pilate heard this, he was more afraid than ever. ⁹ He entered his headquarters again and asked Jesus, "Where are you from?" But Jesus gave him no answer. ¹⁰ Pilate therefore said to him, "Do you refuse to speak to me? Do you not know that I have power to release you, and power to crucify you?" ¹¹ Jesus answered him, "You would have no power over me unless it had been given you from above; therefore the one who handed me over to you is guilty of a greater sin." ¹² From then on Pilate tried to release him, but the Jews cried out, "If you release this man, you are no friend of Caesar. Everyone who claims to be a king sets himself against Caesar."

¹³ When Pilate heard these words, he brought Jesus outside and sat on the judge's bench at a place called The Stone Pavement, or in Hebrew Gabbatha. ¹⁴ Now it was the day of Preparation for the Passover, and it was about noon. He said to the Jews, "Here is your King!" ¹⁵ They cried out, "Away with him! Away with him! Crucify him!" Pilate asked them, "Shall I crucify your King?"

The chief priests answered, "We have no king but Caesar." **16** Then he handed him over to them to be crucified.

✤ The Crucifixion of Jesus

So they took Jesus, **17** and carrying the cross by himself he went out to what is called the Place of the Skull, which in Hebrew is called Golgotha. **18** There they crucified him and with him two others, one on either side, with Jesus between them. **19** Pilate also had an inscription written and put on the cross. It read, "Jesus of Nazareth, the King of the Jews." **20** Many of the Jews read this inscription because the place where Jesus was crucified was near the city, and it was written in Hebrew, in Latin, and in Greek. **21** Then the chief priests of the Jews said to Pilate, "Do not write, 'The King of the Jews,' but, 'This man said, I am King of the Jews.'" **22** Pilate answered, "What I have written I have written." **23** When the soldiers had crucified Jesus, they took his clothes and divided them into four parts, one for each soldier. They also took his tunic; now the tunic was seamless, woven in one piece from the top. **24** So they said to one another, "Let us not tear it, but cast lots for it to see who will get it." This was to fulfill what the scripture says,

> "They divided my clothes among themselves,
>   and for my clothing they cast lots."

25 And that is what the soldiers did.

Meanwhile, standing near the cross of Jesus were his mother, and his mother's sister, Mary the wife of Clopas, and Mary Magdalene. **26** When Jesus saw his mother and the disciple whom he loved standing beside her, he said to his mother, "Woman, here is your son." **27** Then he said to the disciple, "Here is your mother." And from that hour the disciple took her into his own home.

28 After this, when Jesus knew that all was now finished, he said (in order to fulfill the scripture), "I am thirsty." **29** A jar full of sour wine was standing there. So they put a sponge full of the wine on a branch of hyssop and held it to his mouth. **30** When Jesus had received the wine, he said, "It is finished." Then he bowed his head and gave up his spirit.

✤ Jesus' Side Is Pierced

31 Since it was the day of Preparation, the Jews did not want the bodies left on the cross during the Sabbath, especially because that Sabbath was a day of great solemnity. So they asked Pilate to have the legs of the crucified men broken and the bodies removed. **32** Then the soldiers came and broke the legs of the first and of the other who had been crucified with him. **33** But when they came to Jesus and saw that he was already dead, they did not break his legs. **34** Instead, one of the soldiers pierced his side with a spear, and at once blood and water came out. **35** (He who saw this has testified so that you also may believe. His testimony is true, and he knows that he tells the truth, so that you also may continue to believe.) **36** These things occurred so that the scripture might be fulfilled, "None of his bones shall be broken." **37** And again another passage of scripture says, "They will look on the one whom they have pierced."

✤ The Burial of Jesus

38 After these things, Joseph of Arimathea, who was a disciple of Jesus, though a secret one because of his fear of the Jews, asked Pilate to let him take away the body of Jesus. Pilate gave him permission, so he came and removed his body. **39** Nicodemus, who had at first come to Jesus by night, also came, bringing a mixture of myrrh and aloes, weighing about a hundred pounds. **40** They took the body of Jesus and wrapped it with the spices in linen cloths, according to the burial custom of the Jews. **41** Now there was a garden in the place where he was crucified, and in the garden there was a new tomb in which no one had ever been laid. **42** And so, because it was the Jewish day of Preparation, and the tomb was nearby, they laid Jesus there.

CHAPTER 20

✦ The Resurrection of Jesus

 **arly on the first day** of the week, while it was still dark, Mary Magdalene came to the tomb and saw that the stone had been removed from the tomb. ² So she ran and went to Simon Peter and the other disciple, the one whom Jesus loved, and said to them, "They have taken the Lord out of the tomb, and we do not know where they have laid him." ³ Then Peter and the other disciple set out and went toward the tomb. ⁴ The two were running together, but the other disciple outran Peter and reached the tomb first. ⁵ He bent down to look in and saw the linen wrappings lying there, but he did not go in. ⁶ Then Simon Peter came, following him, and went into the tomb. He saw the linen wrappings lying there, ⁷ and the cloth that had been on Jesus's head, not lying with the linen wrappings but rolled up in a place by itself. ⁸ Then the other disciple, who reached the tomb first, also went in, and he saw and believed, ⁹ for as yet they did not understand the scripture, that he must rise from the dead. ¹⁰ Then the disciples returned to their homes.

✦ Jesus Appears to Mary Magdalene

¹¹ But Mary stood weeping outside the tomb. As she wept, she bent over to look into the tomb, ¹² and she saw two angels in white sitting where the body of Jesus had been lying, one at the head and the other at the feet. ¹³ They said to her, "Woman, why are you weeping?" She said to them, "They have taken away my Lord, and I do not know where they have laid him." ¹⁴ When she had said this, she turned around and saw Jesus standing there, but she did not know that it was Jesus. ¹⁵ Jesus said to her, "Woman, why are you weeping? Whom are you looking for?" Supposing him to be the gardener, she said to him, "Sir, if you have carried him away, tell me where you have laid him, and I will take him away." ¹⁶ Jesus said to her, "Mary!" She turned and said to him in

Hebrew, "Rabbouni!" (which means Teacher). **17** Jesus said to her, "Do not touch me, because I have not yet ascended to the Father. But go to my brothers and say to them, 'I am ascending to my Father and your Father, to my God and your God.'" **18** Mary Magdalene went and announced to the disciples, "I have seen the Lord," and she told them that he had said these things to her.

✣ Jesus Appears to the Disciples

19 When it was evening on that day, the first day of the week, and the doors were locked where the disciples were, for fear of the Jews, Jesus came and stood among them and said, "Peace be with you." **20** After he said this, he showed them his hands and his side. Then the disciples rejoiced when they saw the Lord. **21** Jesus said to them again, "Peace be with you. As the Father has sent me, so I send you." **22** When he had said this, he breathed on them and said to them, "Receive the Holy Spirit. **23** If you forgive the sins of any, they are forgiven them; if you retain the sins of any, they are retained."

✣ Jesus and Thomas

24 But Thomas (who was called the Twin), one of the twelve, was not with them when Jesus came. **25** So the other disciples told him, "We have seen the Lord." But he said to them, "Unless I see the mark of the nails in his hands and put my finger in the mark of the nails and my hand in his side, I will not believe."

26 A week later his disciples were again in the house, and Thomas was with them. Although the doors were shut, Jesus came and stood among them and said, "Peace be with you." **27** Then he said to Thomas, "Put your finger here and see my hands. Reach out your hand and put it in my side. Do not doubt but believe." **28** Thomas answered him, "My Lord and my God!" **29** Jesus said to him, "Have you believed because you have seen me? Blessed are those who have not seen and yet have come to believe."

✦ The Purpose of This Book

30 Now Jesus did many other signs in the presence of his disciples that are not written in this book. **31** But these are written so that you may continue to believe that Jesus is the Messiah, the Son of God, and that through believing you may have life in his name.

CHAPTER 21

✦ Jesus Appears to Seven Disciples

**fter these things Jesus** showed himself again to the disciples by the Sea of Tiberias, and he showed himself in this way. **2** Gathered there together were Simon Peter, Thomas called the Twin, Nathanael of Cana in Galilee, the sons of Zebedee, and two others of his disciples. **3** Simon Peter said to them, "I am going fishing." They said to him, "We will go with you." They went out and got into the boat, but that night they caught nothing.

4 Just after daybreak, Jesus stood on the beach, but the disciples did not know that it was Jesus. **5** Jesus said to them, "Children, you have no fish, have you?" They answered him, "No." **6** He said to them, "Cast the net to the right side of the boat, and you will find some." So they cast it, and now they were not able to haul it in because there were so many fish. **7** That disciple whom Jesus loved said to Peter, "It is the Lord!" When Simon Peter heard that it was the Lord, he put on his outer garment, for he had taken it off, and jumped into the sea. **8** But the other disciples came in the boat, dragging the net full of fish, for they were not far from the land, only about a hundred yards off.

9 When they had gone ashore, they saw a charcoal fire there, with fish on it, and bread. **10** Jesus said to them, "Bring some of the fish that you have just caught." **11** So Simon Peter went aboard and hauled the net ashore, full of large fish, a hundred fifty-three of them, and though there were so many, the net was not torn. **12** Jesus said to them, "Come and have breakfast." Now none of the disciples dared to ask him, "Who are you?" because they knew it was the Lord. ¹³ Jesus came and took the bread and gave it to them and did the same with the fish. ¹⁴ This was now the third time that Jesus appeared to the disciples after he was raised from the dead.

✦ Feed My Lambs

¹⁵ When they had finished breakfast, Jesus said to Simon Peter, "Simon son of John, do you love me more than these?" He said to him, "Yes, Lord; you know that I love you." Jesus said to him, "Feed my lambs." ¹⁶ A second time he said to him, "Simon son of John, do you love me?" He said to him, "Yes, Lord; you know that I love you." Jesus said to him, "Tend my sheep." ¹⁷ He said to him the third time, "Simon son of John, do you love me?" Peter felt hurt because he said to him the third time, "Do you love me?" And he said to him, "Lord, you know everything; you know that I love you." Jesus said to him, "Feed my sheep. ¹⁸ Very truly, I tell you, when you were younger, you used to fasten your own belt and to go wherever you wished. But when you grow old, you will stretch out your hands, and someone else will fasten a belt around you and take you where you do not wish to go." ¹⁹ (He said this to indicate the kind of death by which he would glorify God.) After this he said to him, "Follow me."

✦ Jesus and the Beloved Disciple

²⁰ Peter turned and saw the disciple whom Jesus loved following them; he was the one who had reclined next to Jesus at the supper and had said, "Lord, who is it that is going to betray you?" ²¹ When Peter saw him, he said to Jesus, "Lord, what about him?" ²² Jesus said to him, "If it is my will that he remain until I come, what is that to you? Follow me!" ²³ So the rumor spread among the brothers and sisters that this disciple would not die. Yet Jesus did not say to him that he would not die, but, "If it is my will that he remain until I come, what is that to you?"

24 This is the disciple who is testifying to these things and has written them, and we know that his testimony is true. **25** But there are also many other things that Jesus did; if every one of them were written down, I suppose that the world itself could not contain the books that would be written.

✦ The Coming of the Holy Spirit

2 When the day of Pentecost had come, they were all together in one place. ² And suddenly from heaven there came a sound like the rush of a violent wind, and it filled the entire house where they were sitting. ³ Divided tongues, as of fire, appeared among them, and a tongue rested on each of them. ⁴ All of them were filled with the Holy Spirit and began to speak in other languages, as the Spirit gave them ability.

⁵ Now there were devout Jews from every nation under heaven living in Jerusalem. ⁶ And at this sound the crowd gathered and was bewildered, because each one heard them speaking in the native language of each. ⁷ Amazed and astonished, they asked, "Are not all these who are speaking Galileans? ⁸ And how is it that we hear, each of us, in our own native language? ⁹ Parthians, Medes, Elamites, and residents of Mesopotamia, Judea and Cappadocia, Pontus and Asia, ¹⁰ Phrygia and Pamphylia, Egypt and the parts of Libya belonging to Cyrene, and visitors from Rome, both Jews and proselytes, ¹¹ Cretans and Arabs—in our own languages we hear them speaking about God's deeds of power." ¹² All were amazed and perplexed, saying to one another, "What does this mean?"

Acts 2:1–12 (NRSVUE)

✦ The Multitude from Every Nation

7 ⁹ After this I looked, and there was a great multitude that no one could count, from every nation, from all tribes and peoples and languages, standing before the throne and before the Lamb, robed in white, with palm branches in their hands. ¹⁰ They cried out in a loud voice, saying,

> "Salvation belongs to our God who is seated on the throne
> and to the Lamb!"

¹¹ And all the angels stood around the throne and around the elders and the four living creatures, and they fell on their faces before the throne and worshiped God, ¹² singing,

> "Amen! Blessing and glory and wisdom
> and thanksgiving and honor
> and power and might
> be to our God forever and ever! Amen."

¹³ Then one of the elders addressed me, saying, "Who are these, robed in white, and where have they come from?" ¹⁴ I said to him, "Sir, you are the one who knows." Then he said to me, "These are they who have come out of the great ordeal; they have washed their robes and made them white in the blood of the Lamb.

> ¹⁵ For this reason they are before the throne of God
> and worship him day and night within his temple,
> and the one who is seated on the throne will shelter them.
> ¹⁶ They will hunger no more and thirst no more;
> the sun will not strike them,
> nor any scorching heat,
> ¹⁷ for the Lamb at the center of the throne will be
> their shepherd,
> and he will guide them to springs of the water of life,
> and God will wipe away every tear from their eyes."

Revelation 7:9–17 (NRSVUE)

Biblical Maps

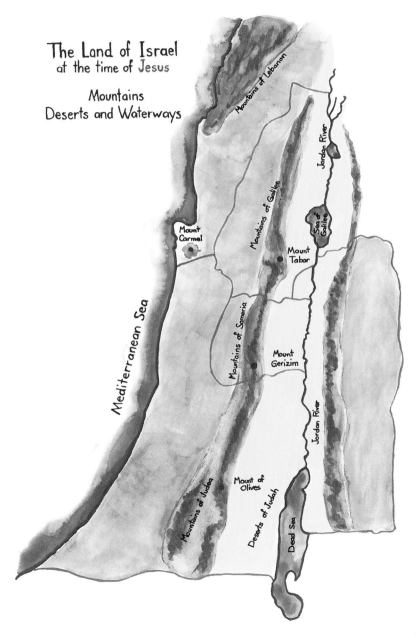

The Land of Israel
at the time of Jesus

Mountains
Deserts and Waterways

Mountains of Lebanon

Jordan River

Mountains of Galilee

Sea of Galilee

Mount Carmel

Mount Tabor

Mediterranean Sea

Mountains of Samaria

Mount Gerizim

Jordan River

Mountains of Judea

Mount of Olives

Deserts of Judah

Dead Sea

The Land of Israel
at the time of Jesus

Principal Cities

Caesarea Philippi

Capernaum • Bethsaida
Sea of Galilee

Cana
Nazareth
Nain

Samaria
Sychar

Jordan River

Arimathea

Jericho

Emmaus

Bethphage
Jerusalem • Bethany

Bethlehem

Dead Sea

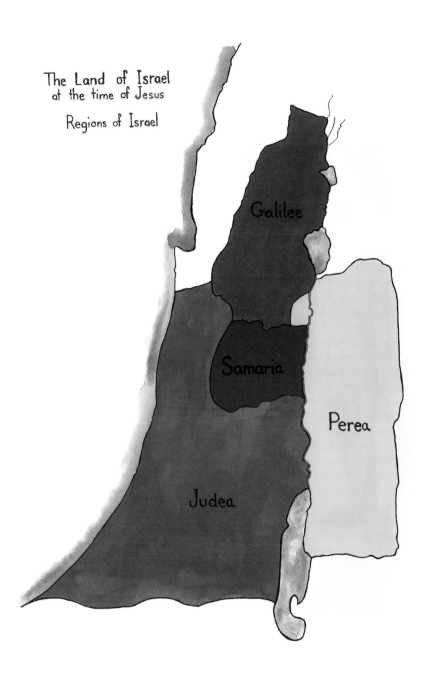

The Land of Israel
at the time of Jesus

Regions of Israel

Galilee

Samaria

Perea

Judea

Journey of the Magi

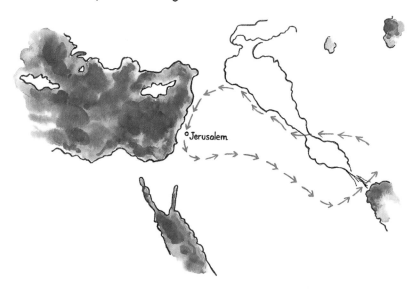

Jerusalem

BIBLICAL MAPS

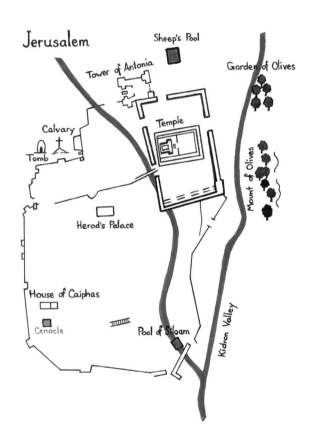

Jerusalem

Sheep's Pool

Tower of Antonia

Garden of Olives

Calvary

Temple

Tomb

Mount of Olives

Herod's Palace

House of Caiphas

Cenacle

Pool of Siloam

Kidron Valley

Index of Scripture

❖　❖　❖

Narrative	Matthew	Mark	Luke	John
The Birth and Childhood of Jesus				
The Annunciation			1:26–38	
The Visitation			1:39–56	
The Nativity and the Adoration of the Shepherds	1:18–25		2:1–20	
The Presentation in the Temple			2:22–38	
The Adoration of the Magi	2:1–12			
The Flight into Egypt	2:13–16			
The Return to Nazareth	2:19–23		2:39–40	
The Finding of Jesus in the Temple			2:41–52	

Narrative	Matthew	Mark	Luke	John
The Passion, Death, and Resurrection of Jesus				
The Messiah Enters Jerusalem	21:1–11	11:1–11	19:28–40	12:12–19
The Last Supper	26:17–35	14:12–31	22:7–34	13:1–38
The Agony in the Garden	26:36–46	14:32–42	22:39–46	
Jesus is Arrested	26:46–56	14:42–52	22:47–53	18:1–12
Jesus before Caiaphas	26:57–75	14:53–72	22:54–71	18:12–27
Jesus before Pilate: The First Time	27:11–14	15:1–5	23:1–7	18:28–38
Jesus before Herod			23:8–12	
Jesus before Pilate: The Second Time	27:15–31	15:6–20	23:13–25	18:39–40, 19:1–16
The Crucifixion	27:32–66	15:20–47	23:26–56	19:17–42
The Resurrection	28:1–8	16:1–8	24:1–12	20:1–10

Narrative	Matthew	Mark	Luke	John
Appearances of the Risen Jesus				
To Mary Magdalene	28:8–10	16:9–11	20:11–18	
On the Road to Emmaus	16:12–13	24:13–35		
To the Disciples (Cenacle)	20:19–23			
To the Apostles (Cenacle)	16:14	24:36–43	20:24–29	
By the Sea of Tiberias	21:1–17			
On a Hill in Galilee	28:16–20	16:15–18		
At Jerusalem	24:44–49			
The Ascension	16:19–20	24:50–53		
Pentecost	Acts of the Apostles 2:1–13			

The Parables of Jesus				
The Good Shepherd				10:1–16
The True Vine				15:1–11
The Mustard Seed	13:31–32			
The Pearl of Great Value	13:45–46			
The Leaven	13:33			
The Hidden Treasure	13:44			
The Seed		4:26–29		
The Sower	13:3–8			
The Ten Bridesmaids	25:1–12			
The Wedding Feast	22:1–14			
The Net	13:47–48			
The Wheat and the Darnel	13:24–30			
The Talents	25:14–30			
The Workers and the Vineyard	20:1–16			
The Good Samaritan			10:30–37	
Lazarus and the Rich Man			16:19–31	
The Found Sheep			15:3–7	
The Found Coin			15:8–10	
The Loving Father			15:11–32	
The Debtors	18:23–35			
The Insistent Friend			11:5–8	
The Pharisee and the Publican			18:9–14	
The Judge and the Widow			18:2–5	
The Rich Fool			12:16–21	

About the Art

✤ ✤ ✤

From cover to cover, this book features images of a grapevine, an image treasured by many children in Catechesis of the Good Shepherd atriums worldwide. This image speaks of the love between Jesus and all of us, according to the parable of the True Vine in John 15. In this parable Jesus tells us that he is the Vine; that we are the branches; and that his Father, who is also our Father, is the Vine Grower taking care of all of us. Jesus offers an image from nature that helps us better understand the nature of our relationship to him, and our relationships with one another. Jesus invites us to *abide*—that is, to remain in him, to live in him. He also says that if we remain in him, we will bear fruit because we are a part of him, sharing in the same sap that flows through the entire vine, the same risen life with him. We will know his joy so that our own joy may be complete. Whenever you reflect on this image of the True Vine, may you be reminded of how close Jesus is to you. As you read the Scripture, may you also be reminded of the Person who loves you and delights in conversation with you.

Before the digital age we live in now, the writing and illumination of the sacred text of the Gospels had been the work of human hands. Copy and illuminate the Gospel texts that delight your heart or give you strength. May this be a way of prayer for you to listen to God's Word and respond lovingly.

Our deepest thanks to our artists for the art that adorns this book: Kathy Ann Sullivan created the cover art, the illuminated letters, the flourishes of the grapevine, and the four living-creature portraits of the Evangelists. Loretta Tedeschi-Cuoco lovingly restored the maps of the Holy Land that were originally drawn by Gianna Gobbi and displayed in the first CGS atrium in Rome, Italy.